USS Lake Champlain

CV/CVA/CVS-39

Turner Publishing Company
Paducah, KY

Just before ending a forty-year career heading up a busy insurance agency in New York City, Jack Sauter tried his hand at writing. His initial effort (at age fifty-nine) produced an article about his Naval Early Warning squadron in Korea. This was published in THE HOOK, the magazine of the Tailhook Association. His next literary effort was a full-length book: SAILORS IN THE SKY, a memoir of his naval service as a radar/combat aircrewman during the Korean War. Among others, he has also written for USA TODAY, AMERICAN LEGION MAGAZINE, SEA CLASSICS, THE HOOK, and the OCEAN LINER GAZETTE. He lives with his wife, Marianne, and son Keith, in Manhasset Hills, New York.

TURNER PUBLISHING COMPANY
Publishers of America's History
412 Broadway•P.O. Box 3101
Paducah, Kentucky 42002-3101
(502) 443-0121

Publishing Consultant: Keith R. Steele
Project Editor: Charlotte Harris
Designer: Peter Zuniga

Copyright©2002 Turner Publishing Company
All rights reserved
Publishing Rights: Turner Publishing Company

This book or any part thereof may not be reproduced without the express written consent of the publisher and/or author.

Library of Congress Catalog No.
2003101779
ISBN 978-1-63026-951-7
LIMITED EDITION

TABLE OF CONTENTS

Publisher's Message 4
Ship History 5
Special Stories 63
USS Lake Champlain CV/CVA/CVS-39 Veterans 83
Photo Gallery 113
Index 120

Publisher's Message

The USS *Lake Champlain, (CV/CVA/CVS -39)*, one of the famous Air Craft Carriers in the history of the US Navy, is also one of the most colorful. From her commissioning on June 3, 1945 by Rear Admiral C.H. Jones, the USS *Lake Champlain* traveled the world in the name of freedom.

This book is dedicated to those of you who proudly served aboard the USS *Lake Champlain*. Through your actions, you created the history of the USS *Lake Champlain* which is held in such high esteem today. The USS *Lake Champlain,* existing only in your memories, will never die as long as one person remains who can tell the story of her sacrifices made and victories won.

We especially thank Jack Sauter (whose reliable assistance proved invaluable during the publication of this volume) and John Printy for their help in making this project become a reality. We thank all of you who submitted your photographs, personal experience stories and biographies for inclusion in this book. Without your help, this volume would not have been possible.

We thank the many brave veterans who called the USS *Lake Champlain* their home. Without you, our history might have indeed told a different story. Finally, we would like to thank Mr. Keith Steele, Turner Publishing Consultant, whose dedication to publishing Naval history helped make this volume a success.

Dave Turner, Founder
Turner Publishing Company

Todd Bottorff
President, Turner Publishing Company

HISTORY OF USS LAKE CHAMPLAIN

A PERSONAL NOTE

It is a both a privilege and an honor for me to write the history of USS LAKE CHAMPLAIN. I had the rare opportunity to serve in CVA-39 during her only combat deployment during the closing months of the Korean War, and my vivid memories of that extraordinary voyage remain bright and lasting. She carried me across the seas to another world. Viewing the ancient Acropolis, the temples of Ceylon and Japan, and the spectacular harbor of Hong Kong, that cruise became the benchmark of my enlistment. More important to our purpose, in that summer of 1953 we engaged the enemy forces in Korea, breaking records with Task Force 77. In those eight months, along with most of my shipmates, I experienced a maturing process unmatched in civilian life. We grew up in a hurry.

Flying in an early-warning Skyraider, (AD4W) as a radar-navigator, Combat Aircrewman, (AT2-CAC), I was one of the few enlisted men who were given the awesome responsibility of being one of the sentinels of Task Force 77. The Navy was a tough taskmaster, but those lessons served us well in civilian life.

In 1990, I became a charter member of the USS LAKE CHAMPLAIN ASSOCIATION and served as its historian. Later, I took over the editorship of THE CHAMP, our magazine, and in 1998, the presidency. Writing and editing THE CHAMP has been a labor of love. Reading all those fabulous letters has brought my own memories to the fore, and I've made scores of new friends. That's a privilege accorded to few, especially at this time of our lives, and for that I'm grateful.

I hope this fine book will not only rekindle the memories of every man who served in our great carrier, but will become a valued family remembrance to be passed on to future generations. This is a living record of what our young men can do whenever their country calls. Men of the Champ—be proud!

-Jack Sauter

THE CHAMP

Writing the history of USS LAKE CHAMPLAIN is not an easy task. Trying to piece together all the events of our carrier's life more than thirty years after the fact is a bold undertaking. While there is no way to determine the exact number of officers and men who once called CV-CVA-CVS-39 their home, it's estimated to be close to 50,000. So, to a large extent, during the twenty years she was in service, there are 50,000 stories to tell, not one. Each of us has his own recollection of these events, and I can only attempt to highlight some of them. This book will be an attempt to catalog and distill those experiences into what I hope is a concise, and yet encompassing treatment of the saga of the Champ. In doing so, perhaps this account will revive some long-dormant and I hope, mostly happy memories of your time on board.

I have taken the liberty of dipping in to the vast number of letters I've received as editor of THE CHAMP to give this chronicle the intimacy of your personal experiences. Just as a human life is more than a collection of statistics, the real story of the Champ must relate directly to those who made up her living and breathing crew. Everyone is important to this telling, from the admiral who flew his starred flag, to the mess cook who ladled your hash. In the end, it is these men who bring life to the ship and her memory. They came from all forty-eight states, with a sprinkling from Hawaii and the Philippines. Some were professional career officers, and others were enlisted men with red service stripes crowding their sleeves. But to the vast majority, LAKE CHAMPLAIN would be the only ship of their enlistment, often coming right on the heels of boot camp, and immediately launching them on their own personal voyages of discovery. Perhaps it is these sailors, of all of those who served in her, who have the most cherished memories. For most of them, their time on board was a true rite of passage.

For many who walked her decks from World War II, through Korea and into the Sixties, our carrier would take the place of a college campus or a trade apprenticeship. A new word would enter their vocabulary: "shipmate." There is no similar expression in civilian life. And for some, LAKE CHAMPLAIN would be the defining influence in their lives. For the first time, other lives would depend on their skill and knowledge, and the responsibility was a heavy one. That move from home and Mom's cooking was a rough one, often compared to a bucket of ice water in the face—the main consolation being that we had a lot of company. But soon, faster than most of us thought possible, LAKE CHAMPLAIN became a home away from home. It was, in truth, a love-hate relationship, as anything that intense must be, but most of us now only recall the happy times, the crazy times.

As time passed, we'd discover that we were part of a great fraternity—those who had served their country in the military. Being a member of this special group would always set us apart and trigger a thousand sea stories. And, after forty or fifty years, some of us still use the words "head" and "deck," and expressions like "squared away" in our daily conversations. And I'll bet many of you still ask your wife: "Honey, what's for chow?"

Unlike today's Navy, there are only men in this story. But just about all of them had women; in love with them, married to them, or glad to see them go. Most of the conversations on board revolved around the opposite sex, and just about every locker boasted a wife or girlfriend's photo taped to the door. But of necessity, the one heroine who completely dominated their lives would be the ship itself.

This is her story.

BACKGROUND AND EVOLUTION OF CARRIER AVIATION

An aircraft carrier is a hybrid. If one thinks about it for a moment, a less likely designed vessel never went to sea. The very idea of flying and landing planes on a moving deck is mind-boggling. I guess we'd have to compare this unique concept to the revolutionary Polaris missile program developed by Admiral Rickover—guided missiles launched underwater to surface and fly thousands of miles to targets well inland.

And like the missile program, carrier aviation had to operate on two levels simultaneously: developing both the aircraft and the ships and technology to both launch and recover them. The nearest commercial corollary I can think of is the automobile industry where not only the engines had to be perfected, but the oil refined into gasoline, and tires, batteries, and roads improved to accept this new mode of transport. For most of the early decades of the 20th Century, most of the admirals had little faith in the value of these ships. Big-gun battleships and cruisers would always carry the battle to the enemy fleet, their main batteries hurling tons of explosive power up to twenty miles away. What these older officers didn't realize, however, was that the carrier's main "battery" was her air group, and that air force would eventually have the potential to carry twenty times the destructive power of the largest battleship's broadside hundreds of miles, not twenty.

Oddly, it all began with the French. The concept of an aircraft carrier—a ship capable of launching and recovering aircraft is as old as the military use of flying machines. The first detailed proposals for an aircraft carrier were published in 1909, the same year the U.S. Army accepted the world's first flying machine for military service. The aircraft carrier was first described by French inventor Clement Ader in his book L'Aviation Militaire. Ader, whose genius produced many innovations in telephonic communications and ground transportation, built several steam-powered flying machines during the last two decades of the 19th century. Few of these actually "flew" in our sense of the word, but he created the real possibility of flight. But his greatest spur to carrier aviation appeared in his book in this quote: "an aircraft-carrying ship becomes indispensable. These vessels will be constructed on plans very different from those now in use. Firstly, the deck will be clear of all obstacles; flat, as wide as possible, without spoiling the nautical lines of the hull: it will have the aspect of a landing field. The speed of the vessel shall be equal to at least that of a cruiser, and even exceed it. The housing of the planes will necessarily be arranged below the deck. This between-deck space will be reached by a freight elevator sufficiently long and wide to receive a plane with its wings folded. To one side there will be the service personnel workshop, charged with the repair and maintenance of planes in constant readiness for take-off. The deck field should be clear of all obstacles. On launching aircraft the forward end should be completely free. When returning, the after part will be free." So, in 1909, a Frenchman had grasped just about every principle of carrier aviation. However, it would be other nations that would take up the challenge.

Still, aircraft were not yet ready to take off from the pitching deck of a ship at sea. The United States was first in flying off and landing aircraft on a ship, but the actual development of aircraft carriers as a distinct type of ship would be initiated by Great Britain. The U.S. Navy sent two officers to watch Orville Wright conduct demonstration flights for the Army at Fort Myer (near Washington, D.C.) in September 1908. The following August, the U.S. Naval Attaché in Paris, Commander F.L. Chapin, was directed to attend an aviation meet in Reims. He was impressed by the men and machines he observed, and submitted a proposal that the U.S. Navy modify one of the new 16,000-ton CONNECTICUT-Class battleships to launch a Wright airplane. He also recommended that auxiliary ships be constructed with flight decks for aircraft operations. His report, which also discussed the possibility of aircraft making night attacks on warships, was duly filed by the Navy Department, apparently without arousing any interest.

The Navy's interest in aviation was spurred by Glen Curtiss. In 1908, the thirty-year-old Curtiss designed, built and flew his own airplane. Talk about a "one man band!" He won wide publicity in May 1910, when he flew the 143 miles from Albany to New York City in two hours and fifty-minutes to capture the NEW YORK WORLD'S $10,000 prize. Jumping the gun, the WORLD claimed, "The battles of the future will be fought in the air! The aeroplane will decide the destiny of nations."

The newspaper set up a bombing range near Hammondsport, New York, arranging floats to simulate the 500 x 90-foot shape of a battleship. Curtiss flew over in his plane, and dropped 8-inch lengths of lead pipe. Rear Admiral William Kimball, one of the observers declared: "There are defects for war purposes: lack of ability to operate in average weather at sea; signally its approach by the noise of its motor; the impossibility of controlling its height and speed to predict accurate bombing ranges, and the difficulty of hitting from a height great enough to give a chance of getting within effective range."

The press interpreted the results quite differently, contrasting the price of "an aeroplane (costing a few hundred dollars) being able to destroy a battleship (costing many millions)." THE NEW YORK TIMES acknowledged a "new menace to armored fleets of war." The aircraft versus battleship controversy was fired before the Navy had its first flying machine. The U.S. Army had but one plane!

Captain Washington Irving Chambers, assistant to the Secretary of the Navy, was instructed to keep abreast of aviation matters. In a few months, learning that the Germans were planning to conduct experiments launching aircraft from the liner AMERIKA, he obtained approval to fly an airplane from a Navy ship. On 9 November 1910, the cruiser BIRMINGHAM was made available for the experiment. Next, a plane and pilot were needed. Captain Chambers hurried to an air meet at Halethorpe, Maryland, in the hope of inducing Wilbur Wright to make the flight. But Wright had already left the field, and attempts to convince him by phone were futile. Walking away from the phone, Chambers encountered Eugene Ely, an exhibition pilot who worked for Curtiss. Chambers explained his project to Ely, and the aviator reportedly exclaimed, " Let me fly off your ship!" The flight was scheduled for 14 November.

If the sailors on board BIRMINGHAM wondered why they had to work on a Sunday to construct a wooden platform 83 feet long and 24 feet wide over the ship's bow, they no doubt thought the entire U.S. Navy had gone mad when an airplane was hoisted aboard the next morning. In his first attempt to take off from a ship, Ely was using a Curtiss pusher biplane, which had been fitted with floats in the event he would have to come down on the water. No one really trusted these newfangled machines!

On 14 November 1910, BIRMINGHAM steamed out into Hampton Roads, Virginia, followed by four destroyers. The BIRMINGHAM was to cruise in the Chesapeake Bay and head into the wind at about ten knots for the take-off. The destroyers would be stationed along the route the plane was to follow up the Elizabeth River towards Norfolk Navy Yard. Shortly after noon BIRMINGHAM got underway, but heavy rain squalls forced a postponement, and she anchored until the weather cleared. At about three o'clock, the weather seemed to be easing, and the order was given to weigh anchor and proceed with the flight. Ely started up the plane's 50-horsepower engine. The anchor came up very slowly, and Ely grew impatient. Giving his mechanic the signal to release the plane, he raced the engine at full power. There were only 57 feet of deck in front of his plane as it started rolling down the inclined ramp at 3:16 P.M.

When the plane reached the end of the ramp, it disappeared over the edge and glided down to the water 38 feet below. Ely pulled back on the stick, but it was too late. The plane's wheels, floats, and propeller tips touched the water. Both blades of the propeller were damaged, but the wooden prop never stopped turning. Neither the speed nor the control of the aircraft was affected. Slowly, the plane began to climb skyward. The sailors on the ship cheered, and BIRMINGHAM'S whistle announced the feat to nearby ships and small craft.

Once airborne, Ely became lost because of the poor visibility and some water that had splashed on his goggles. He landed as soon as he could, coming down at Willoughby Spite, near Norfolk, 2 1/2 miles from BIRMINGHAM. The first flight from a ship was now history.

The year 1910 ended on another bright note for naval aviation. On 23 December, the Navy took up an offer by Glen Curtiss to teach a naval officer to fly without charge. Lieutenant Theodore Ellyson was ordered to report for flight training to the Curtiss camp at North Island, San Diego, California.

The next logical step was to land an airplane on a ship. After consultation with Curtiss and Ely, Captain Chambers made arrangements to use the 13,600-ton armored cruiser PENNSYLVANIA for this experiment. In the Navy Yard at Mare Island, California, a sloped wooden platform 120 feet long and 32 feet wide was built over the ship's stern and after turret. Lieutenant Ellyson suggested the use of an "arresting gear" of sandbags to halt the plane within the limits of the landing platform. Utilizing a system similar to that used to check automobiles at racing meets, Navy men installed 22 pairs of 50-lb. sandbags along the flight deck at three-foot intervals, each pair connected by a line stretched taut 12 inches above the deck. Three pairs of hooks were fitted to Ely's biplane to snag these lines as the plane skimmed over the deck. A canvas screen barrier was erected at the forward end of the platform to prevent the plane from crashing into the ship's superstructure in the event the arresting equipment failed. (One must remember that these planes were very light indeed.) And in case of emergency, life preservers and expert swimmers were made ready aboard the ship, and lifeboats stood by alongside.

On 18 January 1911, Ely took off from a San Francisco airfield and flew out to the PENNSYLVANIA moored in the bay. It was planned that the ship would be underway for the test, but the captain felt there was insufficient maneuvering room, and the ship remained at anchor. Big ship skippers were not very receptive to these new ideas.

Just as during the take-off from a ship two months earlier, the weather was poor. Ely flew over the PENNSYLVANIA and then made a long, low approach to the ship's stern. With the wind behind him (a dangerous situation), Ely pulled the plane up to clear the stern of the cruiser and then cut his engine. Tailwinds carried him over the first eleven arresting lines. At this point, his hook snared a line and with a deck run of scarcely 30 feet! Ely's plane came to a halt at 11:01 A.M. Scores of sailors had crammed the cruiser's superstructure, and a great roar filled the air. Ely's wife greeted him and rewarded him with a hug and a kiss, exclaiming, "I knew you could do it!" The commanding officer of PENNSYLVANIA declared: "This is the most important landing of a bird since the dove flew back to the Ark." Later, he wrote to the Navy Department in tortured prose: "I desire to place myself on record as positively assured of the importance of the aeroplane in future naval warfare, certainly for scouting purposes."

Ely had lunch aboard the cruiser, and at 11:58, with the arresting gear removed from the wooden deck, he reversed the procedure and took off without incident. He flew to the airfield without delay and landed successfully.

The birth of carrier aviation was assured.

More experiments took place, this time using seaplanes. Somehow, the Navy wasn't quite convinced of the safety of landing land planes on a wooden deck. But in March 1911, Congress appropriated $25,000 for the Navy "to be used for experimental operations in the development of aviation for naval purposes" This led to the Wright Brothers offering to train a naval pilot contingent upon the Navy buying one aeroplane from them for $50,000. Lieutenant John Rodgers was ordered to report to their field for training. He became the Navy's second aviator. Captain Chambers then arranged to purchase three planes—two from Curtiss and one from the Wright Brothers with the money Congress had allotted. On 11 July 1911, the Navy's first aircraft, a Curtiss A-1 hydroplane, was flown successfully. (For those of you with vivid memories of World War II, Curtiss Aircraft Company produced one of the most famous fighters of the war, the P-40. This plane became famous as the mainstay of the Flying Tigers in China.)

All this rapid growth was not without loss, however, and Eugene Ely was killed in an air crash only 18 months after his initial flight.

Naval aviation was "blooded" in Mexico in April 1914 when in response to a revolution in that country, 12 hydroplanes based on the battleship MISSISSIPPI and our old friend BIRMINGHAM made reconnaissance flights over the enemy lines near Vera Cruz, Mexico. Some were hit by ground fire, but no casualties were sustained.

When the First World War started, Congress authorized more money for naval aviation, and the pace quickened. On 5 November 1915, an AB-2 flying boat was successfully catapulted from the stern of the battleship NORTH CAROLINA while she was anchored off Pensacola, Florida.

Like all wars, the First World War accelerated the development of every weapons system. The British, who possessed the world's largest fleet, were slow at first to embrace the idea of flying planes from ships. After observing the results of America's efforts and the first German attempts, the Royal Navy finally joined the ranks. In 1912, Parliament called for the establishment of the Royal Flying Corps, which would have both a military wing and a naval wing.

In August 1914, war came to Great Britain, and aircraft were dispatched to France. The naval wing was given responsibility for the aerial defense of the island. The Germans had made great strides in the development of huge Zeppelins, and their use as bombers wasn't lost on the British. On 22 September 1914, a four-plane raid was organized with 20-lb. bombs against the Zeppelin base at Düsseldorf. Three soldiers on the ground were killed, but no damage was sustained by the airships. This was the first combat use of aircraft in the war. On 8 October another raid had better luck, destroying an airship hangar and the Zeppelin inside. This was the first time that aircraft of any nation had struck beyond the battlefield. These attacks were the beginnings of what would become known as strategic bombing.

It was in the Mediterranean that the first real air-sea action took place. Torpedo-carrying seaplanes had been perfected by the Royal Naval Air arm just prior to the war, and on 11 August a Turkish ship was sighted on the north side of the Sea of Marmara. Flight Commander C.H. Edmonds maneuvered into an attack position, cut his engine and glided in for the kill. He released his torpedo from an altitude of 15 feet when he was 300 yards from the ship. Edmonds saw his torpedo strike, and the ship began to settle in the water. A few more attacks took place, but with the end of the Dardanelles campaign, the action shifted once more to the North Sea.

On 15 November, Flight-Sub-Lieutenant H.F. Towler flew a Bristol Scout with a wheeled undercarriage from the flying deck of the seaplane carrier VINDEX. There were no landing facilities, so the plane "ditched" alongside. During the Battle of Jutland, naval aircraft attempted a few attacks but were unsuccessful. It wasn't until 1917 that the first combat strikes were launched from ships. Platforms were ordered built on a number of battleships and cruisers, and soon Sopwith "Pups" were flying from these decks regularly. On August 21st, a Sopwith Pup flying from the cruiser YARMOUTH attacked a Zeppelin and shot it down in flames. While these missions had some success, there was a need for a ship that could carry multiple aircraft—a true aircraft carrier!

In March 1917, a flight deck was built on what had been planned as a light cruiser: FURIOUS. She was a huge ship for that modest designation, carrying an 18-inch gun! (These gigantic weapons wouldn't be utilized again until the Japanese YAMATO and MUSASHI appeared in World War II.) FURIOUS was 787 feet long and displaced nearly 20,000 tons. Her power plant could move her at 31 knots, ideal for launching heavier planes. Her "air group" consisted of four seaplanes and six wheeled aircraft. A hydraulic-operated elevator could move the aircraft from the flight deck to the hangar below. Unfortunately, she only had the ability to launch planes, not recover them. Her aircraft had to fly to land-based airfields after their mission. She was a hybrid—half cruiser, half carrier.

This situation proved intolerable for the Flight Commander, E.H. Dunning. On 2 August 1917, he approached the stern of FURIOUS flying a Sopwith Pup. The carrier was steaming into a 21-knot wind at a speed of 26 knots. This, in effect, put a 47-knot wind across the flight deck. As this was just about the landing speed of the little fighter, the plane would practically hover over the deck. Commander Dunning flew along the side of the ship, and when abreast of the bridge, he sideslipped to port and cut his engine as he came over the flight deck. When his plane got close to the deck, several crewmen grabbed straps attached to the plane and brought it to a stop. It was the first landing of a plane on a warship underway.

Unfortunately, conditions wouldn't always be ideal, and a few weeks later during another landing, the wind was too strong for the crewmen to secure his plane, and Dunning was blown over the side and crashed in the sea. The impact apparently knocked him unconscious, and he drowned before a boat could reach him. Modifications continued to be made on FURIOUS in 1918, but she was neither fish nor fowl. As an aircraft carrier she was a total failure. The hot stack gases affected the density of the air over her stern and her bridge superstructure created dangerous eddies, making landing extremely difficult. In the end, FURIOUS was used solely as a "take-off" carrier.

In the fall off 1918, the British began building the first of their "real" carriers: ARGUS, HERMES and EAGLE. They either were completely flush deck, like ARGUS, or had an "island" on the starboard side. But the war ended before either ship could be employed in combat. They would be invaluable as training vessels in the Twenties and Thirties.

Britain wasn't the only nation experimenting with aircraft carriers. Soon the United States, France and Japan joined her.

We went through the same growing pains as the British, utilizing platforms built on gun turrets in battleships and cruisers, but this system was soon abandoned in favor of a real carrier. The platforms later became steel tracks that were used to launch seaplanes for observation. Those aircraft were launched by the energy from a five-inch shell.

Our first "aircraft carrier" was a converted collier, or coal ship, the JUPITER. In 1922, she was changed into USS LANGLEY, CV-1, and became a floating classroom for US naval carrier aviation. With a length of only 534 feet and a speed of barely 15 knots, she soon became too small and slow to keep pace with the development of naval aircraft. And yet, LANGLEY was invaluable in the perfection of launching, recovering and the storage of all the early planes.

Langley CV-1

She could carry and operate over double that of any carrier of her day. In her holds, she could carry 55 planes, an air group which has never been bettered for a carrier of her tonnage. The rectangular flight deck, not tapered at the bows (as in the British flat-tops), assisted in arranging more aircraft on deck. In was also in LANGLEY that the art of tying down aircraft on deck, rather than fencing them in with a palisade to prevent them from being blown over the side, was perfected. As a result of experience gained in LANGLEY, parallel cross-wires were substituted for fore and aft arrester wires. Later, it was on her flight deck that the first barriers were designed, enabling aircraft to be serviced forward on deck. Through her 15 years of service, LANGLEY has to be remembered as the most successful experimental carrier of all time.

In a harbinger of future events, most of the opposition to our carrier development and naval aviation in general, came not from Congress but from another service. After the war, the leading proponent of a separate air force was the Army general, Billy Mitchell. Mitchell came into conflict with the Navy when, in the early 1920's, he stated that air power would render surface ships incapable of operating as they had before. During a Congressional hearing a little while later, he challenged the Navy to test his claim. Actually, the Navy was very interested in performing these tests for other reasons. They wanted to see the effects of aerial bombs on the armor of their warships.

While agreeing with Mitchell that enough planes carrying large enough bombs could sink surface warships, Admiral Sims, the CNO, felt that this was a perfect argument for the construction of a fleet of aircraft carriers. The battle between the Army and the Navy continued.

A series of tests were held on various obsolete American vessels and captured German warships, culminating in the famous bombing raid on the 22,800-ton German battleship, OSTFRIESLAND. This ship was considered the equal of anything afloat.

First the Navy and Marines dropped a series of 600-pound bombs. Two scored direct hits, but there was no serious damage below decks.

On the morning of 21 July 1921, eight Army MB-2b bombers dropped six 1000-pound bombs—three scoring direct hits, but there was still no appreciable damage. Finally, the Army planes flew out with specially designed 2,000-pound bombs. There were a few near-misses, and one direct hit. The OSTFRIESLAND sank later that day. In spite of the headlines, the Navy was convinced that a modern battleship, underway and manned with a capable crew, could withstand a great deal of damage before sinking. The critical issue was a moving ship as opposed to a stationary one. The controversy continued unabated until Mitchell went over the edge with inflammatory statements impugning the integrity of other high-ranking naval officers. He was later court-martialed and left the service.

In an odd turn of events, the very peacetime tightening of the purse strings led to the buildings of some of our largest carriers.

Carriers in the Pacific 1944

The Washington Naval Conference of 1921 was an attempt to limit the size of capital ships of all nations. The main targets of this disarmament were the battleships and battle-cruisers, which at that time ruled the seas. As a means of "recycling" these giant warships already under construction, the treaty allowed the allied nations to swap carriers for the battle-cruisers that were close to completion. Initially, these ships were to be limited to 27,000 tons, but because of severe unemployment in the shipyards, a concession was granted to go to 33,000 tons. Hence, LEXINGTON and SARATOGA were born. Both were completed in 1927.

Never before had carriers on this scale ever been attempted by any navy. Their design was exceptional for its audacity and far-sightedness. With a flight deck of 888 feet and a huge hangar deck that could accommodate 90 aircraft, these vessels proved capacious enough for the largest and heaviest monoplanes of World War II. Their boilers could deliver 180,000 horsepower through turbo-electric engines driving four shafts and developing an astonishing speed of 34 knots. This made these giants the fastest warships of their displacement in the world. Their size wouldn't be equaled until the MIDWAY Class arrived on the scene after the war. The newer "super flat-tops" even imitated the large square funnels of LEXINGTON that were so distinctive in their silhouettes. After the war, a movement for an independent air force was spearheaded by General Billy Mitchell.

In the 1930s, President Roosevelt initiated a building program that included RANGER, YORKTOWN, ENTERPRISE, WASP, and HORNET. In tandem with the earlier LEXINGTON and SARATOGA, these fleet carriers would form the backbone of our striking power across the Pacific. In spite of a great depression that shrunk the budgets of the Army to dangerous levels, FDR's love of the Navy gave the senior service the flat-tops it would need in that critical first year of the war.

Fortunately, none of our carriers were at Pearl Harbor on 7 December. ENTERPRISE had been scheduled to arrive the day before, but heavy seas delayed the refueling of her destroyer screen for 36 hours, and she was saved. She would go on to become the most decorated ship in the Navy, acquiring twenty out of a possible 22 battle stars—far more than any other ship.

RANGER had too limiting a cruising range for the Pacific, so she remained in the Atlantic, carrying out raids on Norway and covering our landings in North Africa. The brunt of meeting the Japanese onslaught fell to the remaining six flattops. Brutal clashes at Coral Sea, Midway and Guadalcanal whittled down this force until in October 1942, we were left with just one serviceable flight deck: ENTERPRISE (SARATOGA was laid up from damage incurred by a torpedo). Fortunately, help was on the way.

In 1940, FDR's pet project, a Two-Ocean Navy, was laid down and none too soon. Conservative Congressmen didn't want to spend the money, but the fall of France forced their hand. It was a huge building program—the largest ever attempted in history: ten fast battleships and battle-cruisers, scores of cruisers, hundreds of destroyers and submarines, and countless auxiliaries. But the centerpiece of the program, and one that would change the course of naval warfare, was the ESSEX-Class carrier.

As our carrier construction progressed through the years, from LEXINGTON-SARATOGA; RANGER; ENTERPRISE-YORKTOWN, and finally WASP-HORNET, each new ship incorporated improvements over her predecessor. As a result the ESSEX-Class CVs were the most advanced carriers of their time. As the long line of giant flat-tops joined the fleet, additional modifications were made to take advantage of the battle experience gained in that first, hard year of the war. 1942 cost us four fleet CVs plus our original CV-1, LANGLEY, later converted to a seaplane tender. These ESSEXs would have vastly improved fire-fighting protection, as well as double-bottoms against torpedo damage. In spite of the horrific destruction rendered by the kamikazes, not one ESSEX-Class CV was lost.

These new ships would be fast and highly maneuverable. Weighing in at 36,000 tons—full load, with a flight deck of 888 feet, they carried an air group of up to 110 planes, depending on aircraft type. Originally they were armed with 12 five-inch dual-purpose guns, as well as 72 40mm and 52 20mm anti-aircraft weapons. Powered by four shafts generating 150,000 horsepower, their eight boilers could speed them at over 32 knots. With greatly increased fuel storage, the ESSEXs were ideal platforms for the vast reaches of the Pacific, and guaranteed their usage when newer, faster and heavier aircraft were developed in later years. As originally designed, the vessels had an aviation fuel capacity of 240,000 gallons, but as the later CVs were built that was increased. Remarkably, some of these ships were still in active service close to forty-years after their commission! Twenty-four ESSEX-Class fleet carriers were completed, and they, more than any other weapons system, changed the course of the war against Japan.

CV-39

The keel of the 15th ESSEX-Class ship, USS LAKE CHAMPLAIN (CV-39), was laid down on 15 March 1943 at Norfolk Navy Yard. Constructed entirely in a dry-dock (a breakthrough concept at that time), she was named for the Battle of Lake Champlain during the War of 1812. At that time, aircraft carriers were named for famous fighting ships (RANGER, INTREPID, ENTERPRISE) and battles (LEXINGTON, YORKTOWN, VALLEY FORGE).

THE BATTLE OF LAKE CHAMPLAIN

The battle of Lake Champlain was a pivotal one for the Americans engaged. The British knew that this was an important lake where victory might be bought cheaply. Lake Champlain—the water highroad to the heart of New York, was ideally located for imperial strategy, since its seizure would cut New England off from the rest of the states. Both sides prepared for battle by building frigates and sloops from scratch. Cutting down trees in the surrounding forests, they went to work with a fury. Commodore McDonough, the officer in charge, had a new type of vessel built for him—a corvette named SARATOGA, carrying 26 guns. On September 11, 1814, along with three other small brigs and a force untrained for the sea, he faced a well-armed British force of Royal Navy men with a first-class frigate CONFIANCE with 38 guns and three other sloops.

The battle went bad for the Americans early on, but as the afternoon progressed, the new British mounts began to work loose, causing their shot to ride high over the American ships. McDonough's long gunnery training sessions paid off, as his men shot low and straight. The British commander was killed, and with their frigate badly smashed, her crew ceased fire. It looked like a draw, but McDonough had prepared for this moment. With anchors off the bow and long cables to the stern, he set the crew to heaving on those cables, turning SARATOGA around and offering a fresh battery to fire broadside after broadside into the CONFIANCE. The British tars broke and forced their commander to haul down their flag. The battle of Lake Champlain and the War of 1812 was decided. Captain Thomas McDonough sent this message to the Secretary of the Navy: "The Almighty has been pleased to grant us a signal victory on Lake Champlain, in the capture of one frigate, one brig, and two sloops of war of the enemy."

CARRYING THE NAME TO SEA

The first ship to bear this name was a small ammunition carrier that served during the First World War. Her career spanned less than two years, and as a result, there's little information about her. However, in 1997, I was fortunate enough to receive a letter from one of her ex-crewmen, Oscar Barcliff. At the time, he was 96 years old and living in a retirement home. Before he died, he sent me a letter describing his time on board.

"After my enlistment, I was sent to San Diego, California, to the Naval Training station. Upon completion of boot camp, approximately ten weeks, I was sent across country by train to Norfolk, Virginia. While I was awaiting assignment, I was awakened very early on 22 October 1918, and told to report to USS LAKE CHAMPLAIN, an ammunition ship."

"Before daylight, that very same day, we sailed under darken ship conditions. No one appeared to know our destination until we were well out at sea. Then we were told that we would be part of a large convoy bound for the North Sea. Later, we were detached from the convoy and told to sail independently for Inverness, Scotland. Since we were carrying munitions, we were always kept far away from other ships, and often out of sight of the convoy."

"We followed a zigzag course and were always on the alert for U-boats, mines, and other ships. LAKE CHAMPLAIN had been a coal-burning freighter prior to the war, and had been converted to an ammunition ship. She carried provisions for about 30 days in a large walk-in icebox. The crew was small, but tightly knit and friendly."

"Approaching the North Sea and Scotland, we encountered a large storm which knocked our short-wave radio. Radio communication was at that time unreliable at best, and we sailed on, oblivious to all outside news. LAKE CHAMPLAIN therefore didn't receive any news about the Armistice, which occurred on 11 November."

"Coming out of a fog bank near Scotland, we sighted three German battleships. Everyone could feel the hair stand up on the back of their neck, expecting at any moment to get blown to bits. When they failed to open fire, we thought we might be too close for them to fire without endangering themselves, and that they were just waiting until the range opened. Just then, our radio operator received a garbled message that the war was over. Everyone was overjoyed with relief and happiness. The first thing we did was turn on all the lights. We continued on to our port, and moored at Inverness. Because the war was over, no one seemed to know what to do with our ammunition, but eventually it was all unloaded. Everyone in town was celebrating. Horns and sirens were blowing, bells ringing, and even in tight Scotland, none of us in uniform could buy a drink."

"After a long layover, we took on fresh supplies and finally got underway for home in January 1919. We all expected to be home real fast, with a light ship and a straight course, but it was not to be. A terrible storm hit us, with tremendous seas turning us every way but loose. A large range broke free, and it battered back and forth until it was secured with much difficulty. The storm raged on for three days, and no one got any sleep or hot food. Then, just when the sea calmed, our steering cable parted, and we drifted 300 miles off course, mostly in the fog. The return voyage to Norfolk took 27 days!"

"When we arrived in port, we went into the yards to make necessary repairs. Sea-worthy once more, LAKE CHAMPLAIN was re-loaded with ammunition and we sailed for Guantanamo Bay, Cuba. Our shells were unloaded and later used for naval maneuvers. We then returned to Norfolk, where the ship was decommissioned, much to the crew's regret." Oscar Barcliff died a few years after sending us this only account of the first LAKE CHAMPLAIN. We're indebted to him for this fine chronicle.

USS LAKE CHAMPLAIN CV-39

THE EARLY YEARS: 1945-47

Our carrier was built from funds derived from a War Bond drive in New York State, which borders on Lake Champlain. Because of this generosity, the Champ's first skipper adopted the state's motto, "Excelsior," as her own. A handsome bronze plaque commemorated this on the starboard side of the hangar deck. Rear Admiral C.H. Jones, Commandant of Norfolk Navy Yard, commissioned the ship and gave the welcoming address. Not showing any favoritism, the wife of Vermont's U.S. Senator, Warren Austin, was invited to christen the carrier (Vermont also borders Lake Champlain). The yard workmen hastily completed their tasks, and CV-39 was ready on 3 June 1945.

The ship was built in dry-dock, for which reason the conventional christening ceremonies were postponed until the date of commissioning. Perhaps there is no better description of the emotional impact of these ceremonies than a letter from Lt. Al White to his parents. It was discovered in his personal effects by his grandson after he died. "Dear Mother and Father: I sincerely wish that you could have been here for this day and that I might have arranged it. It's a thrill for me to have witnessed this inspiring event, and I'm most assuredly pleased and proud to be on board. As I feel this great pride, I can't help wanting you both to know that wherever we go, it will be part of America."

"Each state is represented on board among the officers and men. I will often think of you and know that if I am able to do a creditable job it is because of my upbringing, your love and the traditions of my family."

The Champ's first skipper was Captain Logan Ramsey, a man famous in his own right. On 7 December 1941, then Lieutenant Commander Ramsey was the Operations Officer of PATWING TWO serving on Ford Island at Pearl Harbor. He had received a message about 0715 about a PBY dropping a depth charge on a submarine at the harbor entrance, and he was trying to confirm it while laying out a search plan. At 0755, he was standing at colors when a plane flew very low over his position. At first he thought it was some Army pilot "flat-hatting," but when he saw the plane drop a bomb, he exclaimed, "That's a Jap!" With that, he raced into the radio room and told the startled operator, "Send this in plain language to all stations and ships: AIR RAID PEARL HARBOR. THIS IS NO DRILL!" His message electrified the nation and the world.

Now, he was taking his first aircraft carrier command to sea. During June and July, CV-39, now affectionately known to the crew as "THE GREAT LAKE," embarked on her shakedown cruise to the Caribbean. She carried out simulated attacks on Culebra Island, near Roosevelt Roads, Puerto Rico. The Champ's first "foreign" liberty was held for all hands at Guantanamo Bay, Cuba. For some shipmates, this was their first encounter with island rum, and it produced the carrier's first "casualties." Air operations were carried out in the next few weeks, unfortunately costing the lives of some of the pilots, as the wings tore loose during their dive-bombing runs. Another day, a freak accident took the life of an innocent bystander, if such a phrase is possible on an aircraft carrier where just about everyone is vulnerable. Artis Chastain described what happened: "On the flight deck the planes were being readied to be stowed below and their wings were folded. On this plane, a Grumman Hellcat, this meant that the leading edges of the wings, where the machine guns were located, were facing downward. I recall the incident vividly because I was standing next to the sailor who was killed. We had just come out of the shower, and gone to our lockers to get dressed when he was hit. Someone who was sitting in the cockpit inadvertently pressed the firing button for the guns, which were supposed to be empty. But there were three 50-caliber rounds in the 6th gun, and they were discharged into the flight deck. One of the bullets went through the deck, and hit the sailor in the back of the neck and exited through his abdomen. Modern day sailors may find it difficult to believe that a bullet could pierce this deck, but the flight deck was wood, just like the other ESSEX-Class Carriers. Our flat-tops wouldn't have armored flight decks until the arrival of the MIDWAY Class just after World War II."

Often, in all the statistics surrounding a shakedown cruise, it's easy to forget what this meant to a young sailor experiencing his first days aboard ship. Bill Katz had these humorous memories to share. "Ah, the sailor goes to sea and he's at peace at last. I can at last realize the great thrill a sailor gets exploring the vast wonders of the ocean. Don't look now, for if you do, you'll find me hanging over the side feeding the fish! As for the waves, we haven't left the Chesapeake yet, and it's like a swimming pool out there. Oh well, maybe I should have joined the Army."

"As for the chow, delicious, brother, delicious! Fried pork chops sizzling in hot grease, with creamy mashed potatoes, covered with brown greasy gravy. For dessert, you get a delicious pudding topped with a luscious-looking syrup. Oh! Oh! My poor stomach." After settling down, Bill discovered the joys of living out of a sea bag. "You have to understand the problems of living out of a sea bag. Picture yourself in a room with all your possessions, including your toilet articles. You're wondering where you're going to store all this stuff. Suddenly, someone enters and hands you a bag, which is approximately five feet deep and two feet wide. The bag is made of canvas with a drawstring on top. The problem is what you should put in the bag first, considering that all your stuff must go in there and you must live out of it. Regardless of what you place on the bottom, invariably it's the first thing that's needed. I have no solution to this problem. No matter how much my shipmates and I mulled this over, it remains one of the great unsolved mysteries of the world! Hammocks weren't much better. I remained pretty comfortable, until one night when I had a little accident. My hammock was slung above a table at which several of my shipmates were playing cards. One swabbie bid seven spades and found me in his lap. Once I became more secure, things improved, but not too much. Our compartment was just outside the Boiler Room, thus our space stood at 110 degrees, day and night! I was a rather thin person and after two weeks in Dante's Inferno, I began to resemble a Japanese prisoner of war!"

"Around the first of July, we shoved off for our shakedown cruise. Our destination was unknown, although scuttlebutt had it pretty well that Cuba was our destination. The Captain, after giving us the official dope, stated emphatically that we would all have to work hard to become a well-trained fighting team. With that, he ends and the drills begin. When I say 'drills,' I mean DRILLS!"

"Upon wakening at 0530 (that is if you could get any sleep with aircraft engines going full blast on the hangar deck all night) you're immediately thrust into 'war' by the sounding of General Quarters. You finish that just in time for a fire drill, which of course is just a little smoke bomb thrown by some slaphappy officer. In the middle of breakfast, you are again interrupted by an

USS Lake Champlain CV-39, September 1945

3 June 1945, A Champ Is Born!

BUILD FOR VICTORY
WORK SAFELY

alarm sounding Torpedo Defense, and you charge up to a gun mount and load dummy ammunition into the gun. What about breakfast? Well, you didn't want it anyway, did you? After a week of running around like maniacs we sight Cuba. The countryside was beautiful, and I was just about losing my mind thinking about setting foot in a foreign country. Boy, just wait for Liberty Call. I'm going to be the first one off the gangway. Well, I certainly was the first one off the ship, but I stepped into a boat, and, armed with a paintbrush and a paint bucket, spent my first day in Cuba painting the outside of the ship."

"The next day, I finally made it ashore and proceeded to walk to a store to buy some souvenirs. After walking miles through clouds of dust, I finally found a ship's store and decided to see what it held. But the place was mobbed, and after waiting for hours, I finally reached the counter only to be told that they were closed for the day! The next day I finally made it to a canteen. In spite of the usual mob scene, I finally elbowed my way to the bar and after yelling, 'Joe' at the Cuban bartender, I order a steak sandwich and a Coke. Of course I got just what I ordered, a ham sandwich and a bottle of Cuban beer!"

"After engaging in more drills, we were congratulated by Captain Ramsey. But before we could relax, the captain said we had to undergo one last drill: a Battle Problem, and have it witnessed by the Admiral and his inspection party. Ramsey said he wanted to make it realistic by turning on the hangar bay sprinklers. We picked up the Admiral, and with General Quarters sounding we ran to our battle stations. From the loud speakers we hear 'bombs' hitting the ship, so we figured everything was going as planned. We secured from General Quarters, and started down the ladder to the hangar deck. And there before us was the sprinkler system going full blast. Water was flying all over the place, with about five inches on deck. We soon learned that the admiral and his party had become so drenched that he ordered his plane and flew off in a hurry. Commanders were screaming at each other; Lieutenants were arguing with Ensigns, and of course the Ensigns were chewing out the crew. If nothing else the Battle Problem was too realistic, but we knew that if all else failed, those sprinklers were going to make like Niagara Falls! There was about $50,000 damage, but I guess it was better to find out now that the system didn't work in battle."

"But all things come to an end, and that included World War II. Soon our planes were gone and thousands of portable racks were installed on the hangar decks. We took off at full speed to pick up our troops and pretty soon I sighted England. But Captain Ramsey said that because of tight troop schedules, we only have one day of liberty. You guessed it. It wasn't my day! But just so I could say I was in England, I carried a trashcan to the dock. Boy, am I clicking off countries, or what?"

USS Lake Champlain

"After three more voyages to Europe to pickup the troops, we finally returned to Newport News and the LAKE CHAMPLAIN is laid up. I imagine that some day they'll pour concrete around her and declare her a state shrine in the remembrance of all those they hated so much. On the bow they will print in large red letters: 'HERE LIES THE WORLD'S BIGGEST DOGHOUSE.'"

"I beg upon you readers to look upon this episode as entirely humorous, and I feel that once I'm released, I'll look back and have one big laugh over the whole thing. If you disagree with my conclusions, remember that I have approximately three million sailors to back me up! And as they say, majority rules."

Captain Ramsey trained the crew hard, since LAKE CHAMPLAIN was destined to join our forces massing off the Japanese home islands for a planned invasion of Kyushu in September and October: OPERATION OLYMPIC. From past experience at Okinawa, they knew the Japanese were holding hundreds of kamikazes in reserve to fly against our ships, and carriers were the prime targets. Putting her pilots and men through the paces between 23 June and the end of the war, her Air Group accomplished the following: 1977 take-offs, 1178 catapultings, 3173 recoveries and 7,016 hours flown.

The crew was as ready as long hours and sweat could make them, but it was not to be. In mid-August, the atomic bombs were dropped on Hiroshima and Nagasaki, and World War II ended.

But the cessation of hostilities didn't mean the end of operations; only now her task was much more pleasant. Returning to the east coast, she held "open house" for more than 200,000 visitors, demonstrating that their tax dollars and War Bonds had been wisely spent. LAKE CHAMPLAIN was the first ship open to the public since the war started and she was a big hit. Philadelphia, Boston and New York were the cities that hosted our carrier, and many memorable liberties were held.

The following month it was back to work. In Norfolk Navy Yard, the air group was off-loaded, along with many unessential personnel. To make additional room for their new "guests," 3,600 folding bunks were installed in the hangar bays. LAKE CHAMPLAIN was about to initiate OPERATION MAGIC CARPET, the swift return of the millions of troops in Europe and the Far East. Nearly every conceivable naval vessel was employed in this happy endeavor, and the intricate logistics were handled so efficiently that just about all of our troops were back in the U.S. by March 1946.

The first voyage took the ship to Southampton, England, where she arrived at noon on 20 October. By 1600 the same day, 3,664 soldiers began crossing the gangways. This continued for eight hours until the last man was aboard. The next morning, LAKE CHAMPLAIN sailed at 0930 with bands playing and hundreds of deliriously happy GIs waving goodbye to England and war.

LOGAN C. RAMSEY,
Captain, USN
Commanding Officer

L. L. KOEPKE,
Commander, USN
Executive Officer

M. MILLER,
Commander, (SC) USN
Supply Officer

R. L. STEVENS,
Lieutenant, USNR
Commissary Officer

F. B. TYCZKOWSKI,
Acting Pay Clerk, USN
Assistant Commissary Officer

D. G. GOODSON,
CCS, USN
Chief Commissary Steward

B. A. HADDON,
CCS, USN
Assistant Commissary Steward

U.S.S. LAKE CHAMPLAIN (CV-39)

Menu for Christmas Day Dinner

Soup

Olives Sweet Pickles Celery Stalks

Roast Young Turkey

Giblet Gravy Cream Whipped Potatoes

Sage Dressing

French Peas Cranberry Sauce

Brick Ice Cream

Fruit Cake Candy

Assorted Fruit

Cigarettes Coffee

Christmas Day menu 1945

Jitter bugs Jacob Thompson, STM 2/C, and W.A. Dean, STM 2/C, first happy hour aboard USS Lake Champlain

First day activities, men waiting on dock with sea bags

Capt. L.C. Ramsey

First day activities, cookies coming out of bake shop oven

Although the carrier only spent one day in England, for one man that was enough to launch a memorable leave. Jim Harper shared this remembrance of that long-ago time.

"As you may know the 'Great Lake' as we called her was assigned to the Magic Carpet run in the fall of 1945 and our first assignment, after being speedily fitted out as a troop ship, was to sail to Southampton, England, to embark troops returning from the European Theater. Our return destination was New York. Since I was due some leave and lived in New York anyway, I applied for two weeks leave in Britain. Miraculously, it was granted, and I stood alone dockside one dreary morning in October and watched the ship gradually disappear into foggy Southampton water and the Solent with her cheering passengers."

"My two weeks in post-war Britain went quickly among friends from college days and family known to us because their children had been evacuated to the States during the Battle of Britain, and wound up with friends of my family. When my two weeks were up I reported to the U.S. Naval Command Center in Grosvenor Square, London, only to be told that the USS LAKE CHAMPLAIN was not on the horizon. At this point, as you can imagine, I was broke and fairly desperate. However, I was able to join forces with a shipmate, Lieutenant Halsey, who was in similar, but not quite so strained, circumstances. To avoid being over-leave, I reported in regularly, and finally we were told that the 'Great Lake' would be making its next Magic Carpet run to Naples, Italy. Here is where the real adventure began!"

"We were flown from London to Paris in Admiral Hewitt's (CINCLANT) personal plane. Upon arrival in Paris, we were put up in separate rooms with bath in the deluxe Parc Monceau Hotel, formerly the headquarters of the German Occupation Staff. The next day, we reported to the Military Transport Command Headquarters in the Place Vendome and asked that our transit orders be stamped with the highest priority that would still not fly that day."

"Well, we had a wonderful time in post-war Paris, returning to M.A.T.S. for our Class 3 priorities every day before taking on the city and its very friendly inhabitants. At a cocktail dance, I found myself on the dance floor with a most attractive young lady. I started out in my best schoolboy French, but she soon interrupted me saying, 'Oh, speak English, can't you?' Well, from that time on we had a wonderful evening winding up in a small café, with complimentary Champagne and entertainment."

"It turned out that her father was a French industrialist who, before it was nationalized, owned the entire electric power grid for Southwestern France. As a result, she knew the country well, and was active during the war helping allied airmen escape through the Pyrenees into Spain and freedom. We agreed to meet the next day and we'd managed to commandeer a jeep for our party, which included another newly found girlfriend. It was the eleventh of November, Armistice Day, with a big parade along the Champs-Elysées, the first since the occupation ended."

"Well, all good things have to come to an end sooner or later, and Halsey and I became concerned that we would miss the ship in Naples. Consequently, we asked for priority orders and were flown to Rome (then to Naples), but not before tearful farewells from our Parisians. Yes, I did see her again, when I visited France three years later, at which time she introduced me to her fiancé! But that, as they say, is another story." (WAR IS HELL!)

"In Naples, as the ship had not yet arrived, Halsey and I were billeted in a gorgeous villa on the Via Crispi with a view of the harbor. While we did make ourselves somewhat useful advising the dock master how to set up for our carrier's arrival, we had plenty of time for sightseeing. The Canadians, whose occupation zone we were in, took us on a spectacular tour of the Amalfi Drive, as far as Salerno. One evening we attended a USO show where Gracie Fields sang. Finally, LAKE CHAMPLAIN made her dramatic appearance and our sojourn was over."

Perhaps the crew knew that these groups of war-weary soldiers were very anxious to return home in a hurry, because LAKE CHAMPLAIN broke the existing trans-Atlantic speed record for warships on her initial voyage from Virginia to Southampton. Her time was four days, 11 hours and 26 minutes. She was just a little shy of QUEEN MARY'S Blue-Ribband speed. Bad weather prevented another try on the east-west return.

During the transit, the GREAT LAKE did everything possible to make the troops feel at home. Movies were shown constantly, and whenever the weather allowed sporting events took place on the flight deck. Below decks, jam sessions were the order of the day, while our band serenaded the long chow lines. The Army couldn't believe the wonderful food heaped on their trays. Most said they'd join the Navy in the next war!

As a post-script, the Commissary Department requested the birth dates of the troops from their personnel officers, and provided large cakes for those men whose birth date fell between 23 to 27 October 1945. Captain Ramsey had earlier started this practice for his crew.

On her return, the port of entry was New York, and in spite of carrying all those troops, our carrier's arrival was almost lost in the shuffle. CV-39's entrance coincided with the great Navy Day celebration in New York's Hudson River. President Truman welcomed the major units of the Pacific Fleet fresh from their victory over Japan. Rather than interfere with the ceremonies in the Hudson, LAKE CHAMPLAIN sailed up the East River and tied up at the Brooklyn Navy Yard. There, she disembarked her happy passengers to awaiting trains.

Thanks to George Purdy, we have a first-hand account of how it felt to be one of those returning servicemen. After spending nearly 18 months on an LST that took part in the Normandy invasion, George was a passenger in the Champ's memorable crossing. "We docked in Brooklyn Navy Yard, and were met by the Salvation Army with fresh donuts, milk and coffee, which we thoroughly enjoyed after shipboard food. We were ushered into a barracks to await our papers for our much-awaited 30-day leaves. The OOD welcomed us with the news that since this was Navy Day, and a holiday, there were no personnel available to type our paperwork. We'd have to wait until Monday. This was met with a loud groan, and he departed promising to see what he could do. An hour later, he returned with a full commander and the news that if we could find enough typists among us, we could process our own leave papers and he'd sign them. Luckily, there were enough Yeomen and Storekeepers (I was a SK 2/c) to do the job. We all turned to and gave the completed forms to the commander for signature. I typed about 150 sets of papers, and when mine came up, I took it to the three-striper, and he asked me who this man was. 'It's me,' I said. He signed it, handed it back, and said, 'Thanks, Purdy. Now get the hell out of here!'"

"Phones were made available to call home and trucks carried us to Pennsylvania Station, where I got my ticket to Philadelphia, no charge. Arrival at Philly was a grand event. Crowds of people were locked in tearful embraces, and I finally located my parents who took me to a fine restaurant for dinner. When my father asked for the bill, he was told, 'No charge!' That Navy Day 1945 will be forever locked in my memory."

From 17 October until 8 November, the carrier remained at the U.S. Army Port of Embarkation, Staten Island, New York, where modifications to the installations for passengers were made by the New York Navy Yard. If anyone thought that this crossing was memorable, that feeling was quickly put to rest as CV-39 embarked on her second MAGIC CARPET run. On 8 November, she sailed for Naples, Italy, and the return city was Newport News, Virginia. This time she carried 5,109 veterans (along with Harper and Halsey) back to the States, departing the Bay of Naples on 19 November. You'll notice that I didn't say "men" because twelve Army nurses were part of the contingent. There was some talk that this was the first time that female passengers were crossing the ocean in a US Navy warship (as opposed to hospital ship or transport), but there was so much else going on that this event fell into the cracks. All of these nurses had been overseas for more than two years.

Three days after bidding Europe farewell, Thanksgiving Day was observed in typical Navy fashion. A full turkey dinner with all the trimmings was served, followed by a special program of sports and entertainment. The only downside of the crossing was the tremendous vibration coming from the four shafts turning furiously. What most of the troops were unaware of was the fact that, a few days before, LAKE CHAMPLAIN had been damaged by a huge rogue wave upon entering the Mediterranean close to Gibraltar. Some of the hangar bay exterior-rolling doors were smashed, and the ship radioed ahead for repair parts to be picked up in Naples. It was critical that those doors were secure and tight-fitting, as hundreds of men would be berthed on the hangar decks, and the December weather in the North Atlantic is usually brutally cold.

Normally, these troop-carrying runs were made at full speed, because of the tight schedules with the trains meeting the ships stateside. But after leaving Naples, welders had to work outside doing the repairs, and the GREAT LAKE slowed to 15 knots until she reached the Atlantic. When she passed Cape Spartel off Morocco, Captain Ramsey called the Navigator and ordered him to give him a course and speed to reach Hampton Roads on schedule. This was done, and the Captain rang down Full Ahead.

All the way across, CV-39 ran like a wild stallion, churning out maximum revolutions, and only slowing when sea conditions required it. Four days later, the Chesapeake Bay sea buoy was sighted bringing the speed run to a close. LAKE CHAMPLAIN had averaged 32.048 knots all the way across, eclipsing the liner QUEEN MARY'S Blue Ribband record! This mark stood until our liner UNITED STATES broke the speed mark for all time in the summer of 1952. When the engineering department was congratulated, the Commander said, "It was easy. All I did was open the throttle and pour in the soup!"

Captain Ramsey ordered that a broom be lashed to the top of the mast signifying a clean sweep. From that time on, the ship was known as the "CHAMP." Needless to say, the more than 5,000 troops were ecstatic at being transported home for Christmas in record time.

On the third MAGIC CARPET run, it was back to Southampton. This time, our carrier transported 5,191 men back from Europe again just in time for Christmas, hitting port on 17 December. The new year signaled another voyage, and Southampton was again the port of entry and exit for CV-39's final troop-carrying assignment, leaving England with 5,286 soldiers—her largest load yet. It was a fitting end to an unusual, but very necessary and joyous task. Nearly 20,000 Army veterans had been brought home in comfort and safety.

One soldier volunteered this remark to a four-striper: "Well Sir, this ain't my idea of no magic carpet, but I'm sure glad to be on it!" With the war over, and most of the servicemen home from overseas, the defense budget was drastically reduced, rendering most of our ships redundant. But (unlike the end of World War I) most of the modern units, especially the battleships, carriers and cruisers, were deactivated and placed in the "mothball" fleet rather than scrapped. LAKE CHAMPLAIN was one of these vessels, and she was placed in reserve in February 1947. For her service in World War II, LAKE CHAMPLAIN earned two decorations: American Theater and World War II Victory Medal.

She was to experience one more brief adventure on her last short run from Berth 42, Norfolk Naval Shipyard to Newport News. ENS Jack Lemmon had just reported aboard from Harvard. The OOD seeing the word "Harvard" assumed that Lemon was fresh out of Communications School (which was based there), and made him Assistant Communications Officer. Lemmon knew nothing about navigation or communications (he'd graduated from the V-12 program with the lowest marks ever!), but things were moving fast, and no one questioned his assignment. Learning that the ship was about to be deactivated and placed in mothballs, and that all unessential material was to be off-loaded, Lemmon saw a way out of his problem. He stripped the Navigation Division of everything that was essential, including all its signal flags, lights, and decoding machines. This way, how could he do his job? He hoped they would send then him somewhere else, perhaps back to school. When the Chief Quartermaster returned from liberty, he flipped, but figuring it wasn't his problem, kept a low profile

Unknown to Lemmon, the carrier had one last voyage to complete, from Norfolk to Newport News. It was a short voyage, but it involved a narrow channel crowded with other ships, but now they had nothing to signal other ships with! Getting underway, the EXEC yelled down to Lemmon something about an underway ensign. Jack had no idea what he was talking about, but he made the motions of looking in the flag locker and found one flag hidden in the corner. By some miracle, it was the right one.

As the LAKE CHAMPLAIN was rounding a turn in the channel, a tanker was heading straight for them. She was obviously in trouble: yawing badly, horns and sirens blaring, flags flying, and her crew running about the decks. Captain Ramsey demanded to know what flags they were flying. Knowing she was in trouble and thinking quickly, Lemmon yelled that she had lost her right propeller and was out of control. She had the right of way. Ramsey immediately ordered the carrier up against the muddy bank and the tanker passed the Champ with inches to spare. Ramsey summoned Lemmon to the bridge where he complimented him on his swift thinking and promised him a 4.0 in his fitness report!

The next time he wore an Ensign's uniform it was on a Hollywood set where the only damage he could do was to the Captain's palm tree!

Now, LAKE CHAMPLAIN would sleep with many of her sisters in a Virginia backwater for five years, never dreaming that she'd once more be called to duty.

BETWEEN WARS

The Navy had attempted to "mothball" its inactive fleet after the First World War, but failed miserably. When we transferred fifty old destroyers to Great Britain in 1940 in the "destroyers for bases" deal, the reactivation crews found little but cracked deck plates, running rust, and frozen machinery. Almost none of the ships had been usable in their intended role as convoy escorts. This time, the Navy wanted to get the preservation right. Now we had plastic coatings, rubber seals, and dehumidification techniques that would guarantee results.

However, as always happens after a big war, budgets were cut and cut again. Most of the mothball fleet would never sail again. Some were lucky, the Champ being one, since carriers, as we will soon see, would again be in great demand

LAKE CHAMPLAIN SETS RECORD

A new world's record for the trans-Atlantic trip from Norfolk, Va., to Southampton, England, was set by the USS LAKE CHAMPLAIN, as she sped across the ocean to Bishop's Rock in four days, 11 hours and 26 minutes. The average was 29.1º knots for the trip.

While the previous record for the distance is not available, the mark set by the ship is just a little short of the 31.8 knot average set by the British liner, Queen Mary, from New York to Southampton in 1938. Since the LAKE CHAMPLAIN did not sail with the record in mind but only to meet the schedule required of her in picking up her first load of troops, she did not reach the full sped not reach the full speed en route which would have enabled her to shatter the Queen's mark as well.

On the return trip, the LAKE CHAMPLAIN again sailed without the intention of setting a record. However, the press of both England and the United States, raving at her speed made on the West-East run declared that she would beat the Queen Mary's record of 30.6 knots on the return East-West trip. In the early hours of the voyage, the LAKE CHAMPLAIN did reach a speed that would have broken the old record to pieces, but bad weather which made the Atlantic a sea of rolling ground swells, forced her to slow down and ended for the time being at least the United States' chances to claim the blue ribbon championship of the Atlantic.

''BUY VICTORY BONDS''

A NEW WAR

Between 1945 and 1950, the Navy had to fight another war. This one wasn't against some foreign enemy, but a much more insidious foe, a budget-cutting Congress and President, and a sister service: the Air Force.

Japan didn't surrender because she was invaded by ground forces, nor did she capitulate because the Navy had starved her into submission. She gave up because two planes had dropped two nuclear bombs. With that one stroke, the Air Force became the most influential offensive branch of our armed forces. Future wars would be fought with long-range bombers carrying nuclear weapons, they reasoned. There would be no need for expensive fleets of aircraft carriers and their supporting ships; no need for Marine amphibious troops or landing craft; and no need for a large standing army or an unpopular draft. In the post-war years, the Air Force public-relations blitz carried this message successfully to a cost-cutting Republican Congress and the Truman administration. The public was only too eager to embrace the lower taxes, and to forget the military after a long world war. Truman's misguided appointment of a political hack, Louis Johnson, as Secretary of Defense nearly ended the Navy's role in global defense planning. As for the Marines, who needed amphibious forces when our main adversary was Russia? She possessed no islands to conquer and her navy was no threat.

Military budgets were cut and cut again in the name of lower taxes. Ships were undermanned, maintenance suffered, and most of the experienced officers and chiefs had retired or returned to civilian life. ESSEX-Class carrier strength was cut from eight to four, carrier air groups from 14 to 6, and Marine Corps squadrons from 23 to 12. With the 1949 defense budget cut to 13

Champ goes into mothballs

billion, the Navy could no longer procure new aircraft. Our defense of Europe would rest on the nuclear bomber. The Far East was pretty much forgotten.

On June 25th, 1950, while the Champ and most of her sisters were asleep a half a world away, hostilities commenced not in Europe where it was expected, but in an unknown country: Korea. In spite of having the greatest navy the world had ever seen only five years earlier, our force was only a shell of its former glory. When the North Koreans surged across the 38th Parallel, the United States Navy had only ONE fleet carrier in the western Pacific: USS VALLEY FORGE CV-45. She was, of course, an ESSEX-Class, but she only had one flight deck. The second carrier to appear on the scene was the British Royal Navy's TRIUMPH. Starting small, an old adage would soon be proven. Since the birth of our nation in 1775, control of the sea had been the decisive element in the winning of every war. In Korea, the United States Navy would be the essential component of success, and the repeated salvation against disasters.

Suddenly, we needed all kinds of ships. Korea was 5,000 miles from San Francisco, but Pusan was scarcely 225 miles from the 38th Parallel. BOXER was waiting to go into a west coast yard for an overhaul. She was quickly turned around and headed west. PHILIPPINE SEA was scheduled to relieve VALLEY FORGE in October; she too was sent hotfooting to join Task Force 77.

The big bomber Air Force was perfectly designed to smash the industrial power base of North Korea, but it turned out that the Koreans had no industrial base. Our problem was their army butting up against the Pusan perimeter, where our forces were hanging on by their fingernails. Their supply lines were extended and vulnerable, however—a job tailor-made for carrier-based aircraft.

Close support of our ground forces was the order of the day, but the fuel-guzzling Air Force jets, operating from distant Japanese bases, had such limited time over their targets that they were ineffective. Then too, the Navy had been flying ground support for the Marines all through World War II, and were well suited to their task. Our carriers could range up and down the Korean coast, with the air groups pounding the North Korean supply lines, railroad bridges and supply dumps.

At both the Inchon invasion in September 1950, and the Hungnam evacuation from the Chosin Reservoir in December, carrier air provided the critical air cover. PRINCETON, LEYTE and VALLEY FORGE flew hundreds of sorties allowing us to evacuate every soldier, alive or dead, his equipment and thousands of refugees. It was in the words of one Admiral, "an invasion in reverse!"

By 1951, with finally enough money in hand, the Navy reordered its priorities. Fleet carriers were needed, but there wasn't enough time to build new ones. Besides, the Korean War was becoming a conflict fought on both sides with World War II weapons. Enter the ESSEX-Class CVs that were laid up across the country.

In order to be able to handle the new jet aircraft, extensive modifications had to be made to these ships, which were laid down for a different enemy and a different time. All the ESSEXs were modernized with 27C conversions, LAKE CHAMPLAIN being one of these. In most cases, the twin five-inch gun mounts were removed and replaced by 14 three-inch 50-cal. guns. Flight decks were strengthened, island structures were streamlined, and aviation fuel capacity was increased. Also altered were the catapults to handle heavier aircraft, enlarged bomb elevators, increased aircraft elevator capacity, and Mk V arresting gear. The Squadron Ready Rooms were relocated from the 02 level to the second deck, requiring the installation of an escalator on the starboard side to move the equipment-laden pilots to the flight deck. In the course of enlarging her blister voids, the Champ's hull was widened by eight feet to provide increased buoyancy. This last change made any future Panama Canal transit impossible. In an unforeseen development, this structural alteration would also transform a normal deployment into a memorable odyssey. A total of nine ESSEX-Class carriers received this modernization.

Work started on the Champ in the spring of 1951, and would continue until her recommissioning in September 1952. In a rare coincidence, LAKE CHAMPLAIN was fitted out in Newport News next to the new liner, UNITED STATES, which was being readied for her record-breaking maiden voyage. The Champ was about to lose her trans-Atlantic laurel.

THE KOREAN DEPLOYMENT

During a recommissioning ceremony on 19 September 1952 at Norfolk Naval Shipyard, Captain George Mundorff took command. After a shakedown cruise to Guantanamo Bay, Cuba, LAKE CHAMPLAIN (now designated an attack carrier—CVA-39) returned to her new homeport, Mayport, Florida. Here, intensive preparations were made for her first combat deployment. In the early months of 1953, CVA-39 returned to Norfolk, where most of her new crew was integrated into the ship's routine. In mid-April her airedales arrived; Carrier Air Group Four under the command of CDR John Sweeney. This group was comprised of the following squadrons: VF-22, VF-62, VF-44, and VA-45. Rounding out this mixed-bag of aircraft were four VC teams—specialized bands of three-plane units that handled photo-reconnaissance, airborne early warning, anti-submarine, electronic countermeasures and nuclear capability.

The aircraft embarked were F2H-2 Banshees (VF-22 and VF-62), F3D Skynights (VC-4), AD-4s (VA-45), AD4Ws (VC-12), F2H-2Ps (VC-62 Photo), AD4Ns (VC-33) and VF-44 F4U-4s (VF-44). This writer joined the ship as an air crewman/ Radar-electronics technician (AT3 AC) with VC-12.

Most of us, at sometime in our lives, have had the unenviable experience of packing up all our personal gear and moving from one place to another. At other times, we've had to prepare for a long trip, worrying that we've forgotten to take something vital. Multiply that by three-thousand, and you have some idea what CVA-39 was like as she prepared to embark two-thirds of the way around the globe.

Pier Seven was a sea of packing crates loaded with spare parts, canned goods, fire-extinguishing foam, cigarettes, paint, soap, bags of flour, vacuum tubes, powdered milk, sugar, and those easy-to-forget items like rubber bands and toilet paper. The latter caused a real storage problem, for we wouldn't have access to a U.S. Naval depot for nearly six weeks, and our final complement was more than 3,500 officers and men. All that final, frantic weekend, conveyer belts moved carton after carton onto the hangar decks, where forklift trucks hauled them God knows where. Massive steel hatch covers had been removed, revealing a cutaway view of the lower decks. Gazing down into this abyss, we could grasp for the first time the tremendous size of this carrier. When it appeared that all the supply spaces were filled, there were still tons of potatoes and apples stacked on the decks. These were finally stowed into overheads and gun tubs, or were lashed along the catwalks. These fruits and vegetables appeared early on in the ship's menus, and apples were always available crossing the Atlantic.

One sailor, John Robben, described his feelings the day LAKE CHAMPLAIN cast off for the Far East. "I vividly recall the day the ship sailed for Korea in April 1953. Our carrier had been moored to a pier in Norfolk, and every day trucks arrived bringing us supplies. We all pitched in bringing all those boxes and crates aboard. One day, I helped load 10,000 rolls of toilet paper! Another day, thousands of cans of fruit juice, powdered milk, sugar, salt, pineapples and coffee arrived. Then it was the bombs and shells—tons of them. I helped roll 250- and 500-pound bombs across the hangar deck to the magazine elevator. The bombs made us realize that we were going to war, and not on a pleasure cruise. Finally, the ship was fully stocked and we were ready to depart. A mail truck was waiting on the dock for one final pickup."

"I was working in the Mail Department then, and one of my jobs was to put a leather mailbag over my shoulder, and go from mailbox to mailbox collecting the last letters. Some sailors were still furiously writing letters when I arrived. 'Hey mailman!' they'd shout. 'Give me another minute to finish this, will ya?' 'Hurry up,' I'd reply, 'that mail truck isn't going to wait forever.' I knew just how that sailor felt because I was feeling the same way. To all of us it seemed as if we were going away forever and this was our last opportunity to say a few words to those we loved."

"Finally, I had all the mail and was walking down the gangway to the waiting truck when a voice rang out, 'Mailman! Mailman!' An officer was running towards me waving an envelope. His was the last letter to leave the ship that day, and, as I brought it to the truck on the dock with all the others I'd collected, I felt as heroic as if I'd just preserved the lifelines of hundreds of sailors and their families. The look on that officer's face told me I was right. Now, everyone was gone except a few wives and girlfriends waving goodbye to their sailors on the ship. I felt like kneeling down and kissing the dock beneath my feet as a way of saying farewell to America, but I felt too self-conscious to do it. Instead, I walked up the gangway and disappeared inside the carrier. It would be a long time before I set foot on American soil, but as they say, 'The longest journey begins with the first step.' And I had just taken mine."

On all naval vessels, all the men who are not actively engaged in running the ship fall in for "quarters" when we enter or leave port. The crew lines the flight deck in a neat formation. For those of us outboard, we had a bird's-eye view of the proceedings. A ship's departure has all the earmarks of high drama, especially for those in it.

On 12 January 1952, the *United States* is in the midst of a visit from her little sister. The *America* is undergoing her off-season overhaul; in the background, workers continue to fit out the *United States*. Between them is the aircraft carrier *Lake Champlain*, undergoing an SCB-27A modernization. (Photo courtesy of the SSHSA Collection, University of Baltimore Library)

Modernized 'Champ' to join AIRLANT

Four tugs had taken up position on the bow and stern to move this 40,000-ton giant out into the stream. Just across the pier was another carrier that would accompany us across the Atlantic: USS CORAL SEA CVA-43. Brisk orders were passed between the ships, as the hawsers took up the strain. Three long blasts from our whistle reverberated across the harbor, bells jangled in the tugs' pilothouses, and white water boiled up beneath their sterns. At first nothing happened, but slowly, very slowly, the distance from our hull to the pier widened. Then from our band, which was stationed on the flight deck, came the strains of "Anchors Aweigh." We were on our way!

As we cleared the pier, a group of wives and sweethearts moved forward, not wanting to let go. They knew our destination, and for many there was the unspoken fear that this might be a last goodbye.

Once we were out in the stream, we felt the throb of our own engines take hold. We bid our tugs farewell with a few more blasts on our whistle, and they headed for CORAL SEA. Soon we were released from quarters, and all hands went to work.

It was only natural that some fraying of tempers occurred as the nearly one-thousand men of the air group were gradually absorbed into the ship's routine. The ship's company had only been on board for a few months, and was just becoming familiar with a vessel still reverberating to the sound of workmen putting the finishing touches on the reconversion. Crowded themselves, they now had to adjust to a horde of strangers who spoke a different language and wore wings on their ratings. The ship's company was akin to the residents of a Florida resort who have to contend with a swarm of tourists every winter. The town couldn't survive without them, but you'd have a difficult time convincing the natives. But adjust we did. We had no other choice.

A few days before, we'd taken a brief (but to the crew, unnecessary) VIP run to Mayport. Now, at last, we were on our way. We sailed across the Atlantic in company with CORAL SEA CVA-43 and the destroyers PURDY, MOALE, INGRAHAM and SUMNER. Our first day at sea was anything but routine when we collided with USS SABINE AO-25, the tanker that was carrying our aviation gas. Luck was with us, however, and we got off with little more than a mangled forward catwalk. The tanker fared worse, having its after superstructure banged up a bit, but nothing serious and thankfully no injuries. A tanker is the last ship you want to collide with!

After refueling, our flat-top settled into a routine that, except for a few ports of call, would remain monotonously unbroken until we reached Japan nearly six weeks later. CVA-39 would cross the Equator, span nineteen time zones, three oceans, countless seas and gulfs, and even transit the Suez Canal, but the daily pattern wouldn't vary. This was a tried and true regimen of work and watches and sleep that the navy had been perfecting since the days of sail. Once immersed in this nautical time capsule, Monday could be Friday and May could be December. In spaces like the boiler rooms, night could be day.

In spite of being cut off from land, LAKE CHAMPLAIN was a complete American community, self-sufficient in nearly every way. We had our own police, fire, and sanitation departments, a post office, a movie theater, and a well-equipped hospital. To keep us informed and entertained, our weekly ship's newspaper, The Champ, kept us abreast of shipboard activities and featured many photographs. Our radio station carried the news, as well as such popular singers as Patti Page, Nat King Cole and Bing Crosby. Our restaurants were open all hours and served more than 10,000 meals a day. Although there were some complaints, I never saw anyone eating elsewhere!

A walk around the decks would reveal a fresh-water plant, a huge laundry (which always mangled your dungarees and lost your socks), two churches, a library, a post-office, an ice-cream parlor, a barbershop, a printing press, and our very own shoemaker. Of course, in the middle of all this, there was a very busy airport.

We may have been self-sufficient in many ways, but we were still missing some important items—women being just one of them. On board, we resembled a monastery—all male and serving under similar vows, obedience and chastity (at least out of sight of land). Also, there were other things we lacked that wouldn't become apparent right away. None of us could get behind the wheel of a car for eight months, and for those who enjoyed a beer or a scotch, it soon became a fond memory. Perhaps that's why we tended to become a bit wild when we finally went ashore on liberty.

Like all towns, we had our own neighborhoods, and each compartment resembled a street, with a major exception: these neighbors knew nearly everything about each other. There weren't any doors or curtains to close. Enlisted men literally rubbed shoulders (and other things) in their cramped quarters. Living spaces were squeezed anywhere that there was room, and often where there wasn't. The average "bedroom" was fifteen feet wide, twenty-five feet long and eight feet high. To about thirty men, this was home.

Departing Norfolk for Korea

It might seem odd to refer to this floating piece of cold steel as "home," but CVA-39 would soon became as familiar to us as every room in the home or apartment we'd left behind. Each of us would discover the best spots to watch the sea, play cards, eat a geedunck or just crap out. Moreover, we could locate these spaces and make our way around them in total darkness. This phenomenon was known as sailor's ESP. We slept on steel racks that held canvas like a sail. On this stretched canvas was a two-inch thick mattress. Usually there were three racks fitted from deck to overhead, with the distance in between measuring about twenty inches. If the man above you was in the 200-pound range, he would often sag into your "air space." Our lockers were miniscule, barely holding our underwear, socks and dungarees. We usually "stored" our whites or blues between the mattress and the canvas, as hangers were practically unknown. Our pea coats were kept in a separate locker.

Drachma - Greek money

LAKE CHAMPLAIN was sailing east instead of west for a very good reason. As I previously mentioned, her reconversion had resulted in an increase in her beam, making a Panama Canal transit impossible. Just about all the post-war CVAs were the same. Strategically, we now had enough flat-tops to protect both oceans, unlike the early days of the Pacific War where we frantically shuttled carriers back and forth. Ten days out of Norfolk, we anchored in the shadow of Gibraltar's rock. CORAL SEA left for service with the Sixth Fleet, and we proceeded eastward in company with our destroyers. During our initial air operations in the Mediterranean, a plane handler was killed when he was struck by a prop. He would be the first of nine men who wouldn't return to the States. When the last notes of "Taps" echoed and died during his memorial service on the hangar deck, so did any illusion that this was a pleasure cruise. In our heart of hearts, each one of us said, "This could have been me."

Athens was our first liberty port, and our last one in Europe for more than six months. With raging inflation, we lit cigars with 20,000-drachma notes and climbed up a steep hill to view the Parthenon. Some of the crew discovered ouzo, much to their regret, but regardless, Greece was a welcome break. In the evening, as liberty wound down, a large contingent of knowing locals congregated in the cafés near the Fleet Landing to watch the aftermath of too much sun, ouzo and wild spirits. Trucks had been commandeered to gather up those who were no longer ambulatory, and they headed for the liberty launches in various stage of exotic dress and undress. Fur hats were the rage, along with some of those skirts that the Greek Army wore. There were some big heads the next morning at quarters, but Athens was a break we all needed.

The Suez Canal beckoned. It was a very hot, slow journey that all of us were glad to see end. We'd sweat and sweat, and when we thought we couldn't take it anymore, we'd turn around and sweat some more. Occasionally we'd see a camel or a truck, but mostly there was just a blazing sun and a bleak desert that stretched endlessly to the horizon. With the Champ in the van, our five warships resembled some sea borne caravan right out of the Arabian Nights. Relentless in her flair to gain singular honors, we later discovered that we were the largest ship to transit the Canal's 108 miles.

Except for a refueling stop at Aden, we sailed uninterrupted through the Red Sea and Indian Ocean to Colombo, Ceylon (now Sri Lanka). The humidity soared, and we looked forward to any opportunity to get out on deck and breathe the open air. We watched flying fish break the surface of the flat, blue sea, gliding out at right angles from the bow wave, their silver wings glistening in the sun. These sights and spectacular sunsets were our only rewards. In this climate, the hull itself sweated and the compartments were transformed into saunas. It didn't take long for the perspiration to affect our bedding. The interior atmosphere in our compartments took on all the trappings of an unemptied hamper. As a result we were ordered to "air bedding." This entailed removing the sweat-stained canvas pieces from their racks and lowering them over the side from the lowered deck-edge elevator. We were issued long lines to secure to the eyelets of the canvas. The turbulence of the rushing sea took the place of a washing machine, and a few hours in that tropic sun removed all the stains along with the odor.

One of my shipmates, viewing this, thought that this would be an ideal way to clean and bleach his dungarees. He fastened a line through the belt loops and dropped them over the side, securing the line to a stanchion. An hour later he pulled up his line and discovered a few, sparking clean—belt loops!

Ceylon brought us into the Far East with both feet. Elephants, wild monkeys, ancient temples, and warm beer (it was a British Crown colony) greeted us in this most exotic of ports. Here, everyone wore a skirt, and women carried huge baskets balanced on their heads. The capital, Colombo, contained a number of sights seen nowhere else, but it was brutally hot and crowded, and the smart sailors headed inland to Kandy, the ancient capital, or to the Mount Lavinia Hotel on the Indian Ocean. This locale was later featured in the movie, "The Bridge on the River Kwai." In spite of it's oriental "charms," after three days we were glad to be on our way.

The Champ sailed east into the waters of the Malay Barrier. Moving past Sumatra, we skirted the archipelago of Indonesia, its islands dangling like some necklace adorning the Equator.

The shortest route to Manila would have carried us about fifty miles north of the Equator, but our Navigator, CDR Wiseman, endeared himself to the crew by slightly diverting, allowing us to touch the sacred mark. More than ninety percent of the crew partook of that most treasured of all nautical ceremonies—Crossing the Line. A massive canvas pool was rigged up on the flight deck, and a wooden platform adjoined it. It was here that the sentences were issued and carried out. Prior to the Crossing, dire messages were exchanged between most of the crew (pollywogs) and those who would be in charge (shellbacks). But in spite of much posturing, the outcome was a *fait accompli*. All the high-ranking officers were shellbacks. Shorn of much hair, walloped by canvas strips, and finally dunked in a makeshift pool or drenched by a high-pressure hose, we were all initiated into the "Solemn Mystery of the Ancient Order of the Deep," at last becoming "Shellbacks." 30 May 1953 would be a day long remembered.

Manila was a washout, literally as well as figuratively. With a third of the crew ashore, a typhoon changed course and CVA-39 had to get underway to safely ride out the storm. The next morning, it was a sodden and forlorn bunch of sailors who rode an LCI back to the ship. Some were so worn out that they had to be hauled aboard by a cargo net! John Willet recalls one man clad only in his bathing suit because his uniform was stolen (that must have been a great story in itself!). He was climbing the cargo net with two water buffalo horns tied to his shoulders! Two other guys had a case of San Miguel beer they thought they could bring aboard, but they were caught by the OOD and had to throw it into Manila Bay. For those who were trapped in the deluge, it was a night to remember!

Finally at 1437, 9 June 1953, LAKE CHAMPLAIN moored to buoy #11 in Yokosuka harbor, Japan. Liberty was extremely brief—36 hours; just long enough to take aboard RADM W.D. Johnson, Commander Carrier Division ONE and his staff. Then, as the flagship, we rushed to join Task Force 77, which was engaged in an all-out effort to stem the current Communist offensive. VF-44 was replaced by VF-111 from BOXER, which brought us a squadron of F4U Corsairs in place of jets, and VC-4's huge F3D Skynights were flown to Korea to operate from land airfields. The heavy aircraft were taking a toll on our flight deck.

On the morning of 13 June, we entered the war zone. Soon we joined the task force, which was now comprised of CVAs PRINCETON, BOXER and PHILIPPINE SEA, the heavy cruiser BREMERTON and nine destroyers. We immediately commenced air operations, and soon discovered that the 13th was a "lucky" number for the Champ. A landing Banshee from VF-22 had neglected to fire off all its remaining ammunition, and upon catching the wire, its 20mm guns discharged into a parked sister aircraft nestled in the pack on the flight deck. A fuel tank fire instantly broke out, and disaster was only avoided by the heroic efforts of the flight deck crew, who contained the blaze and minimized the damage. Incredibly, the pilot of the parked plane just managed to jump free before the flames engulfed his F2H. Two planes were lost, but miraculously no lives.

The following men were decorated at a Commendatory Mast the following month: Elton Balch DDC, Samuel Black AD1, Madison Compton AD2, Ralph Pasquale AO3, John Gercnack AO3, Gerald Gumpper AO3, Thomas Green AO3, Roy Batchell AD3, John Kruitoff AD3, Thomas Reeves AO3, Duane Brickson AN, Harold Cole AB1, Robert Smith AB1, John Adams AB1 and Andrew Motika AB2. Heroes all!

Equator crossing ceremonies

Most of the crew never had an opportunity to test their mettle in such dramatic fashion. They toiled day after day, night after night, standing watch, cooking 10,000 meals, tending the boilers, servicing, directing and launching the planes, often in close proximity too whirling props and jet intakes, doing the laundry, sorting the mail, and the hundred and one other jobs that keep a 40,000-ton attack carrier on the line. Were these men not "heroes" as well? The dictionary describes the word "hero" as a man known for his special achievements. Who back home in the comfort of civilian life wouldn't call what we did special? Would they put a price on it?

But the Champ wouldn't always be so lucky. Danger and death are constant companions in an aircraft carrier, and especially on the flight deck. If anyone ever deserved hazardous duty pay, it was the flight deck crew, especially the aviation bosun mates.

Lake Champlain CVA-39

From a distance, the launching and recovery of an air group doesn't appear too difficult. The planes are catapulted or roll down the deck and fly off. Looks simple? It isn't. First, there's the limited space to consider. On land, airports are usually built out in the countryside. There are acres and acres for all the aircraft to park, taxi, take off and land. On board a flat-top, the landing and storage area resembles that infamous stateroom in the Marx Brothers classic, "A Night At The Opera." Space is at a premium; that's why Navy planes have wings that fold. It doesn't matter how sophisticated the ship or its aircraft are; at some level, carrier aviation is just a clumsy, primitive undertaking. It involves a great deal of stuff—stuff that weighs a lot, costs a fortune, and has to be moved, often at the most inopportune time.

During launches and recoveries, the flight deck is the most dangerous place in the navy. The sailors to whom this is home not only need eyes in back of their head, but must also be blessed with the proverbial nine lives of a

Fire on flight deck

cat. This innocent looking stage could turn into a vicious killer when the bugle sounded "flight quarters." Whirling props could lop off an arm or worse, or jet intakes might suck you into a thousand spinning razor blades. Other times, one could be blown over the side by a jet blast or mauled by a broken arresting cable. These horrors (and more) all occurred during this deployment. When the command, "Start engines" is given, each pilot looked to his plane captain to give a thumbs-up signal, signifying "all clear." When ready, other airedales crawled under the wings to remove the wooden chocks that held the plane in place. If a pilot gunned his engine, the airedale could be blown away by the slipstream. Once the aircraft were ready for launching, other airmen wearing yellow shirts, directed the jets and props forward. The jets moved onto the catapults. It was here that some of the most hazardous work took place.

Some of the Aviation Bosun's Mates attached a steel bridle, or launch bar, to the undercarriage. This bar was secured to the catapult, which was powered by tremendous hydraulic pressure from deep below decks. This device effectively became the slingshot that propelled the ten-ton Skyraider or Panther jet into the sky in a couple of seconds. Just before the planes were launched, the pilots turned up full power and put pressure on the hold-back bolt. It was at this time that an AB crawled under the landing gear to make certain the bar was set securely into the catapult slide. Lying under this screaming and vibrating twenty-thousand pounds of aircraft had to be one of most frightening experiences I could imagine. When it came to displaying courage, those ABs were in a special class. And yet, they accepted these heart-stopping hazards as "all in a day's work."

At the other end of this operation, the flight deck could become a roadway of danger. A jet hurtling in to land at 125 miles an hour may suddenly miss the arresting gear, and turn as wild and murderous as a runaway bomb. Barriers, both steel and nylon were in place to stop this type of accident, but there were times when aircraft floated right over these barriers and smashed into the parked planes forward. This type of mishap fortunately never happened to us, but we did experience errant hung rockets that broke loose upon landing and skidded up the flight deck at close to 80-100 miles an hour. One broke a plane-handler's leg. When the air group came home to roost, it was time to refuel and respot them.

Aircraft that were crowded in the forward part of the flight deck were towed back in the same sequence they'd be launched in the next operation. Most minor repairs were performed on the flight deck, while more serious problems required that the plane be moved by an elevator to the hangar deck. It was critical that all the planes be gassed, armed, and respotted as quickly as possible. In combat, this could mean the difference between victory and defeat.

Never is a carrier more vulnerable that when she's rearming and refueling her air group. One bomb, no matter how small, in the middle of all those rockets, napalm, and avgas, would turn the flight deck into an inferno. This is exactly what happened to the Japanese carriers at Midway when our dive-bombers found them in the midst of changing bombs to torpedoes.

Now, LAKE CHAMPLAIN was in full wartime mode. Darken ship routine was executed just after sunset, and many hatches remained closed to insure watertight integrity. During air-ops, the bomb elevators ran through the mess decks. Often a swabbie found himself eating chow next to a 1,000-pound bomb. More adventurous types would straddle these canisters of TNT and pose for photos. It was enough to give a mother heart failure!

Day after day, we launched our squadrons against targets in North Korea. The Chinese, believing that the truce line would be based on the final position of the respective fronts, were engaged in a full-scale offensive. LAKE CHAMPLAIN was one of four ESSEX-class CVA's trying to stop them. Our jets and props ranged far and wide, attacking troop concentrations, fuel depots, supply trains—anything that moved.

We tasted the inconvenience of war

Our air group had been flying so many missions and delivering such prodigious amounts of ordnance that we were refueling and rearming almost every night. On top of their normal day's work, the ship's company was up well into the early hours of the morning, manhandling supplies and ammunition. This was back-breaking labor, and after two or three consecutive nights, it started to take its toll.

At their peak, the four air groups of Task Force 77 were using more than 9,000 barrels of aviation gas a day. Tankers, it seemed, were constantly alongside. These replenishments took place under the most adverse weather conditions, with visibility down to a hundred feet in fog and mist. Searchlights were often employed, and "darken ship" went by the boards. The need outweighed the risk.

Watching a refueling or replenishment was never dull. We marveled at the navigational and ship-handling skills exhibited by both helmsmen. Keeping the ships exactly on station required the utmost concentration. We were moving at 14 knots, and allowing for currents, wind, and tremendous difference in size, the slack in the oil lines was barely a hundred feet. This exact distance and speed had to maintained for nearly two hours. This was the kind of naval expertise that wins wars, every bit as much as launching an air group or firing a broadside. No matter how often we refueled or replenished, it always provided a good show for all hands.

Sometimes during these replenishments, hundreds of cartons of foodstuffs and canned goods would be manhandled across the deck to be stored below. It wouldn't be the Navy if some enterprising sailors didn't "accidentally" drop a carton spilling its contents, or "misplaced" a case completely. Then a few of us would have a "cocktail hour" in one of the dark gun tubs with some Dole pineapple or tomato juice. Eating that "forbidden fruit" was doubly delectable for beating the system. We had precious few opportunities to thumb our noses at the Navy.

On 16 June, Belvin Hudson of VF-44 fell over the side while climbing a catwalk during flight operations. A search was carried out by our plane guard destroyers, but he was never found. The fall from the catwalk to the sea was over seventy feet, so the drop alone was enough to kill a man. He would not be the last man on this deployment to die that way.

The 19th was another sad day for CVA-39. During the launching of 101 sorties, the starboard catapult was put out of action due to a runaway shot. Worse still was the loss of Lt. (J.G.) D.E. Brewer of VA-45. While engaged in a bombing run, his plane was seriously damaged by flak. He attempted a low altitude bailout, but his chute failed to open in time and he was killed on impact. The next day, the battleship NEW JERSEY, flagship of the Seventh Fleet, joined us. Later, our chopper brought VADM "Jocko" Clark aboard for operational planning. But fog closed in, and flight ops were severely restricted or cancelled. This weather pattern persisted until the 24th, when we launched eighty dive-bombers and fighters. And, that night, fate struck close to home.

At 0245, on a pitch-black flight deck, an AD4N from my sister squadron, VC-33, was catapulted. Immediately, something failed in the catapult machinery, and the Skyraider crashed just about a hundred yards in front of CVA-39, churning out more than 30 knots. The pilot, Lt. Keown, and one of the radar men, Chief Peloquin, exited the sinking plane on the port side away from the hull. Bob Nault, the other crewman, went out the starboard hatch as seawater gushed in on him. All this had taken about ten seconds. Bob inflated his Mae West, and to his horror, found the moving side of the hull right next to him. He knew the pounding screws were but seconds away, and he saw no way out. But then a miracle

July 1953 AD Skyraider launches against North Korea

happened. The big, fearsome side suddenly pulled away, leaving him in the turbulent wake, choking on what seemed to be half the ocean. Quick action on the part of the quartermaster had saved their lives. The three of them crowded in a raft and tried to get the attention of some of the ships in the task force. But it's very difficult to see a small raft at sea, even in daylight, and this was a pitch-black night. Most of the flares they'd carried with them as part of their "Mae Wests" were duds. Finally, though, the last one ignited, and they were eventually picked up by our plane guard destroyer, USS MOALE DD-693.

One of our aircrewmen, George Walls, became concerned over these inoperative flares, so he contacted our Parachute Rigger, Kevin Woods, who outfitted him with a dozen flares, a heavy-duty flashlight, and some extra shark-chaser. George felt pretty secure, until one of the other aircrewmen remarked, "You won't have to worry about being picked up, George. Once you hit the water, you'll sink like a rock!" Those of us who flew nearly every day from these decks, could always find humor in any situation.

This catapult breakdown, coupled with the other one a few days earlier, effectively put an end to our flight operations, and we proceeded to Yokosuka for repairs.

Some of us felt as if we were letting the rest of the task force down, retiring so rapidly just after our arrival, but the old-timers reminded us that no one would be shedding any tears if the situation were reversed. In the Navy, you take what comes. It's the luck of the draw.

LIBERTY IN JAPAN

There was some question about including liberty in a history of LAKE CHAMPLAIN. But this is essentially a book of remembrance and entertainment, and our hours ashore are among our most vivid and treasured recollections.

In Yokosuka, we had the distinct advantage of being moored at a pier, rather than waiting interminably for liberty launches to carry us ashore. Our appetites had been whetted by only the briefest glimpse of this mystical country, so we all looked forward to our first real taste of Japan. For close to two months, we had sailed more than 20,000 miles to reach here, and then just when we were about to enjoy its riches, it was whisked away from us. During all that time, we'd had a total of seven days in port. Considering the necessities of port and starboard watches, most of us had spent barely 36 hours away from the ship during the past ten weeks.

Our host country did not disappoint us. Japan was exotic, but there were plenty of American overtones. Eight years of American presence made us comfortable, but left just enough mystery to stir our imagination. There was little doubt that this was a foreign country.

The Naval Operating Base itself had more amenities than the entire complex of installations on the ocean we'd left in April. Everyone remarked that we'd been in the wrong fleet. The Pacific command certainly knew how to take care of whitehats—not to mention chiefs and officers.

A huge cafeteria greeted us. After drinking only powdered milk on board, we reveled in the real thing, along with hot dogs, hamburgers, pie and ice cream. This is not to say that we didn't imbibe our quota of beer and stronger spirits, but first things first, at least among the younger members of our crew.

Each group, from enlisted men to petty officers to chiefs and those wearing gold braid had their own clubs. In our P.O. Club, we could sit at a table with starched linen and real plates and be served like gentlemen. Two waiters hovered, anticipating our every wish. A steak dinner set you back a dollar. Upstairs there was musical entertainment, with bands that had a remarkable resemblance to Benny Goodman or Harry James. Better still, there were American girls to ogle—mostly Waves or civilian employees from the base. Of course there were plenty of "babysans," as the young Japanese girls were known.

We soon had our first experience with MPCs (Military Payment Certificates). To avoid counterfeiting, our government issued us script rather than dollars. This was the coin of the realm at the clubs, restaurants and the PX. These MPCs (which had an uncanny resemblance to Monopoly money) could be exchanged for yen at a bank near the Main Gate. Mixed drinks were 25 cents, beer 15 cents. One purchased tickets for drinks, and we soon learned to pile them in the center of the table for the waiter. Once he had our orders, he would continue serving us without interruption. Most of us thought we had died and gone to heaven! The base also included ball fields, a swimming pool, a large movie theater that showed first-run films free, and a well-stocked PX.

Once outside the Main Gate, the real Japan beckoned. Of course, those nearby shops were designed to cater to every sailor's wish. Would you like your blues or whites tailored while you wait? Your portrait painted? A set of china to be shipped home to your parents or girlfriend? Or help in choosing a gift for your mama-san, papa-san, or girlfriend-san?

Once past this "strip," Yokosuka was a typical small Japanese city. The real excitement lay elsewhere.

An hour or so's train ride carried one to Yokohoma or Tokyo. The capital was huge—more than seven million, and had enough diversions to last a lifetime. But many sailors were content to find a bar with friendly faces and just unwind after many days at sea. For the more inquisitive, there was the Emperor's Palace, ancient temples galore, the Tokyo Baths, scores of nightclubs and restaurants, the glitter of the Ginza after dark, and the Ernie Pyle Club—a popular spot for all servicemen. Best of all, the exchange rate practically made us millionaires. With all this yen, it was only natural that we'd soon meet some of these baby-sans.

The initial appearance of these teenage Japanese girls came as a bit of a shock. None of the wartime movies or newsreels prepared us for these narrow-waisted, doll-like creatures. Always smiling, they answered every question with, "Never hoppon, Joe!" Regardless of whether you wanted to know them better or not, they remained smiling, and most looked indistinguishable from their teenage American counterparts.

One of the aircrewmen from our team discovered the Tokyo Baths right next to the Ginza. He was so entranced that he decided to take a milk bath, a lemon bath and a Turkish bath. Later, he joined a Japanese family in a communal bath. They were so fascinated by his stories that they invited him to breakfast.

A couple of sea going mountain climbers-Mt. Fuji Sept. 1953

Sailors and crewmen of VC-12

Task Force 77, Korea 1953

We soon discovered that sailors were in a minority on the streets of the Japanese capital. The Army outnumbered us about five to one. Sometimes this was an advantage. When we were being billeted in an Army hotel, the sergeant behind the desk, impressed by our "wings," assigned us to the better rooms with marvelous views. Later, I noticed his pale blue ribbon, denoting the Medal of Honor. Service in the dining room was so elegant that some of the swabbies nearly went into shock! The room was a dollar a day and three meals were the same. Everyone admitted that the Far Eastern Command certainly knew how to lay on an R & R.

More adventurous types traveled to Kamakura to surf, or marvel at the giant Buddha built in 1252. Others went further afield, by taking R&Rs to Karuiazawa in the Japanese "Alps," or attempting to climb Mount Fuji.

While most of the crew was ashore enjoying the sights, work progressed on our catapults, as well as other parts of the ship. A new teakwood flight deck was laid by Japanese shipyard workers, and repairs were made to our damaged catwalk from the tanker collision outside of Norfolk. With so many cables snaking throughout the ship, most of the air group was just in the way, so ball games between the squadrons were organized.

BACK TO THE LINE

On the morning of 11 July, it was farewell to fun and games and back to the line. This time, only PRINCETON and BOXER were our consorts, along with our usual tin-cans. Fog still plagued the task force, limiting our air ops. During the entire stretch of two weeks, only on the 17th did we launch over a hundred planes. As a footnote to operations on this date, another record was set; one that could have made it into Ripley's "Believe It or Not." Lt. T.A. Francis of VF-22 made the 5,000th landing on the Champ since she was commissioned. One might wonder, "So what?" Well, he also made the 3,000th on 29 April, and the 4,000th on 14 June!

On the 22nd, an arresting gear cable parted seriously injuring R. Kilgrove. That same afternoon, returning from a strike, a Banshee, disabled by flak over Korea, couldn't make it back to the ship, but the pilot managed to reach the coast, where he bailed out and was recovered by a chopper from USS BREMERTON.

Flight quarters sounded at 0430 on 23 July. From every sector of the front came calls for air-support. The Chinese had mounted a strong offensive, and Task Force 77 responded in spades. At 0908, ENS H.K. Wallace lost his port wing tank as he was being catapulted. This caused his Banshee to flip over as it left the deck, crashing upside down into the sea. The aircraft sank in seven seconds. The pilot stayed with her.

Task Force 77 broke its record that day, and the Champ chimed in with 157 launches to hold up her end. That record didn't stand for long, as the 24th brought a new achievement: an even 600 sorties, with CVA-39 contributing 156. All this activity in the air meant a maximum effort on the part of the squadron personnel: "mechs," metal smiths, electricians, electronic technicians and parachute riggers. Hangar bay lights burned well into the night, as planes were readied for the next day's missions.

During the next afternoon's recovery, the bullhorn announced, "Plane in final approach has hung rocket." This had happened before, and the missile had remained firmly in its rack. As a result, few, if any on the flight deck moved. The Skyraider landed, caught a wire, and came to an abrupt stop. Its rocket, unfortunately, didn't, and scooted down the deck at close to 80 knots. It struck a plane captain and left him with a compound fracture of the leg. The following day, the same thing happened, but this time the deck was clear in seconds.

In Korea, the Chinese were exerting their last big effort, and General Maxwell Taylor had thrown two American divisions into the line to close the gap. All of our prop aircraft engaged in close support—our Corsairs and Skyraiders bombing, strafing and rocketing the enemy. The battleship NEW JERSEY, accompanied by the cruisers MANCHESTER, BREMERTON and ST.PAUL shelled targets deep inland, using spotter aircraft and their naval gunfire observers.

Here is an account of what it was like flying one of those jets over North Korea. This story was submitted by Lt. John Sullivan of VF-62. He and his fellow pilot, Eugene K. Myers, had the unique distinction of wearing both gold Navy wings and badges of the New York City police department. Both pilots had seen service in World War II, prior to joining the Champ as part of Air Group Four. Lt. Sullivan's account is a rare opportunity for the ship's company and the air group support personnel to see the result of their efforts in manning our carrier, and seeing that those planes got airborne and performed their missions every day. Every job was important, from those who serviced his Banshee in the air group, to those who labored in more mundane tasks like pushing planes, serving food, or working in the heat of the engine room. Here is John's story.

"I was recalled to active duty with another New York City policeman, a radio-car operator in the 7th Precinct, Gene Myers, who was a former pilot in my reserve squadron at NAS Floyd Bennett Field, N.Y. We were both fortunate to be able to remain together, and we were both assigned to VF-62 at Jacksonville, Florida. From the old 'war weary' Hellcats we stepped into sleek, lightning fast Banshee F2H jets. My first hop in a Banshee was probably the greatest thrill I had in flying."

"We trained long and hard until the following April 1952, when we joined Air Group Four for duty aboard USS LAKE CHAMPLAIN for duty with Task Force 77 off Korea."

"On one morning in June 1953, Myers and I were both on our way, and with rockets and bombs slung beneath the wings of our Banshees, we were probably the fastest and best-armed 'patrol cars' New York City ever launched to quell a disturbance. The success of our first mission could best be described in a quip Myers later made. 'It would take the best efforts of the New York City Fire Department to put out the fires we caused!' The Reds had launched an offensive, and our ground forces needed all the help they could get. Our boys were going down to tree-top level with their bombing and strafing, and I know their efforts paid off. The enemy advance was halted, and he later withdrew."

"Our mission was to fly up through what was referred to as 'Death Valley,' a section of mountain passes that extend from the Amlyon Reservoir on the south to Wonson Harbor on the north. Through the valley formed by these Eastern Mountains passed a great deal of the supplies the enemy had to move to the front, so they took great pains to protect it. I imagine that there were more guns emplaced there than any other route in Korea. The mountains made it possible to hide them from snooping jets, and it's only when an air attack is made on the transportation facilities that all hell breaks loose. On the particular day I speak of, I was leading three planes up the same valley. We had just passed the Amylon Reservoir and were flying at about 300 feet, and indicating some 500 miles an hour, when we cut between two mountain ranges and out onto a flat bowl-shaped hollow. Before I could bring my guns to bear, I had flown directly over a marshalling yard containing some thirty boxcars. I passed so close that I could see the laborers unloading the cargo and supplies. I pulled back hard on the stick, sat my Banshee on its tail, and climbed straight up to 10,000 feet where I leveled off for my first attack. We fanned in on the target from three directions and I had the pleasure of

Korea 1953

watching two of my rockets streak home and explode in two boxcars. My wingman dropped four bombs on a string of boxcars and it was almost impossible to assess the damage because of the fire and smoke. My third attack I made from the flat, and walked my 20mm up one row of boxcars hoping to set off a secondary explosion. When this failed, I fired a rocket at the last car, and the whole thing blew right up underneath me. The fragments tore chunks out of my wings and fuselage, and knocked my dive brakes out. Flying a plane with the dive brakes extended is like driving a car with the brakes locked, and naturally enough makes a terrific difference in fuel consumption. I couldn't make it back to the carrier, so I headed for the front lines, hoping to make it to one of the auxiliary airfields close by."

"I just made it to the strip when I ran out of gas. Somebody must have been praying for me that day! The Communist forces didn't care much for jet pilots, and our treatment wasn't the best if we wound up in their hands."

North Korean complex after raid from our planes, July 1953

"Other times we flew Photo Escort hops, covering the unarmed photo planes on their missions, and generally would assign one or two fighters to act as escort unless the mission was going to the Yalu River. Then, we would assign more. Closer to the carriers we'd fly Carrier Air Patrol. Police action to a tee. We would sit at some altitude between 20,000 and 40,000 feet, and guard the task force against air attack. We would wait to be directed to investigate an unknown air target by one of our radar planes. The Chinese had more than 300 bombers capable of reaching us, so this was not one of the most sought after missions, but it would be crucial if the occasion arose."

"Gene and I were flying when the war ended in Korea, and as fate would have it, a New York City cop flew the last combat carrier landing of the war. Our Police magazine in New York played it up big with a headline story, "Cop Blows Whistle on Korean Police Action.""

As a postscript to the flight deck fire on 13 June, John says," I was in Vultures Row (island gallery) observing the recovery of an earlier launch by our squadron. My stateroom mate, Lt. Phil Davis, was flying 208 and had just cleared the barricade and was parked, when four 20mm shells pierced his fuel tank engulfing his Banshee in flames. Phil closed his canopy to ward off the flames while I observed the heroics of the fire-fighters from my perch in the island. I never saw Phil exit the aircraft with all the smoke and I was sick until I saw him in the Ready Room. Even today, he accuses me of breaking a rib when I hugged him."

The 25th of July dawned bright and clear, a rarity on this coast at this time of the year. Again, the Task Force broke its record with 746 flights. Later that day, I was in the backseat of one of our AD4W Skyraiders as we returned from an early-warning flight. We were told throttle back and wait for the last jets to land before coming aboard. The task force carriers were headed into the wind on a course taking them directly towards to coast of North Korea. I asked our pilot, Lt. Williams, why the ships hadn't turned. He surmised that some of the jets were still airborne and didn't have enough fuel to come around again. He said, "Watch closely, Jack, and you'll see some fancy maneuvering." ADM Johnson was running out of sea room, and would soon be within range of the North Korean shore batteries.

At last, the final aircraft touched down, and the entire task force made a 180- degree turn. A dozen ships of all types turned if guided by one hand, their long wakes etching concentric white circles in the deep blue sea. Life magazine later ran a spread on the Champ, and what we saw that day was captured on film. On a more serious note, during this operation a plane handler was sucked into a jet intake and critically injured.

That night, scores of airedales labored over their planes. Our own department had a radar problem that kept us up well past midnight. The last men didn't sack out until close to 0200.

Most of us felt as if we'd just closed our eyes, when the "bong, bong, bong" of General Quarters sounded. In the past, all GQs had been announced in the Plan of the Day, so this one had to be the real thing. Lights were turned on and someone shouted, "This is no drill!" All hands responded in record time, as all battle stations were manned and made ready. Blue night-lights bathed everyone in the Ready Room in an eerie glow, and the teletype reported many bogies closing the task force. The steel deck vibrated, as our engines poured on the coal. Our jets were catted off, and our squadron put up a long-range radar plane. I sat in one of our Skyraiders on the deck-edge elevator waiting for a call that never came. That was as close as I ever came to have someone shoot at me in earnest. It's not an experience I want to repeat, but it gave me an undying appreciation of what my forebears had accomplished in World War II.

Whatever was up there disappeared before our planes could make contact, and exactly who they were remains a mystery to this day. It was a chastened crew who dragged themselves back to their sacks. A few hours later, we were at it again. Air Group Four flew 166 sorties, a Champ and Task Force 77 record. Our planes flew deep into North Korea, cratering airfields and blasting communication centers. One of our Skyraiders from VA-45 ditched in the sea after an engine failure, but the pilot, Lt. Brumbach, was recovered by our chopper uninjured. On the flight deck, Airman L. Woods was seriously injured when he was blown into a tractor by jet blast. When the last aircraft returned that day, they brought the sad news that ENS Broyles of VF-22 failed to

Douglas Skyraider landing U.S.S. Lake Champlain 1953.

rendezvous after a bombing run. He was last seen in a 40-degree dive at 6,000 feet. No ejection was observed, and he was listed as missing in action.

Often when we weren't flying, we'd find a spot on a catwalk in the "island" and watch the planes return. No matter how many times we witnessed a recovery, it was never dull. These pros made it look easy, but of course it was anything but. After a bone-jarring catapult shot, these pilots had been flying over enemy territory, dodging flak and searching out targets. They knew that if they bailed out over North Korea, their chances of survival were very slim. Many troops, after being subjected to strafing and napalm attacks, are in no mood to observe the niceties of the Geneva Convention. Now, physically and emotionally drained, they had to find their way back to the Champ and land on her pitching deck. During all those hectic weeks of combat, the air group had no barrier crashes. All our aircraft landed safely, except one AD that ran out of fuel and ditched alongside. The pilot was picked up by our helicopter. More than anything else, this record demonstrated not only their exceptional skill, but also the fortitude and unfailing devotion of every airman.

If there were any doubts about the ability of carriers to carry out any assignment, the Korean War quickly dispelled them. Banshee pilots boasted that there was no enemy target that they could not hit within twenty minutes of launch from eighty miles at sea. The jets were too fast for much of the enemy's anti-aircraft, and both the Banshee and Panther proved to be gratifyingly rugged and durable. Our pilots worked around the clock, keeping the enemy forces off balance. And they lived in what writer James Michener called "a profession in which men must expect to die."

Landing Signal officer, 1953

Their skill, when one examines it, was astonishing. Imagine cutting a rail line (a major target in Korea) that measured no more than sixty inches wide, while zipping by at four-hundred knots. No easy task. Close air support became a naval aviation specialty. Sometimes the planes of Task Force 77 were flying as many as 500 close-support missions a day. Launch, strike, and recover—day after day, night after night.

All of this, while achieving marvelous results, did not come without cost. In the last two years of the war alone, the Navy and Marines lost 384 tactical aircraft. Of these, 193 Corsairs and 102 Skyraiders were victims.

In spite of many successes, the flying could be frustrating as well. One of Task Force 77's Air Group commanders had these comments: "A pilot would go out one day, do a first-rate bombing job on a bridge or leave several craters in a rail bed, then come back the next day and find that all the damage had been repaired overnight. The war in Korea demanded more competence, courage, and skill from the naval aviator than did World War II. The flying hours were longer, the days on the firing line more, the anti-aircraft hazards greater, the weather worse, and the public appreciation and understanding of the pilot's work and sacrifice was less." This was from a pilot who had flown 102 combat missions in the Pacific.

The next day, while returning from a flight, we heard word on our radio that both sides had accepted the truce terms, bringing the 37-month Korean War to a close.

During her time on the line, LAKE CHAMPLAIN's Airgroup Four flew 2,244 sorties against North Korean and Chinese targets, expending 1,350 tons of bombs, 1,106 rockets, and more than 300,000 rounds of 20mm and 50-caliber rounds of machine gun fire. On the morning of 28 July 1953, the following dispatch appeared in our Plan of the Day: "Upon the occasion of an armistice in Korea this date Commander Seventh Fleet expresses his heartiest congratulations to all ships and units under his command on their individual and collective performance in the fight against communist aggression. During the critical period when the fate of the truce was hanging in the balance, you responded in a manner that is in keeping with the best tradition of the Navy, and you materially aided the cause of freedom by persuading the enemy that war is not in his best interest. We pray that we have achieved a lasting peace, but we must remain ready and alert to meet any future threat to the security of the free world. I am proud of you. Well done to all hands. Signed J.J. Clark, VADM, Seventh Fleet, Commanding." Ten days later, Clark arrived by chopper to preside over a decorations ceremony.

LIFE ON BOARD

While our planes flew from the ship to attack targets hundreds of miles inside Korea, life went on inside CVA-39.

Mornings in that sultry climate brought a routine that never changed. We awakened to the odor of sweating bodies, and, rubbing the sleep from our eyes, we joined the other swabbies shuffling to the showers. Water hours sharply restricted our use of the showers to a brief period just before morning chow and just before lights out. This was usually the case during that summer off the coast of Korea.

Most men were clad in their skivvies or were as naked as the day they were born, but everyone seemed to wear the identical rubber sandals. While shaving in front of those dull-steel sinks, rolling with the ship, the voices of Patti Page or Eddie Fisher were heard throughout the interior deck spaces. Radio Central kept us entertained with the songs of the Hit Parade. Besides music, those odd-shaped gray speakers carried the sound of bells, whistles and bugles. The bells toll for VIP visitors (bong-bong, bong-bong, bong-bong, bong-bong: "COMCARDIV ONE coming aboard" etc.) Bos'n whistles got your attention for an announcement, e.g. "The smoking lamp is out in all authorized spaces," or better still, "Liberty for all hands will commence immediately." The bugler played "Taps" to signal lights out. As we toweled ourselves dry (the sweat returned in a few minutes in that Turkish Bath atmosphere), the smell of frying bacon and sausage permeated the air, triggering our digestive juices. I don't think anyone ever forgot that smell.

Breakfast was a big meal. No coffee and doughnuts here. Besides the usual eggs, cereal, oatmeal or French toast, we never lacked for heartier food. Pork or lamb chops, ham, steak, mashed or fried potatoes, and even spaghetti often found their way on our menu. It pretty much depended on what was left over from the previous night's evening chow. Freshly-baked bread, corn bread or rolls were always at the end of the chow line. Various fruit juices or lemonade accompanied this meal, as well as unlimited coffee.

During working hours, there were water fountains to quench your thirst, with salt pills alongside. In addition, a few Coke machines were strategically located throughout the ship. The latter were so popular that one man, Andy Stein, spent his entire time on board busy replenishing the syrup and cups. During the deployment, the crew drank more than a million Cokes! They also consumed vast quantities of beef, potatoes, vegetables, flour, and sugar. Also, 134,000 hot dogs and a quarter-million cups of ice cream were eagerly devoured. (Unfortunately, there are no figures for Tums!)

LAKE CHAMPLAIN also consumed prodigious quantities of paint, soap and cleaning materials. A common joke was: "We may not win a Presidential Unit Citation (actually we did, a Korean one!), but we'll definitely receive the Good Housekeeping Seal of Approval!" The normal workday was from 0800 to 1600, with an hour and a half for noon chow. A fair chunk of that time was spent on a serpentine queue that snaked across the hangar deck and down to the mess decks. Most men carried pocket books or comics in their dungarees, which helped make the long wait tolerable. One sailor told me that he'd read the complete works of Mark Twain just waiting to eat! To ease this interminable passage, our band was pressed into service every day and played while we shuffled across the deck. A great morale builder.

Once we knocked off work, many men who had been coped up in steaming compartments below decks were glad to get out in the catwalks or up on the flight deck, operations permitting. One advantage carrier duty possessed was the relatively wide-open spaces denied other warships. There was always a breeze underway, and the sunsets were often memorable. In warm waters we could observe

flying fish, porpoises, or an occasional whale. During the late afternoon, on days when flight operations had concluded, we had a chance to take a breather. Those hours just before sunset, when the sea kept reflecting the color of the sky, were among the most enjoyable on board. Standing on the flight deck, with the wind in our faces and the soundless sea stretching out before us, one could almost forget all the hard labor of the past few hours. Watching the broad Pacific swells from the top deck, time takes on another dimension.

One of my favorite pastimes was ocean watching. The sea is always the same, yet always different; deep blue one hour, and green the next, with the changing light spreading stars across the shimmering texture. Whitecaps were the icing in this limitless environment, sometimes turbulent, sometimes placid, and all the while encompassing an ethereal beauty like nothing else in the world. When the sky filled with gorgeous clouds, the combination was unbeatable, and the sunsets at sea were breathtaking. I once read where some Polynesian peoples believed that if you looked hard enough, the face of God could be seen on the surface of the sea. I never lost my love for this most entrancing and mysterious of heaven's creations. Close to land, sea birds accompanied us, some making their nests in the upper reaches of the hangar decks.

Officers not allowed!

When there was no night flying, movies were shown in one of the hangar bays. On other evenings, this area was occupied with one of ship's favorite pastimes: Bingo. Our Catholic Chaplain, Father Joe Kelly, arranged to purchase everything needed for these games in Yokohoma. This was one of the unexpected advantages of having a Catholic Chaplain on board!

For those who thought that Bingo was for little old gray-haired ladies, there were always games of chance in nearly every compartment. Our detachment favored Monopoly, and a game ran continuously for weeks on end. Men dropped out, broke or exhausted, and others took their place. The stakes were a penny to a dollar. That may not sound like much, but if you landed on the Boardwalk with a "hotel," it would set you back twenty-bucks. Acey-deucey was another popular pastime. Other times, when flight operations were suspended, the forward elevator would be lowered to the hangar deck, where it made an ideal volleyball court. In the more humid climates, especially the South China Sea or the Indian Ocean, scores of men brought their blankets and pillows up to the flight deck and slept *al fresco*. There was always a breeze, albeit a moist one, and it was light years ahead of the steaming compartments. Air conditioning only existed in spaces rarely seen by white hats. The sky supplied us with a bonus in the form of the Southern Cross. Actually, on the black flight deck, the night sky was never more revealing, regardless of what part of the world we were sailing in. It resembled a canopy of glittering diamonds. Even without "darken ship," the flight deck was without illumination because of the night vision requirements of the bridge personnel. Sometimes the brilliant phosphorous wake stretched out like a thousand fireflies.

One of the drawbacks of watching the sky and the sea was that it put our distance from home in clear perspective. Out beyond the sight of land (which was the usual case) there was no way to record our passage—no landmarks, no monuments. At times we felt like the Flying Dutchman, just roaming the seas without hitting port.

By far, the most rewarding pastime was reading mail. At sea, our letters and packages would arrive by highline from the tankers and supply ships that refueled and replenished us. Many families sent newspapers and magazines along with their letters, so we had an opportunity to keep abreast of events in the U.S. Letter writers seemed to be everywhere. Once work was secured for the day, they could be found in their racks, in the library, and even perched on the wings of parked aircraft. One of the perks in Korea was postage-free mail.

With loneliness our constant companion, the arrival of mail was a stellar event. All hands not on duty cheered the huge mailsacks, as they were high-lined across the gap of water from the tanker or supply ship. Once delivered, most conversation died as each man looked for a quiet spot to reconnect with family, wife, or girlfriend, thousands of miles away. The letters were read and re-read until they eventually disintegrated in the humidity. Often there would be cause for a celebration when photos arrived of a newborn son or daughter. Sometimes, though, a sailor's letter would be returned, stamped "Addressee Deceased." Whatever the event, the mail always reinforced a feeling of infinite remoteness from the rest of the world.

As welcome as most of the mail was, it had a downside as well. Leafing through a Life or Time magazine, it was pretty evident that this war was on America's back-burner. At home, it was business as usual. Full color magazine ads featured young men cruising along in a new convertible, usually with an attractive blonde sitting next to them. There was no rationing, all the resorts were packed, and yet we knew that just over the horizon, young men were being killed and wounded in a good cause. Forgotten war? You bet.

After a few weeks at sea, the Champ took on all the trappings of a home. It may seem strange to use such a word when describing a huge warship, but LAKE CHAMPLAIN was our home, just as much as that house in Indiana, that farm in Alabama, or that apartment in Brooklyn. Everyone had their favorite hide-a-way, whether it was a gun tub to stand in and shoot the breeze, or a catwalk overlooking the surging ocean. Some sailors enjoyed the quiet of the library in the evening, simply because an aircraft carrier is, if nothing else, one of the noisiest ships in the Navy. One swabbie remarked that living in this ship was like living in an airport.

Friendships were forged that would last a lifetime. These links were far more intense than any group of college students or assembly-line workers. We were engaged in serious work, and often surrounded by life and death situations. Consequently, it was easy to share intimate confidences rarely aired in civilian life. Perhaps the sea had something to do with it.

Out in the ocean, often hundreds of miles from the nearest land, we lost all concept of what life at home was like. Time had a different meaning—always how many days and nights until the next liberty, or more important, until we reached home. We sometimes felt as if we were sailing in some limbo—neither here nor there. Suspended animation would be a good description. It was a perfect place for a sailor to reflect on his life. Where he'd been and where he was going. A lot of my friends made up their minds about the girl they wanted to marry. It was far easier out there than it would be at home with her immediate proximity a major distraction. I later discovered that I wasn't the only sailor to propose by mail.

In the compartments, nearly everyone taped photos to lockers or on bulkheads. Others had carried their RCA 45-RPM phonographs with them, along with a selection of records. Magazines and books could be found under most mattresses, along with all those letters. It may have been the closest quarters anyone could imagine, but once you were in your rack with a pillow under your head, you were snug as a bug in a rug.

During our deployment, we hosted many VIPs; everyone from heads of British Crown colonies to Portuguese orphans. But perhaps the visitor who left us with the most lasting legacy was the writer James Michener, who was on board during the last days of combat. During his time in the Champ, he gathered material for his best selling novel, <u>The Bridges At Toko-Ri</u>. This book became the seminal opus of naval aviation in the Korean War. It was later made into a successful feature film starring William Holden, Grace Kelly, Frederick March and Mickey Rooney. Another "star" was the carrier ORISKANY, a Champ sister, but an image of CVA-39 appeared on the book jacket.

The most famous, and often quoted, line in Michener's book is: "Why is America lucky enough to have such men? They leave this tiny ship and fly against the enemy. Then they must seek the ship, lost somewhere on the sea. And when they find it, they have to land on its pitching deck. Where did we get such men?"

Every night, small groups of men gathered in the gun-tubs holding "bull sessions." Sometimes it was a gripe exercise, but usually the talk revolved around our girlfriends, some of whom we'd marry on our return, and what we'd do with our lives when we no longer wore dress blues. Mail was discussed, especially if we came from the same town. During one stretch, a close friend, John Robben, hadn't received any mail for a couple of weeks, and was really down over it. Some of his shipmates teased him that his next letter would be a "Dear John," but in reality every letter he received was a "Dear John," including the ones from his parents! Eventually, he was buried in letters. His fiancée had forgotten to change the Fleet Post Office address.

Another shipmate, Dick Murphy, inevitably complained about being put on report, yet again, for wearing white socks with dungarees: "Boy, you'd think the Communists really worry about that, wouldn't you?"

A NEW ROLE

The shooting stopped on 27 July 1953, but our job continued. We had a scheduled deployment, and we wouldn't depart these waters until our time was fulfilled. But the changes were monumental.

No more darken ship, no more bombs in the mess decks or rockets on the flight deck. Still, our planes took off armed with 20mm and 50-caliber ammunition—this was only a truce, after all, and not total peace. However, there were no more replenishments at sea. Water restrictions were eased—not totally, but increased so that one could take more than one shower a day. Flight operations were cut to a bare minimum in accordance with the new budgetary requirements—just enough for all the pilots and aircrewmen to qualify for their flight pay. Our stays in Japan were longer, and more R & Rs were dispensed.

Lost in the excitement of those last frantic days just before the war's end, LAKE CHAMPLAIN welcomed a new skipper and "Exec." Captain Leonard B. Southerland relieved Captain Mundorff, and our popular Operations Officer, Commander John Lynch, became our new Exec. Maybe it was the new team, maybe it was the end of hostilities, but whatever it was, the pace slackened and the Champ became a happier, more relaxed ship. Southerland was a completely different personality than Mundorff, and it was reflected in the way the ship was run.

After Southerland left the ship, he was promoted to flag rank, and unfortunately lost his life in a helicopter crash in Okinawa in 1958. More to the point, we had only one more memorial service for a fallen shipmate, and that death was an accident.

In late September, we got some great news. Upon our return to Japan, we'd sail south to Sasebo, where we'd on-load over a hundred combat-weary Marines and soldiers for a fabulous ten-day trip to Hong Kong. Just so we wouldn't get too rusty, on the way we engaged in air operations with the Formosan Defense Command. This garnered the ship the China Service Medal.

In carrying these soldiers and leathernecks, the Champ in some respects reverted to her post-World War II role as a major Magic Carpet instrument. The commissary department went all-out with steak and ice cream on nearly every menu. Movies were

Captain Leonard Southerland, Skipper 1953-1954

Commander John Lynch, Executive Officer 1953

shown twice each evening, and sunbathing was encouraged. No cruise ship ever had a happier group of passengers. Hong Kong was everything a sailor could wish for. It brimmed with sights, sounds and experiences. The moment you stepped from the liberty launch, you were susceptible to sensory overload. The nearest thing to China, it boasted an exotic blend of east and west, duplicated nowhere else on the globe. From an exhilarating ride on the Peak Tram to the highest point, viewing the great harbor, to the weird Tiger Balm Gardens, we tried to absorb all the street images, colorful vendors, and mysterious smells of this incredible port. In every alley and by-way there were bird-sellers, jade dealers, wood carvers, and a multitude of shops offering all the world's merchandise at rock-bottom prices. Never did our dollar go further. Nearly every man came home with tailor-made suits or jackets.

When we tired of shopping, there were swims in Repulse Bay, fabulous meals at Aberdeen or the Peninsula Hotel, and floating markets to marvel at. For those who had to remain on board, there were other sights, just as fantastic. One day a group of small sampans came alongside loaded to the gunnels with ship's painters armed with long poles and brushes. What made this so unusual was all the painters were women! They were called, appropriately enough, "Mary Soo's Side Cleaners." We supplied the Navy Gray and they did the rest. When they finished, LAKE CHAMPLAIN looked as if she had just been commissioned!

While we were anchored out in the harbor, the ship was constantly surrounded by bumboats, offering their wares to every sailor manning the rails. They were prevented from tying up for security reasons, but one day everyone was satisfied as the hangar deck was transformed into a huge oriental bazaar. Scores of tables carried all of Hong Kong's treasures right on board. A lively business was transacted, and all involved left with smiles on their faces, if lighter in their wallets.

Kowloon was the part of Hong Kong on the mainland, and because of its proximity to China, the Crown Colony restricted the wearing of military uniforms to Victoria, or Hong Kong Island. As only a few whitehats were far-sighted enough to purchase civilian slacks and sport shirts in Japan, this restricted the competition to officers, who were similarly clad. No saluting. As a result, the best bargains were had here, along with uncrowded restaurants. Unquestionably, the finest hotel in the Crown Colony, and perhaps the Far East, was the Peninsula. Some of us enjoyed the cocktail lounge and the marvelous restaurant. There was a universal feeling, that if we ever won the lottery, this is where we'd head.

Our return voyage to Yokosuka was tempered by the death of Michael Vitztum, who was lost at sea. More bad news awaited us when VC-4 rejoined the ship. On 2 July, while flying from their base in South Korea, one of their F3Ds was shot down by enemy fire. Missing in action were LT (j.g.) Robert Bick, the pilot, and Linton Smith ATC, the radar operator. These were our final fatalities.

More than anything else, though, this detour to a dream port signaled the end of the fighting.

Many on board were deeply disappointed by the lack of a clear-cut victory. It was difficult to appreciate what we (and the rest of the carrier force) had accomplished in this grueling 37 months of what most called a "dirty war." Being used to the smashing victories of World War II, and raised on all its war films, some thought that Korea was a lost cause. But this was the first of the "limited wars" we were to engage in over the next half-century. With both sides possessing enough nuclear power to destroy not only their opposite, but also the entire world, our policy became one of "containment." After more than three years, and a cost of over million and a half dead or wounded, the Chinese and the North Koreans were exactly where they had started—square one. If our goal was the preservation of South Korea, we had won in spades. One only has to compare the two Koreas to find the answer.

After gutting our armed forces in the years after World War II, we recovered far more quickly than anyone could have imagined, and fought a Chinese army that vastly outnumbered us to a standstill. And we accomplished this without the terrible risk of nuclear war. The Navy could be proud of its vital role.

Korea also led to the rejuvenation of all of our military—the Navy's carrier force most of all. We went from four operational ESSEX-Class carriers at the start of the war to twenty-two at the end. All political opposition to our super-carrier program evaporated overnight. Soon, the keel would be laid for FORRESTAL.

LAKE CHAMPLAIN departed Yokosuka on 17 October 1953. On her return voyage, she made port at Singapore, Colombo, Ceylon (again), Cannes, France, and Lisbon, Portugal. With very limited air operations, this was, for many on board, a pleasure cruise, but one that had been dearly earned. Almost in sight of home, there was still one more surprise in store for us: The last Bingo onboard.

Chaplain Kelly had been running regular Bingo games on the hangar deck since the war ended. Unknown to us, he held back $1,500 for a last grand jackpot to generate interest. Did I say generate interest? The turnout so far exceeded the expectations that more than two hundred hopeful players had to be turned away, as there weren't enough cards.

The tension rose, as each game was played. Finally, it was time for the big event: fill the card, and winner take all!

If a writer had scripted this, it couldn't have had a more storybook ending. A married seaman-deuce (the poorest man in the Navy!) won the grand prize. For him, it was more than a year's pay. The chaplain sent his wife a money order, just to make sure that it wouldn't get "lost" along the way. Just about all hands thought this was a good idea, except a couple of old timers who remarked, "That's the trouble having a Catholic priest run these things. A married chaplain would know better than to send all that money to a sailor's wife." In an aside, another sailor wrote to me that he'd been sitting next to the winner all night, doing nothing. Just before the last game, they decided to switch cards. *C'est la vie*!

On 3 December, Air Group Four launched 65 planes for NAS Jacksonville, Florida. The next day, the Champ made her stateside landfall at Mayport to a tumultuous welcome. LAKE CHAMPLAIN would never again venture into the Pacific nor engage in combat. But her future duties would be just as important—the preservation of peace.

During the Korean War, CVA-39 won the following awards:
National Defense Service Medal
United Nations Medal with Korea clasp
Korean Service Medal with one battle star
China Service Medal
Naval Occupation Medal
Korean Presidential Unit Citation
Korean War Medal (foreign decoration)
Navy Combat Action Award

Det 44 - VC-12 USS Lake Champlain CVA-39 Korean deployment 3-53 thru 12-53

Back from Korea-Mayport, Florida- Dec. 1953

Yokosuka, Japan - Oct. 1953

KOREAN DEPLOYMENT SUMMARY

Length of deployment——218 days
Days at sea ——160
Days in port——58
Days "on the line" in combat——28
Days in which air operations were conducted——59
Total distance steamed ——71,780 nautical miles
(Three times around the earth at the Equator)
Combat sorties flown——2,244

TYPE OF ORDNANCE EXPENDED

2,000 lb bombs——315
1,000 lb bombs——902
500 lb bombs——264
250 lb bombs——4,018
100 lb bombs——2,727
Depth bombs——7
Fragmentation bombs——12
3.5" Solid Rockets——121
5" ATAR——429
5" HVAR——408
6.5" ATAR——148
20mm rounds——282,848
50-caliber rounds——61,200

Fueling at sea——27
Reprovisioning at sea——7
Rearming at sea——14
Number of destroyers refueled——57

Miscellaneous Items
Fuel burned ——12,911,990 gallons
Aviation gas——3,687,593
Carrier landings——5,559
Barrier crashes——5
Food consumed——2,642,000 lbs
including: 204,848 lbs of beef, 506,100 lbs of potatoes, 257,600 lbs of flour
134,880 hot dogs, 1,002,100 Cokes, 250,000 cups of ice cream
100,000 cigars, and 50,000 haircuts.
To keep the Champ looking good we used the following:
21,320 lbs of soap
730 swabs
261 brooms
Paint——5,320 gallons

Perhaps the saddest and most telling statistic was the loss of nine crewmembers that made the supreme sacrifice preserving our liberty.

A NEW CAREER

With the end of hostilities in the Far East, LAKE CHAMPLAIN joined the other carriers in the Atlantic, on a regular rotation in the Mediterranean Sea with the Sixth Fleet. Before joining the fleet, the Champ briefly became a movie star. Featured in the second Cinerama film, "The Thrill of a Lifetime," the film crew captured carrier catapult shots and landings in a heart-

1957

stopping manner never before shown to the public. The scenario even included the "rescue" of a downed pilot by our helicopter. With a new C.O. CAPT Edward Hannigan, CVA-39 left Mayport on 22 September 1954, en route to Europe on her first tour of duty. On board was Air Group Eight, comprised of VF-84 (F9FPanthers), VF-61 (Cougars), and VF-82, VC-4, and VC-62, all flying F2H Banshees. Attack Squadron 85 fielded AD6 Skyraiders. Other Skyraiders were used by VC-12 (AD4Ws) and VC-33 (AD4Ns). For strategic purposes, VC-5 was on board, carrying the huge AJ-1 Savages with nuclear capability.

    This deployment was much more pleasant than her Far Eastern service. The main dangers ashore were being distracted by the new bikini (bathing suit?), which caused more than one rented car to be involved in a collision! Gibraltar, Barcelona, Genoa, Naples and Marseilles were just some of the ports visited. After a seven-month span, she returned on 22 April 1955.

    In June 1955, one of the Champ's most popular skippers, CAPT James Flately, took command. After only four months stateside, the Champ was back on station in the Med. Now she carried Air Group Six. Two fighter squadrons: VF-33 and VF-74 flew Furys and Cougars respectively. They were accompanied by two attack squadrons flying AD Skyraiders—VA-25 and a Marine group, VMA-324. On board were the usual VCs-4-12-33 and 62.

    Ports of call were Gibraltar, Barcelona, Rhodes, Naples (Rome), Cannes (Paris), Athens, Palma de Majorca, Beirut, Valencia, Genoa and Izmir.

    This may sound like all "fun and games," but the Sixth Fleet was engaged in serious business. The Russians were slipping submarines into the Mediterranean, so "hunter-killer" operations became standard. In October 1956, following a training cruise to Gitmo, The Champ joined FORRESTAL and 21 other ships off the Azores to stand by during the Suez crisis.

    However, there was no denying that the liberty was outstanding, and sometimes memorable. Many a Champ sailor couldn't believe that he could sign up for a weekend in Paris while CVA-39 was anchored in Marseilles or Cannes. Others took advantage

New York City early 60's

of a visit to the Eternal City, where almost every time the Pope would arrange an audience. Those on board who had studied Italian or French or Spanish in high school had an opportunity to brush up on their "Parley-vous." Many were astonished that the natives could understand them (of course, the reverse was another thing entirely). In the warmer weather, the crystal-clear Mediterranean Sea was a perfect place for a swim or a lunch on the beach. Conditions weren't always perfect, though. On a February 24th visit to Cannes in the Riviera, sailors found two feet of snow among the palm trees! In spite of some anti-American overtones, the sailors were usually welcomed with open arms. For many countries, like Greece and Turkey, where American soldiers were never seen, the Sixth Fleet's presence was tangible proof of America's commitment to a free Europe. One restaurateur in Nice said, "If the Americans would leave and not return, I would weep. But next year, all of France would weep as well."

Space Capsule recovery

Some sailors had vivid memories of their "dream" liberties. Gene Collett had this tale to tell. "I was among the first to fork over my $50.00, imaging that the three-day tour to Paris would be overbooked. But apparently many of my shipmates felt that the wine, the women, and perhaps the songs were just as good in Cannes as in the French Capital. Plus, they would be spared a ten-hour train ride."

"Going along the coastline of the Mediterranean, the views from our compartment window were like something out of a geography book. The sparkling water sharply contrasted with steep granite mountains plunging down to the sea. Pines dotted the landscape, and each curve revealed a pocket beach of pebbles."

"Once we went inland, we passed miles of vineyards and stone farmhouses. There was very little traffic on the roads. Although American Express chartered the train, we made several stops along the way: Avignon, Valence and Lyons. At each station, vendors covered every open window, offering wine, cheese, fruit, cold meats and French bread. By the third stop, the wine had taken its toll, and some of us felt as if we were floating to Paris. I'm sure many of us were."

"Finally, just as dusk was approaching, we pulled into Gare Lyons, our station. Each group was assigned to a hotel on the Left Bank, and off we went in a bus that looked as though it had been through the First World War!"

"I was bunked with two other men from my squadron. After a quick wash-up, we went out on the town. Bob Crandall and I headed for Les Halles, a huge outdoor market on the other side of the river, noted for its good bistros. Our hotel concierge had recommended it."

"We hopped in an old Renault taxi, and I almost expected to see Maurice Chevalier behind the wheel. My high-school French was a bit rusty, but we managed to locate our brasserie. I saved our bill from that memorable night, and I see that we had onion soup, beef Burgundy, some French Fries (natch!) and to finish off, a crepe Suzette. We also had a carafe of wine, and it had a great effect on us."

"The weather was good, and having a street map, we decided to walk back to our hotel. We discovered that hardly anyone goes to bed early in Paris—or alone. Les Halles was a beehive of activity, even at this late hour. It turned out to be the main market of the city; packed with butchers carrying sides of beef, and trucks unloading boxes of produce. The smells were so over-powering we could have been blind and still found our way around. All around us, tourists and locals walked in the street, some arm in arm, others locked in an embrace, oblivious to everything around them. Bob said it reminded him of a movie, only we were in this one."

"The next day started early for us. A lot of the guys were hung over, but we figured we'd probably only have this one chance in a lifetime to see Paris, and we weren't going to pass it up. We signed up for a bus tour, and for three hours took a crash course in French history. By lunchtime, we'd seen enough monuments to last forever, but along the way we noticed some young girls who were definitely monumental in their own way. Unfortunately, the tour didn't include them!"

"We ate in an outdoor restaurant, enjoying some Indian summer weather. There was an afternoon tour, but instead Bob and I decided to wander about on our own. We parted ways, and I took in the Louvre Museum for about an hour, clicking off the Mona Lisa and the Winged Victory. Walking back across the Seine river, I ran into another American, who insisted on taking me to his local American Legion, where we bent the elbow for a couple of hours. There hadn't been too many American sailors in Paris for a while, so I was a bit of a celebrity in this home of ex-GIs."

"That night we all went to the Casino de Paris for a huge dinner with wine that never stopped. This was followed by a three-hour stage show. The comedians were bi-lingual, and the biggest laughs came from the English version. But it was the showgirls that attracted most of our attention. They were shapely and pretty, and if nothing else showed us how deeply the war had affected the French economy. Here it was, ten years later, and the girls were still clad in only half a costume!"

"On Sunday morning, Bob and I were the only two people in the dining room. We'd decided that we wanted to go to Mass in

Notre Dame, and shortly after finishing our croissants and café filter, we headed back to the river. The cathedral's interior was everything we'd imagined, and we met a couple of pilots from a sister squadron. This meeting resulted in a few 'after breakfast drinks,' a first for me. We all took a taxi to the Eiffel Tower, and rode to the top. The view was breathtaking. After that, the officers headed for a private club, but Bob and I decided to try the French subway, which they called the Metro. We found it very clean and efficient, but it was only a short five-minute ride back to our hotel."

"While waiting for our bus to take us to the train, one of us had the bright idea of leaving all our excess Francs for the chambermaids and waiters. Everyone agreed, but the waiters were more interested in the cigarettes peeking out of our top jumper pockets. We broke out a few packs, and this resulted in smiles all around. All of us had stacked up on Sea Stores before leaving the ship, and we got the equivalent of a better than dollar a pack on the street. We'd paid 12 cents! This exchange allowed us to buy unlimited souvenirs both in Paris and in Cannes."

"The train ride back south was anti-climactic, and most of us spent the time sleeping. By the time we reached the fleet landing at Villefranche, we were a grimy lot, but we were still enjoying a 'high' from our marvelous weekend. Out in the stream, the Champ sat at anchor, ablaze with light. We all agreed that while Paris was wonderful, we were glad to be 'home.'"

Our crew, and the thousands of sailors from the other ships, were indeed good ambassadors for the Unites States. We spent money, yes, but we were genuinely interested in the people. There were numerous "open houses" where we welcomed visitors from every country. Other times, our Chaplains would organize groups to help the poor by repairing housing or distributing food and money collected for that purpose. Youngsters from orphanages would be given tours of the ship, followed by a hot lunch and all the ice cream they could eat. On occasion, those on shore would get a real treat when the carrier engaged in Operation Pinwheel. By massing prop planes on the four corners of the flight deck facing outward, the ship could be turned without using the engines. I guess everyone was happy, except the mechs who had to service those engines.

The men of CVA-39 and the other vessels of the Sixth Fleet played their roles well. They could have their ships off any trouble spot in a few days, land their Marines in a few hours, or have their aircraft over a target in a few minutes. While the fleet didn't belong to NATO, they were in essence, NATO's seaborne right-flank. LAKE CHAMPLAIN's third Mediterranean cruise, and final deployment as a CVA, was with Air Task Group 182. She departed Mayport on 21 January 1957 for a six-month operational voyage, Captain Joseph Young Commanding. The following squadrons embarked: VF-81 flying F7U Cutlasses; VA-16 Special Weapons Team, flying AD4 Skyraiders; Marine Squadrons VMF 533, flying F2H Banshees; VFP-62 Photo F2H Banshees; VAW-12 Early Warning AD5W Skyraiders; VAW-33 Electronic Countermeasures AD4 Skyraiders; VAH-7 F7U Cutlasses.

CVA-39 made port at the following places: Gibraltar, Valencia, Spain, Naples, Italy, Istanbul, Turkey, Salonika, Greece, Athens, Greece, Livorno, Italy, Barcelona, Spain, Cannes, France, Marseilles, France and Palma de Majorca.

If this sounds like a pleasure-cruise, guess again. Besides meeting all her operational objectives, the crew had to literally fight for their lives on 3 July 1957.

A serious fire struck while she was anchored at Marseilles, France. It started when a barge came alongside to transport our vehicles ashore. A faulty valve on board accidentally discharged hundreds of gallons of aviation gas into the harbor, which was ignited by a discarded cigarette. Flames reached up high above the flight deck. Five members of the Champ's crew were lost, as well as five French civilian workers. Many others were injured. Only quick action by the crew saved the ship from serious damage and further loss of life.

Ed Chatterton was one those who was trapped by the fire. "I was in RADIO 4, on the starboard side aft with another ETN working on a transmitter. It was a hot day, and we had the hatch propped open to get some air. We heard a dull roar, and then the announcement over the bullhorn, 'Fire in the water, starboard side.' We headed for the hatch, but by the time we got close enough to see outside, the flames were coming through the opening, driving us back. It was so hot that it melted down the steel light cover just inside the door. All the radio handles and meter faces also melted. The blistering heat drove us into the forward compartment, where the only way out was a scuttle to the starboard catwalk. We tried to open it, but the pin sheared and the handle turned without pulling the dogs. That probably saved our lives, because the draft would have surely killed us on the spot. We tried to use the radio to tell people that we were trapped, but nothing worked because of the fire. We went down to the deck and tried to breathe through our T-shirts and handkerchiefs, but the sooty black smoke followed us right down to the deck. We were about ready to chance the flames when we saw a glimmer of light. It was one of the fire parties foaming and fogging. They were astonished to see us. We went up to the middle of the flight deck where we spit and hacked for an hour. Everything came up black."

"It was a lot closer to disaster than most people realized, because there were eleven 55-gallon drums of gasoline on the fantail. One of the fire parties kept a fog hose on them to cool them. Later, a Chief sent the fire party away and he took over the hose alone. The intense heat bowed the drums top and bottom, close to bursting, but he stood his ground cooling the barrels. Had they exploded, they would have set off some of the fueled Skyraiders on the after end of the flight deck, and with the aircraft packed close together, it would have started a chain reaction. God knows what would have happened then. Praise the Lord for our fire parties and the guts in the men who manned them."

Many men jumped over the side to escape the flames and intense heat. Soon, an announcement was made, "Away all boats to pick up survivors." Ed Winslow reported that a friend of his, Matt Matherin from V-6 Division, was on the barge and badly burned on the face and hands. He saved himself by recalling what he had been taught in boot camp about burning oil at the water's surface. He jumped into the harbor and surfaced three times, in each instance splashing away the fuel and then diving under. He finally swam free of the area. He was sent to a burn center in Texas, and later married his nurse.

George Essey was a Hospital Corpsman, one of those very much in demand on that day. "When the General Alarm sounded, I grabbed my medical kit and barreled up the ladders to the hangar deck. As I rounded the ladder I saw red, orange flames flickering over the bulkheads and the open sky. I ran down to Sickbay, and told everyone what I saw and that this was no drill. As I was running to the scene of the fire, a big Warrant Officer, about 6'6," grabbed me, lifted me from the ground, and told me to wait until they brought up the injured men. Then Clyde Null, HM1, led me to the officer's gangway, where they were bringing up the burned sailors. As we were running forward, Clyde said, 'If you hear one bang, run faster, if you hear two, run like hell and start praying, and if you hear a third big bang run with all your might and pretend that there's another carrier attached to the bow of our ship!' I was never so scared in all my life.

"The following days were sheer hell. I was stationed in the temporary morgue until the Fleet Mortician came aboard. The stench from the burns and the formaldehyde really got to me. One dental technician, Bill Murphy, had the unenviable task of identifying some of the burned bodies from their dental records. The Champ was very lucky. If things had gone the other way we could have lost hundreds of men."

The following were among the more than eighty men commended by the Captain for heroic action:

Jim Hammock BMC, whose action was instrumental in preventing the spread of the fire and saving the ship.

Don Clark BM1, who led a fire party down an accommodation ladder in close proximity to the origin of the fire.

John Turley AB3 and Marion Mosley AB3 were among the first men to arrive and hook up the fog and foam hoses, and saw that they were manned. They then donned breathing apparatus and searched below decks for trapped men.

Jim Cobb DC1 and Bill Fant DC2 were commended for proceeding through smoke and flames to throw burning acetylene bottles over the side to prevent an explosion.

George Gillott AD2 and Bob Webb BM2 directed fire-fighting in the critical early minutes, and later fought their way through smoke and flames to cut the barges loose alongside to separate the main source of the conflagration.

The entire V-12 Division was commended for their fire-fighting efforts in keeping the fire from spreading to the parked planes. Finally, all the Hospital Corpsmen were recognized for the long hours treating their injured and burned shipmates. Once underway, the crew turned to and all the damaged planes and burned vehicles were deep-sixed. Welders repaired the catwalks, and, after a thorough paint job, one would never know just how close the Champ had come to destruction.

THE CHAMP BECOMES A CVS

Because the super-carriers were coming on line, and supersonic attack aircraft were finding it difficult to operate from decks designed for World War II planes, most of the ESSEX-Class CVAs were being converted to ASW (Anti-submarine) work. They would carry S2F Furys and helicopters, and they would operate along the Atlantic coast. CVA-39 became CVS-39 in the summer of 1957. But LAKE CHAMPLAIN would have one last fling as an attack carrier. She left for the Med with Marine Air Group 26 on 5 September 1957, only five weeks from returning from her last deployment.

MAG-26 was comprised of VMF-312, VMA-324, VMA-533 and three helicopter squadrons. Our flat-top supported EXERCISE DEEPWATER, a NATO operation involving amphibious landings on the Turkish coast. She returned to Portsmouth, Virginia, where she entered the yards for a three-month overhaul. CAPTs Joseph Young and George Luker commanded the ship during this period.

The Champ returned to Mayport, and became the flagship of an Anti-Submarine task group. On 9 June 1958, CVS-39 sailed from Virginia to Europe with her new squadrons and duties. VS-27 boasted Grumman S2Fs and Trackers, along with HSS-1 Seabats of HU-3. In addition were HUP-2s from HU-2 and FASRON-3.

August of that year found the ship in an enviable position: entering New York Navy Yard for a four-month overhaul, finishing up at the Bayonne Annex on 4 April. When commenting on a New York City liberty, one old salt remarked: "Where else can you enter a port and discover a beautiful woman welcoming you. In one hand she's carrying a torch (for you), and in the other an address book! Her name? LIBERTY, what else!" Then it was off again to the Champ's favorite port (it seemed), Guantanamo Bay, Cuba, for a Caribbean shakedown prior to her last European deployment. Leaving the Old World after a short tour of duty, she sailed to Quonset Point, Rhode Island, her new homeport, arriving on 3 September 1959. There, she became part of a trio of CVS carriers—ESSEX and WASP her partners. With new anti-submarine squadrons and electronics, she polished her ASW capabilities while settling into her New England home. For the next two years, CVS-39 established a regular cycle of three-week operational cruises off the Atlantic coast.

Her new skippers were CAPTs Penland and Weymouth.

Probably in the entire career of our carrier, this duty was never more pleasurable. Short times at sea, usually arranged to sail in warm waters in the winter, and operate off Canada and the New England coast in the summer. Quonset Point was an ideal liberty port, well used to sailors from World War II, and the proximity of a huge Seabee complex next door at Davisville. Providence was a half hour away, Boston an hour and even the Big Apple was within weekend range.

At sea, the Champ and her consorts honed their skills. By 1959, the Russian submarine had become our biggest threat. The Soviets were beginning to produce nuclear submarines to go with the German-inspired, top-of-the-line diesel electrics. ASW (anti-submarine) techniques—air search, sonar ranging, electronic countermeasures and the like, had now been invalidated by higher underwater speeds and greater endurance. The CNO readily admitted that ASW was his greatest concern. LAKE CHAMPLAIN was once again on the cutting edge.

In January 1961, for the first time in our nation's history, a former naval officer moved into the White House. His tenure would bring LAKE CHAMPLAIN further challenges and glory.

Later that year, on 5 May, our carrier was chosen to play a humble, yet significant role in the first chapter of the United States in outer space. America's first astronaut, Navy Commander Alan Shepard, was recovered by the Champ from the Atlantic, 302 miles down-range from Cape Canaveral, Florida. Shepard's FREEDOM SEVEN Project Mercury space capsule was plucked from the ocean after a dazzling 5,500 mph dash from beyond the earth's atmosphere. The Champ was stationed with three newly-arrived Marine HUS-1 helicopters from MAG-26. The three USMC helicopters were joined by two HSS-1Ns from HS-5. As LCDR Shepard's capsule approached the splashdown area, LTs Wayne Koons and George Cox in a MAG-26 helo were on hand, and secured a line to the space vehicle while retrieving America's first astronaut. Hovering nearby all the while were LT JGs Dan Manningham and Richebourg Gaillard III of HS-5.

America's first space triumph was marked by a thunderous reception for the astronaut by the crewmen of the Champ. One could almost hear the scratching of history on the page of time. The U.S. had succeeded in space. Oren Peterson, a Lieutenant Commander, and the Officer in Charge of VC-12, wrote this moving letter to his family. "Well it's all over, and I was there, viewing the historic first U.S. manned space flight. If you thought it was exciting and suspenseful on television, you should have been here! Just picture us, 2,000 men on the open decks of LAKE CHAMPLAIN, up since the early hours and awaiting the arrival of our visitor from space. Tension mounted steadily as the countdown went through its several delays. Then finally came those last interminable seconds. The air was electric! Rockets away! A great cheer went up from all our throats."

"Then we waited. Announcements came over the loudspeakers that the flight was going just as programmed. An attempt was made to feed in Shepard's radio transmissions over the loudspeakers. We could make out his voice although it was mostly static. Then came the word, 'He's coming down from 75 degrees up and off the port quarter, and will land about six miles dead ahead of the ship.' All eyes strained. Then came the sonic boom from high in the air where the capsule decelerated through the speed of sound. People pointed up high in the clear sky off the port bow, and there was a small white puff of smoke. Soon after, this was followed by another boom to add sound to the smoke which we had already seen; no doubt this was an attention-getting device to bring eyes to the area where the parachute would be seen. And sure enough, soon afterward we saw the chute—orange in color. Another spontaneous cheer. About three minutes later the capsule hit the water and the chute fell clear. Shortly after, the recovery helicopter was hovering overhead. 'Commander Shepard has left the capsule and is being hoisted into the chopper,' came the report. The helicopter completed its hookup, and the capsule began to rise, water pouring from the bottom vents of the capsule. Minutes later, the capsule was lowered to its resting pad on the flight deck. The chopper landed as well and Commander Shepard stepped out."

"You probably saw the rest on television; how he was greeted by the press and NASA technicians, how he strode to the capsule and checked something inside, and then went below for extensive debriefing and medical tests. As he left, a great cheer went up from all of us, but he didn't hear it due to the noise of the choppers. And so, it's history now. I thought I'd write this down and share this moment with you. Someday this letter may prove a cherished prize for your grandchildren."

As the chopper approached the flight deck, Alan Shepard told one of the aircrewmen: "This is one of the best carrier landings I've ever made!" As naval aviator Shepard was welcomed aboard by CAPT Ralph Weymouth, the crew went wild with enthusiasm. The ship's post office achieved some notoriety by issuing first day covers of the event for every man, no doubt making this a collector's dream come true. Although millions joined the echo of her cheers that day, the crew aboard the capsule-catching carrier will always hold the added thrill of distinction of being the very first citizens to welcome America's first astronaut back from outer space. We will never forget the unique advantage we enjoyed that sun-drenched, history-making morning in May 1961. The Champ was there!

During the summer, newer choppers were seen on deck: among them the Sirkorsky HSS-2 Sea King, but more ominous events would soon involve LAKE CHAMPLAIN.

After Castro took over Cuba in 1959, he soon consolidated his relationship with the Soviet Union. He felt that Guantanamo Bay was Cuban soil, and made threatening gestures to eject us. We in turn increased our Marine strength, and the situation deteriorated. Advisors and MIG fighters were one thing, but nuclear missiles were another completely. When our intelligence revealed an increase of 50 percent in arriving Russian merchantmen, U-2 flights were authorized. On 29 August 1962 the photo recon plane brought back incontrovertible proof of Russian missile sites. The fat was in the fire. The Navy went on full alert.

Various contingencies were explored, and a "quarantine" or blockade of the island was ordered. LAKE CHAMPLAIN joined a force that consisted of Task Force 135, built around the giant CVAs INDEPENDENCE and ENTERPRISE, and Task Force 136, led by the carrier ESSEX, three cruisers and a screen of destroyers. Soviet subs had been detected along the route, and ASW carriers, CVS-39 among them, utilized their aircraft. Their planes, mostly S2Fs, were employed to monitor the Russian freighters.

Dwight Lubich, one of pilots, related how his reconnaissance flights carried him directly over the Soviet freighters. "We were embarked from at least 29 October through 1 December 1962, during which my crew flew eight night surveillance missions from 10 through 20 November. We would have flown one more, except that during the pre-flight for another launch, it was announced that the blockade had ended, or at least our participation therein."

USS Lake Champlain

"I do recall some of the details from this period. First, I learned of our impending participation and subsequent sailing when returning with a group of pilots from FCLP (Fleet Carrier Landing Practice) at Quonset Point late on the evening of 24 October. We were met by the Duty Officer who told us to go home, pack, and return early the next day for a 'sea cruise in the warm waters of the Caribbean.' Also, different from the normal night ASW operation, we were authorized to drop below the standard 300-foot night minimum altitude 'as necessary' to identify vessels and check deck cargo for the missiles. This required close crew coordination, since the co-pilot operated the searchlight and verbally identified the ship over the intercom, while the crewman recorded the report. All the while I had one eye on the radio altimeter and the other on the gyro horizon, while trying not to hit the superstructure and/or rigging of the target vessel!"

"We were briefed to make as few passes as necessary so as not to provoke an incident, but since many of the ships names/homeports were in the Cyrillic alphabet, this was not always possible. Earlier in the period there had been more moonlight, making our job a little less perilous. Another concern of mine was the seventy-million candle-power searchlight on the S2F that provided a nice target for small arms fire. Since this Grumman product had no armor plating, nor self-sealing fuel tanks, we might end up as another Cold War statistic!" In the end, the Russians backed down, removing all offensive weapons from Cuba.

To demonstrate how well our Navy had perfected its ASW capability, every time a Russian Foxtrot submarine surfaced during the crisis, one of our destroyers was there, and frequently carrier planes from CVSs like the Champ. The Navy certainly played its part well in unnerving the submariners, pinging on them with active sonar and, in at least one case, dropping practice depth charges, which could be particularly unsettling to ears trapped inside a pressure hull.

The solution to the Cuban Missile crisis was, in the end, a diplomatic one. But the Russians, everywhere they looked, could see American forces deployed in brutal strokes in the readied missile wings, the manned B-52s aloft, the deployed Army and Marine units. And they could see our national resolve far out in the Atlantic, in the hundreds of warships, LAKE CHAMPLAIN not the least among them. LAKE CHAMPLAIN was awarded the Armed Forces Expeditionary Medal for this deployment.

In this single harrowing moment, the United States Navy fully justified every penny spent on its ships and men. The whole reverse process took weeks, but by 15 December, the Navy could report that the last offensive weapons (in the form of 15-crated IL-28s) had left Cuba. The Navy kept on eye on these weapons almost every step of the way back through the Atlantic, the Mediterranean and the Baltic. At the height of the crisis, 181 U.S. warships had taken part. The United States had again turned to sea power to wield the iron fist in a velvet glove, and again the ships and men of the Atlantic Fleet had shown that this confidence was not misplaced.

The Champ was getting old. She was now the last straight deck carrier left in the operational fleet. With mostly choppers and Furys, she could recover aircraft without undue concern. On other huge flat-tops, many of which were nuclear-powered, Intruders and other supersonic jets needed the acres of flight deck space offered by this new line of giants with canted decks. CAPTs Bolan and Burgess skippered our carrier through the Cuban crisis and beyond.

In the early Sixties, the Champ locked horns (and other things) with other objects, sometimes ships, sometimes inanimate objects, sometimes raw nature itself. Early in the morning of 16 February 1963, the Champ was battered by a vicious North Atlantic storm. David R. McDonald of Farmington Falls, Maine, was on forward lookout duty of the carrier's 60-foot flight deck when a gigantic wave struck the ship. "I thought I was a goner," McDonald said. "I hung there and looked at that wave." Although he fastened a death grip on that railing, the wave wrenched him loose and hurled him 17 feet downward into a gun tub.

Another crewman, standing inside a passageway from the catwalk, felt the impact of the wave, paused a moment, opened the hatch to see if McDonald was down in the gun tub, and with others climbed down to rescue him. He returned to duty the next morning.

In October of that year, a killer hurricane, Flora, struck the Caribbean, centering on Haiti. With winds upwards of 140 miles an hour, the devastation was incredible. LAKE CHAMPLAIN was selected to help with humanitarian relief after the storm. After taking on a large cargo of CARE packages at Mayport, Florida, the ship steamed to Haiti. On arrival, she found hundreds of dead animals floating offshore. The devastation was immediately apparent upon entering Port-au-Prince harbor—the hillsides looked as though they had been bombed. The carrier stayed a week off-loading the relief packages. Although there was limited liberty, it wasn't recommended because of the desperation of the people. The Ships Company and her Marine contingent quickly delivered food and medicine to the homeless thousands, and our medical staff assisted the local doctors. It was estimated that the Haitian death toll would exceed 2,500.

LAKE CHAMPLAIN also seemed to have a propensity for colliding with other ships and piers. On 6 May 1964, USS DECATUR DD-936 lost steering control as she was breaking away after completing a refueling operation. The destroyer became locked underneath the overhang of the flight deck, and was held in her grip while the pitching motion of the ship acted as a battering ram on DECATUR. Miraculously, no one was killed or injured, but the Champ sheared away everything above the level of the main deck, including the mast, forward stack and most of the aluminum superstructure. Our damage was limited to the starboard catwalks and bow gun tub. DECATUR, seriously damaged, managed to return to Norfolk under her own power, but she was taken out of service.

Less than one month later, on 3 June 1964, while carrying a contingent of Midshipmen to a northern European summer cruise, the Champ ran into thick fog in Chesapeake Bay. In spite of signaling a warning that we were intending to pass a Norwegian tanker, the SKAUVAGG, on the right, she plowed right into our starboard quarter. The tanker hit us on an angle, and caused damage above and below the waterline. Some gas bottles next to the battery shop ignited, starting a nasty fire. Fortunately, no personnel casualties were sustained, but the NROTC midshipmen were transferred to ESSEX, who carried them to Scandinavia. CVS-39 had to go into the yards for twenty days of repairs. End of European cruise.

On another occasion, the Champ rearranged the contours of her pier at Quonset Point. In October 1964, the Champ got underway to participate in exercise STEELPIKE I, the largest amphibious landings held since World War II. Our group provided ASW protection for the task group on the Atlantic transit to the Bay of Cadiz and the following assault on the Spanish beaches near Huelva. From 10 to 30 October CVSG-54 conducted continuous round the clock flight operations compiling 3,446 flight hours in just 20 days. This was LAKE CHAMPLAIN's last overseas deployment. She returned to Quonset Point on 25 November.

On 26 August 1965, CVS-39 was again involved in the space program when she was selected to retrieve the GEMINI 5 astronauts, LTCOL L. Gordon Cooper USAF and LCDR Pete Conrad USN, who had just completed eight days

TOP RIGGER-USS Lake Champlain (CVS-39) claims Atlantic Fleet record for rigging Davis (S2F) barrier with a time of 59 seconds

in orbit. This event held a particular significance for LCDR Conrad, since he'd made his first carrier landing in 1954 on LAKE CHAMPLAIN.

1965 would mark the Champ's twentieth year, and in the fast-moving world of naval aviation, she was having trouble keeping pace. Her proud crew fondly called her, "the straightest and the greatest," but she was beginning to spend more time under repair than at sea. After 65,000 arrested landings, her active life came to an end. On 2 May 1966, at the Philadelphia Navy Yard, her pennant was hauled down for the last time and she was placed in the inactive fleet. But she wasn't ready for the scrap yard. LAKE CHAMPLAIN was given a "special" status to allow the Defense Department to consider alternative uses for CVS-39. For a while, it was thought she might serve a useful purpose as a space recovery vessel or as a training carrier, but the latter would have required the expense of installing a canted deck from ANTIETAM CVS-36.

The ESSEXs were going out of commission one by one, however, and in the end she was sealed and dehumidified and placed back in "mothballs." During the next few years, much of her serviceable equipment was removed and placed in other flat-tops, the J.F.KENNEDY being only one.

In August, 1972, her time ran out and she was towed to a salvage yard in Kearney, New Jersey for cutting up.

While she was being dismantled, one of her former crewmen, Ray Benedict, couldn't let her go. Ray had served on board from April 1960 to March 1962. He was a member of the Marine Detachment and a crewman on one of the 5-inch mounts. He held various other jobs during his tenure, but none as rewarding as the Orderly and driver for Captain Cecil Bolam. It was probably that last experience that inspired him to do what he did, and save a little bit of the Champ for posterity. I'll let him tell his story.

"On a dark, moonless night, just after my wife had given birth to my son, Tim, I climbed aboard the Champ just before the cutting torches and other nasty equipment began their terrible work. I knew at the time that if anything was to be salvaged, it was my job to do so."

"Every night after leaving the hospital to see my wife and son, I would visit the Champ with my tools. If I could have towed her to safety, I would have. So, in my anxiety I removed the Zebra, X-Ray and Yoke identifying plates from the hatches. Also the sprinkler heads from the brig that so many prisoners had polished. Then, the Ready Room placards and the Marine Corps insignia from the Marine C.O.'s door. I have Captain Bolem's chair from the bridge, from which I stood off to one side when he was in command. I never sat in it, as this was his chair as Commanding Officer. I do not own it, and only guard it as I would if he was there. Sometime, it would be my honor to see him back in that chair. I loved serving under him as a crewmember, and truly loved the LAKE CHAMPLAIN. It's gone, but some parts are around. I'd like to believe that as long as any crewmember lives, so does our ship. It took nine months to complete the dismantling of our ship down to the keel. I would pass by and slowly but surely see her disappearing. I didn't feel good stopping as time went by, but I did it as if I were visiting a sick friend. I took some pictures while she was at Kearney, New Jersey in 1972, but none after they started the dismantling. I wanted to remember her as she was."

"I still have the Captain's chair and some other memorabilia. Most crewmen probably never got to see it while they were on board, but it kind of represents the ship. Standing close, it still has the paint and smell of the ship."

So, the Champ faded into history. Yet, as we shall see in the succeeding pages, not completely.

WALKING THE DECKS OF HISTORY:

Discovering the ghosts of the Champ

In 1982, in the New York Times, I saw a photo of another ESSEX-Class carrier in New York City. I took a double-take, but it was true. The carrier INTREPID had been saved from the cutting torch, and she was about to be permanently moored at the foot of 42nd Street in Manhattan as a floating museum. A few weeks later, I had some business on the east side, and, recalling the news item, I decided to see the ship for myself. It was a dreary day as I proceeded across Manhattan, west along 42nd Street, past Times Square to the river. There, as I turned the corner, a great warship filled my vision, and looked for a moment, almost alive. I almost expected to see this gray carrier get underway. That familiar silhouette reawakened within me images and memories going back three decades. The roar of the city traffic faded, replaced now by the high-pitched scream of jets hurtling into the night sky off Korea.

With a multitude of planes crowding her flight deck and an array of signal flags fluttering from the yard, I strained to hear the bosun proclaim, "Set the special sea detail" and "Single up all lines." But there's no bosun, and those lines that held her fast to the pier would never again be cast off for a ship about to get underway. INTREPID stood mute: a dead ship, but also a living symbol of all those brave men who served in her. In a greater sense, for me she represented every carrier and every carrier sailor, ship's company and airedale, officer and whitehat. And, for me, she was the nearest embodiment of the Champ around.

As I approached the stairway on the wharf leading to the quarterdeck, I was humbled by this mighty mass of steel towering over me. Memories flooded back to a sunny afternoon in April 1953, when I stood next to USS LAKE CHAMPLAIN CVA- 39, on Pier Seven, Naval Operating Base, Norfolk. At that time, some of us had serious doubts that anything this big could float, much less move. But, coming aboard, her hangar deck felt even more solid under my feet than the concrete pier alongside. Later I discovered, like thousands of sailors before me, that she would indeed not only move, but would become as one with the great ocean, her true home.

Earlier I had served in other carriers: USS MIDWAY CVB-41 and USS FRANKLIN D. ROOSEVELT, CVB-42. These CVBs (as they were then designated) were the first of the large post war battle-carriers. Later they would be exceeded in size by the FORRESTAL Class, the initial super flat-tops. Nevertheless, at 888 feet and 40,000 tons, LAKE CHAMPLAIN was impressive enough for me.

These superb ships introduced me into the world of carrier aviation, the most exhilarating adventure I could imagine. I was more fortunate than most of my shipmates, having the incomparable opportunity to fly

AD4W Skyraider being launched - Korea June 1953

from and land on these decks. I was an enlisted aircrewman, flying as a radar navigator in an airborne early warning squadron. I operated from the backseat of a Douglas Skyraider, and it was the thrill of a lifetime.

Observing flight deck operations, even as a spectator, was an unforgettable thrill. Few experiences in the next 50 years would ever come close to that spectacular ballet of men and machines, all struggling to maneuver in a space far too small to accommodate them. Screaming jets catapulted into the sky, while other planes slowly eased into position behind them. The blur of multi-colored shirts directing these ten-ton monsters on a narrow deck, the strong smell of burning kerosene, signal flags whipping in the breeze of a great ship at full steam, the incredible cacophony of a score of straining engines: all this was the gist of high drama.

However, if anything topped being on the flight deck, it was observing this same intricate operation from the air, on the final approach before turning into the wind to be recovered. No matter how often I viewed this jumble of planes and men from a mile or two out, I never thought there would be room enough for us to land. Wedged in that tiny compartment, unable to exert even the slightest control over my destiny, I placed myself in God's hands and my pilot's skills, and I learned the true meaning of faith. Carrier landings, regardless of how many you made, were NEVER, but NEVER, routine.

All these memories welled up as I walked the worn and beaten flight deck of CV-11. Late in the morning of a drizzly Monday, I had the ship almost to myself. Aircraft that would never fly again stood mute as statues, tied down to a final resting place. I thought about the pilots and crews who manned these sleek jets and wide-bellied props, and I wondered if any of them have ever returned to their old "friends" who bore them aloft and whispered, "Thanks." I'd give anything to sit in the backseat of one of my Skyraider AD4-Ws, but they've all but disappeared.

Looking aft to the "island," I could almost again hear the high-pitched commands emanating from the bull horn: "Prepare to launch aircraft" or "Clear the deck. Plane in final approach has hung rocket." Images that I don't want to recall force their way into my mind's eye: the mangled, blood-soaked body of the plane handler who walked into a whirling prop, and later, looking down from the deck into the churning sea for a shipmate who was blown over the side by jet blast. We never found him.

Of course, there were happy times too. The crossing of the Equator in May 1953, en route to Korea, when hundreds of men were initiated into the realm of King Neptune in that never-to-be-forgotten ceremony. None of us could forget those humid nights in the tropics, when the flight deck was littered with scores of sailors fleeing their fetid compartments. The sheer immensity of the black star-filled sky quickly brought all conversations down to the level of a whisper, and for awhile we could imagine ourselves the only ship in this trackless sea. Under this celestial dome there was a solemn feeling that we were inside some vast cathedral, and I guess in a very real sense we were.

It was a time out of time.

Somehow, we never talked about death, even though it was our constant companion. In the glorious optimism of youth, we thought we'd live forever.

Those conversations would flow, night after night, whenever we weren't flying or standing watches. More than anything else, it was a communal confession. In the inky darkness, our hopes and fears bubbled to the surface, revealing far more about ourselves than we could or would have done in the daylight. Reassurance was found in the glow of each other's cigarettes, signaling that we weren't suffering a singular loneliness.

Sailors being sailors, though, no exchange could remain totally serious. One night, one of our "inner circle," Dick Murphy, remarked that the last time he'd been in a place this dark, it was in the "Tunnel of Love." John Williford, laughing, rejoined, "Don't get any ideas!"

I moved down the port ladder, onto a catwalk holding a gun mount. I discovered that there was no better place to think, and dream those special dreams of all sailors, than on such a catwalk on a moving ship. I thought, too, of the hundreds of gunners who stood here during World War II, sometimes for days on end, searching the sky for the deadly kamikazes. They had their dreams as well, and I'm reminded that some of them traded their tomorrows for the freedoms we enjoy today.

Climbing all the way down below, I reached the cavernous hangar deck. There, I needed a little time to acclimate myself. Unbelievably, the entire space had been turned over to a myriad of visual displays and running documentaries that continuously rolled, regardless of whether there were viewers or not. It's as if they were playing for my ghosts and had a life of their own. Here, meticulously crafted warship models vied with more planes, some mock-ups from the dawn of aviation.

There was even a restaurant, which brought into sharp recollection the endless hours I spent on chow lines in such a space. I tried to recreate that distinctive atmosphere, but in vain. What I missed most was that unique smell—the evocative blend of frying grease, lubricating oil and the scent of hundreds of sweating men. Finally, I moved out into the open air of the fantail, and it was exactly as I remembered it from the Champ.

It was here that we marked the progress of our long journey, observing the mighty screws etch their message on a slate of blue. Crossing the Atlantic, the Mediterranean, or the Indian Ocean, it became a rendezvous perch to watch the last rays of the dying sun. Other times, the chaplain held communal prayer services, and it was an ideal spot to make new friends, as our rates and ranks disappeared in a mutual bond of loneliness. Some of those links remain unbroken nearly fifty years later, as my shipmate and good friend John Robben can attest to. Sadly, some of the men who shared those evenings were later shot down or disappeared at sea. Watching the long wake somehow put the monumental distance we were covering into context, and gazing at the dying swirls of spume could mesmerize even the most hardened sailor. It's hard to recapture that special feeling on a moored vessel, but I try. Screaming gulls broke my trance, and I retreated once again back into the hangar deck.

I began to walk forward, hoping to retrieve that old sense of place, but there were just too many distractions. To survive, INTREPID must be a tourist attraction. There aren't enough old sailors to support such an expensive venture. It's hard to imagine that, within the confines of this steel chamber, hundreds of men fought and died amid exploding planes, smoke and fire.

Some think this is not a dignified way for a ship to end her days. Better to be sunk as a target like SARATOGA and NEVADA at Bikini, or chopped up into razor blades as most of INTREPID's sisters were, including the Champ. I disagree. Historically, the Navy has always come out on the short end. America is dotted with battlefield memorials, from Bunker Hill to Gettysburg, from Appomatox to the Alamo, but there's no way to mark a site at sea where noble events occurred, and brave men died. All too often, the greatest ships of those battles lie below the surface along with the heroic men who fought in them.

We're fortunate to have such priceless carrier memorials as INTREPID, LEXINGTON, YORKTOWN, and now HORNET. Former sailors are trying to save MIDWAY and FORRESTAL, and I wish them well. America needs constant reminders of those who sacrificed much (and sometimes all) to preserve the freedom we enjoy today. Every school child in New York could learn much from INTREPID. There's no better way to lift history out of the dry pages of a book and make it a living experience.

I found myself all the way forward on the hangar deck, and my journey with the ghosts of my past was almost over. This area, where so often at sea the forward elevator was lowered for volleyball games when the air group stood down, is now a theatre. Here, wide-screen movies of flight deck operations are shown. Ensconced in this dark enclosed space, the sound system is so authentic that the vivid images of catapulting jets shock me with a sharp tingle that sets my hair on end.

Now, I said goodbye to this remarkable ship. There was no officer of the deck to ask permission from, nor was I expected to turn aft and salute the national ensign. There was just a long stairway leading down to the pier, and a reality of a different sort.

As I reached the last step, I turned and took a long, last look at CV-11. The ghosts of my memories had gone now, disappearing back into the hundreds of compartments and spaces above and below deck. But they're still there, waiting for other sailors to come home. Like me.

It was difficult walking away from INTREPID. The smells, the sounds, the sensations of moving through that mighty vessel, brought back recollections of a time in my life that was precious to me. Their effect on me was profound, and it taught me once again about the rich quality of that experience.

EPILOGUE

A NEW BEGINNING

By 1987, USS LAKE CHAMPLAIN had been gone for fifteen years. She only remained as a fond memory in the hearts of her surviving crew. But two events, totally unrelated, would soon bring the name LAKE CHAMPLAIN to the fore once more, on land, at sea, and in the air.

Unknown to but a few people inside the Navy, a new line of ships had been authorized—the TICONDEROGA Class of guided-missile cruisers. This in itself wasn't notable, except that these ships would primarily bear the names of former carriers that had gone to the breakers. LAKE CHAMPLAIN would be one of these.

Of course, none of her former shipmates knew this. As far as we were concerned, our carrier and home was gone. Memories of our days and nights on board grew dim, and we wondered if anything of our ship survived. Aside from the Captain's chair that was rescued from the wreckers, there were few other artifacts.

In July 1987, I was contacted by my Navy League Chapter in New York about the upcoming commissioning of a warship in New York City. Would I be interested in attending this ceremony, and more to the point, would I be inclined to contribute to the crew's welfare fund? After reading a little further, my subsequent answer to both questions was a rousing "Aye, Aye, Sir!" This would be the first such commissioning in New York City since the end of World War II. I'd been to other such events, usually submarine launchings at Groton's Electric Boat Co. in Connecticut, but this promised to be something different altogether. For openers, the name LAKE CHAMPLAIN leaped up at me from the page.

Was I seeing things? LAKE CHAMPLAIN was cut up into razor blades more than ten years before. No, I wasn't seeing things. Yet this wasn't an aircraft carrier, it was a new type of warship: a guided-missile cruiser. Her number would be CG-57. I mailed in my acceptance (along with a check), and shortly thereafter I received a beautifully engraved invitation for my wife and me.

It was a brutally hot August day in New York City, the kind referred to as a "dog day." We were committed, however, and we joined a group of other attendees in the shadow of another ESSEX-Class carrier—the INTREPID. The Navy Band assembled on its deck edge elevator, and we sweltered through interminable speeches by the ship-builder, the Secretary of the Navy, and various politicos, which included Mayor Koch of New York and Senator Patrick Moynihan.

When the last speech ended, Captain Ralph K. Martin, the skipper of CG-57 accepted the ship from the Ingalls Shipbuilding Co. Then came the moment we had been waiting for. The command rang out: "Man the ship!" From seemingly every hatch and opening hundreds of white clad officers and men manned the rails, to the accompaniment of "Anchors Aweigh," courtesy of the US Navy Band.

The screws turned, the helicopter rotors gyrated, the radar antennas revolved, and the 5-inch gun rotated. My wife Marianne and I were invited on a tour of the ship. To my wondrous surprise, what did I discover on the quarterdeck but the original bell from CVA-39! So, this new greyhound would be going to sea with a part of our great carrier. It was a bit like an organ transplant. LAKE CHAMPLAIN was alive and sailing the world's oceans.

Reunions

Captain Martin and I corresponded for a while, and a year later he graciously sent me an inscribed copy of CG-57s first cruise book, commemorating her West Pac deployment. While this cruiser was carrying part of our original home with her, she was home-ported 3,000 miles away in San Diego. We needed something closer to keep our memories alive.

In 1989, that something took shape when the first national reunion of the USS LAKE CHAMPLAIN ASSOCIATION was held in Charleston, South Carolina. A few former crewmembers had created a database of some of the men who had served in the Champ, and placed ads in some military magazines.

Over a hundred shipmates, their wives and friends met for three nights at this charming and historic city, trading sea stories and reliving the days of their youth. We elected officers, and adopted a set of by-laws. We voted to meet the following years at Jacksonville, Florida and Burlington, Vermont, on Lake Champlain itself, a very suitable location.

We had some growing pains, but slowly, the organization expanded. We're now at close to 900 paid, with many more on the edge. A vigorous recruiting program was instituted by Chris Carroll, our Vice-President's wife, with great success.

Through the years we've gathered at such interesting sites as: Nashville, Tennessee; Charleston, South Carolina; Burlington, Vermont; Philadelphia, Pennsylvania; the Catskills, New York; Pensacola, Florida; New Orleans, Louisiana; Virginia Beach, Virginia, Baltimore, Maryland, and Myrtle Beach, South Carolina.

These reunions compressed our time frames. Meeting old shipmates erased the years, and soon it was as if we were sitting in the same mess-deck again, complaining about the appearance of meatloaf yet again. The loss of hair and teeth were compensated by the gain of pounds and inches. All of us, it seemed, were far more concerned with the rise in Medicare than the rise of hemlines. Photos of grandchildren were prominent around the tables, as well as fading cruisebooks. "Did I ever look that young?" was a common remark. We recalled the good times and the bad, the grinding loneliness and the wonderful liberties, and, by putting these memories in context, placed an imprimatur on our lives. In addition, our wives inwardly basked in the memory that their men had done something out of the ordinary with their lives. It was a time for all to be proud.

Through our Ship's Store, members can purchase hats, shirts and jackets, all outfitted with the LAKE CHAMPLAIN logo. Just ask any wife how difficult it is to get one of those jackets or shirts from our backs. Many of the letters I've received reveal that some of our shipmates were buried in them! A quarterly magazine, THE CHAMP, is published for the members. It features stories from the various "lives" of our ship, and is filled with many striking photos. Still, it's the letters that attract the most notice. Everyone has a chance to be heard. These messages could easily be turned into a book (such as the one you're holding right now). If nothing else, it revealed to me how little I knew about the USS LAKE CHAMPLAIN.

We didn't neglect the Internet. A few years back, John Printy established our own website and Champ Chat Room. The thousands of "hits" have been invaluable in attracting new members. In 1998, the ESSEX Class carrier HORNET CVS-12 was spared from the scrappers, and has been transformed into a carrier memorial at Alameda, California. She was the last of the ESSEXs to be saved, the others being INTREPID CV-11, in New York City, YORKTOWN CV-10, in Charleston, South Carolina, and LEXINGTON CV-16, at Corpus Christi, Texas. Dwight Lubich, a former S2F pilot on the Champ, and two other museum volunteers, Pete Clayton and Alan McKean, decided to convert one of the HORNET's compartments into a Champ Room—a hallowed place that would become a repository of LAKE CHAMPLAIN memorabilia, and an ongoing permanent memorial to the Champ. Donations from the Association and its members were solicited, and at this writing the space is well on its way to becoming a living remembrance of our great carrier. One of our shipmates, Keith Sweazy, donated a handsome hutch with two sideboys, that he fashioned himself.

Consequently, with a guided-missile cruiser sailing the seas, a permanent location on another ESSEX Class carrier memorial, and a vibrant association, the Champ's memory is very much alive. Our object is to make old sailors young again, even if only for a few days a year.

As time passes, and we enter this new millennium, one thing is certain. It may be easy to take a sailor out of the Champ, but it's damn hard to take the Champ out of a sailor! Our gallant ship will live as long as one man remains who served in her.

Jack Sauter

Lake Champlain Association Room Aboard Hornet

Compartment B-0208-AEL, frames 113-117. Originally Radio Xmitter Rm. #2; later assigned as Air Group Maintenance Office. Of the twenty four a Essex Class associations, approximately half have committed to a space in Hornet to display their artifacts. Especially with Keith Sweazy's beautiful oak cabinet work, when finished this room will be the premier association compartment.

THE LAST DAY

The following is the mid-watch entry written by LTJG J.V. Connor on CVS-39s last night at sea en route to the Philadelphia Naval Shipyard for decommissioning.

A sad day begins for the Champ and her crew
It's hard for both, but the story is true.
In true Champ style we begin underway,
En route to Philly for a long, long, stay.
We operate alone, but are not to blame,
That soon no active ship will bear our name.
Boilers two, three, five and seven are on line
And Gens two and four are running just fine.
Yoke has been set throughout this proud ship,
NAVALAIRLANT messages direct this trip.
Our Captain is S.O.P.A. and OTC,
The fate of the Champ we all wait to see.
Our speed is One-Two, our course Two "O" Five,
Champ may be doomed but her spirit survives.
Her Captain and crew are the best you can find
To put her away is something we mind.
But true to her name she'll go winning someday,
When once again we hear that Champ's underway.

(S.O.P.A—Senior Officer Present, Afloat. OTC—Officer in Tactical Command)

COMMANDING OFFICERS OF USS LAKE CHAMPLAIN

Logan Ramsey——June 1945 to February 1947
George T. Mundorff——May 1952 to July 1953
Leonard B. Southerland——July 1953 to June 1954
Edward A. Hannigan——June 1954 to June 1955
James H. Flatley——June 1955 to June 1956
Joseph B. Young——June 1956 to July 1957
George R. Luker——July 1957 to August 1958
Robert W. Leeman——August 1958 to October 1959
Joseph R. Penland——October 1959 to August 1960
Ralph Weymouth——August 1960 to July 1961
Cecil A. Bolam——July 1961 to September 1962
Andrew L. Burgess——September 1962 to June 1963
Charles A. Blovin——June 1963 to July 1964
James C. Longino Jr.——July 1964 to June 1965
Elbert H. English——June 1965 to June 1966
Deactivated 2 May 1966
Decommissioned 30 June 1966

DECORATIONS EARNED BY CV-CVA-CVS-39

American Theater Medal
Victory Medal World War II
National Defense Service Medal
United Nations Medal with Korea Clasp
Naval Occupation Medal (Europe-Japan)
Korean Service Medal with one bronze battle star
China Service Medal
Navy Combat Ribbon
Korean Presidential Unit Citation (foreign decoration)
Korean War Medal (foreign award)
Armed Forces Expeditionary Medal
Navy "E"

BIBLIOGRAPHY AND OTHER SOURCES

Bryant, J. AIRCRAFT CARRIER
Field, J. A. U.S. NAVAL OPERATIONS IN KOREA, Government Printing office 1962
Humble, FLEET CARRIERS OF WORLD WAR II
Isenberg, Michael, SHIELD of the REPUBLIC, St.Martins Press 1993
Kilduff, Peter and Clayton, Pete, THE CHAMP: The Straightest and the Greatest, article in THE HOOK, Winter 1978
Morrison, Samuel Eliot, U.S. NAVAL OPERATIONS IN WORLD WAR II
Little Brown 1961 – 1964
Polmar, Norman, AIRCRAFT CARRIERS, Doubleday, 1969
Sauter, Jack, SAILORS in the SKY, McFarland & Co. 1995
THE CHAMP Cruisebooks: 1953, 1955, 1957

Various articles and letters from the association magazine THE CHAMP

USS LAKE CHAMPLAIN

Submitted by Joseph M. Campion

She may not be chronologically the oldest carrier in the fleet but she is the oldest. All the others have been rebuilt. Only the *Lake Champlain* (CVS-39) the *"Champ"* still has her straight flight deck.

And yet with equipment that is, to put it mildly, dated, the *Champ* comes with the E's. She is the ship that is singled out as the best in her class. One wonders, but one wonders not for long.

Her bridge is quiet. An occasional report is made and an order given. The ship is slipping past the Statue of Liberty. Fourteen helicopters fly over in perfect formation.

They curve away from the ship and soon they are headed home again. But the *Champ* now has only a few minutes to take them aboard before docking. Flying in single file, one close behind the other, they begin to land. In a matter of minutes, ten of them touched down on the flight deck. In Pri-Fly the atmosphere is calm. There is a green flag in the windows and the air officer merely nods his head as one after another the copters land.

There are four still in the air, but the deck must be cleared before they can land. Small tractors painted bright yellow and crew members in blue, yellow, brown and white uniforms are already hauling the machines aft.

As the last is towed away, the four copters still in the air land almost simultaneously. From the moment the operation began until the last copter is on deck less than ten minutes have passed.

It looks simple. There are few commands given and those in a quiet voice. Yet this is a complicated maneuver demanding, on one hand, tremendous cooperation from all hands, and on the other, considerable initiative on the part of each individual.

It is because of this cooperation and initiative that the *Lake Champlain* men were able to save the life of a British seaman recently.

Lake Champlain and its task group of destroyers were battling heavy North Atlantic seas and wind-whipped snow. Suddenly, Friday afternoon, February 15, an urgent message was received from the British destroyer HMS Lowenstoft. Emergency assistance was requested for a young sailor with an acute appendicitis attack.

Within minutes of the request, Lieutenants (junior grade) Tom Gillen and Jim McRee of Helicopter Squadron Five, were in the air in their SH34J helicopter, heading for the British ship in a blinding snowstorm. Making their way through winds of 65 knots, the pilots located the destroyer over 30 miles from *Lake Champlain*. Two helicopter crewmen lowered the rescue hoist, and the sick British sailor, David Hoare, was brought aboard.

After an instrument-controlled flight and landing on the *Champ*, Hoare was rushed to the carrier's well-equipped sickbay. At a little after midnight, Saturday morning, Navy doctors Neil V. White, Commander, and Roy Garrison, Lieutenant, operated and removed the sailor's near-ruptured appendix. All during the operation, high winds and violent seas buffeted the ship, but by 4 a.m. Saturday, the ailing sailor was "resting well after removal of appendix."

When notified of the successful operation, the *Lowenstoft* sent this message; "We are most grateful for the very timely assistance in transfer of Hoare by helo in such difficult weather conditions. Many, many thanks to all concerned."

It was also because of this highly motivated and highly trained crew that the *Champ* has managed to pick two consecutive E's.

On September 14, 1962, *Lake Champlain* was officially presented with the U.S. Atlantic

An S2-D Tracker (formerly S2F) about to be catapulted from the flight deck of the Champ.

USS Severn AO-61 fuels the Champ and USS Forrest Sherman DD 931 simultaneously.

Fleet Battle Efficiency E's Award for outstanding performance in her class. This is the second consecutive year the *Lake Champlain* has received this coveted fleet award.

In May 1961 it was the Champ that was selected to be the prime recovery ship in America's first astronaut shot. As the *Champ* cruised down the range in her assigned area and the world held its breath, Commander Alan B. Shepard in his Freedom 7 capsule was blasted into space from Cape Canaveral, the first American to achieve this.

After parachuting into the ocean, the capsule and Commander Shepard were picked up by copters from the *Champ* and delivered safely to her flight deck.

This rescue made the headlines. A less publicized rescue had occurred shortly before

when the *Champ* played rescuing angel to the British luxury line *Queen of Bermuda* with a helicopter delivery of 300 pounds of oxygen for a stricken passenger on the New York bound cruise ship.

The drama began when the *Champlain* received an emergency message relayed by the USS *Decatur* (DD-936) in which the *Queen of Bermuda* requested large quantities of oxygen for a reported congestive heart failure case on board.

The *Champ*, some 200 miles away at the time, immediately changed course and dispatched two HSS-2 turbine powered helicopters to the rescue.

An hour after takeoff, the speedy choppers sighted the luxury line. Hundreds of passengers armed with cameras lined the rails as they made their approach. Despite gale force winds, the HSS-2's lowered the oxygen supply by hoist, just aft of the ship's swimming pool. The passengers cheered excitedly when the transfer was completed successfully.

The *Champ* comes by her name naturally. It is not just an abbreviation of *Lake Champlain*. Following Japan's surrender to the Allies in September 1945, the *Champ* was assigned to the Navy's "Magic Carpet" operation as a troop transport, and helped return thousands of GIs from Europe to the U.S.

It was then, early in her career that, she earned her right to the title of *Champ*. Homeward bound from Europe with more that 5,000 troops aboard, she averaged 32,043 knots (37.175 mph).

She steamed the 3,960.3 nautical miles from Cape Spartel, near Gibraltar, to the Chesapeake Bay sea buoy off Hampton Roads, VA, in only four days, eight hours and 51 minutes. This was the longest speed run on record. Since she is a naval vessel, she was not eligible for the "Blue Ribbon" award commercial vessels for the fastest Atlantic crossing. The *Champ* record stood until the summer of 1952, when it was surpassed by the luxury liner SS *United States* on her maiden voyage to Europe.

Although commissioned on June 3, 1945, the *Champ* did not go to war until April 1953. When she went she traveled 20,000 miles through the Red Sea, Indian Ocean and China Sea, becoming the largest ship to pass through the Suez Canal.

Arriving in Korea in June she became the Flagship of Carrier Task Force 77, delivering daily strikes at North Korean troops and installations. During this time, *"Champ"* pilots flew 2,244 combat sorties, dropping 1,350 tons of bombs and firing 1,106 rockets at the enemy.

The *Champ's* current Commanding Officer is Captain Andrew L. Burgess, USN. She is the flagship of RADM Noel A.M. Gayler, USN.

The *Champ*, the only straight deck carrier now serving with the fleet, is 899 feet o.a. and was built at the Norfolk Naval Shipyard.

SAILOR, WE CAN HEAR YOUR THOUGHTS

by D.H. Boxmeyer, SN

Sailor, we can hear your thoughts; we can see your gripes; you say the chow is either too little, or too bad. But buddy, it could be less and it could be worse. You say it is too hot or it is too cold, but sailor, you know it could be hotter or it might get colder. The lines are long, the pay is small, the flicks are old, the nights are short, the work is hard, and the crackers are stale.

We hear it all, sailor, but it could be worse.

You've been aboard for six months, a year, a year and a half or two; the ladders are still steep, the noise is still too loud, and the milk is still warm. You've made your crow, but the lines are longer yet, the inspections harder, and the days are longer. Your pay is more now, but the week ends are still too short, and the leaves are few and far between.

You've hauled on ten million miles of line; you've pushed a plane twice around the world. You've swabbed, scrubbed, buffed, painted, and chipped, and then it is time to start over. And sailor, you can be sure you'll stand a lifetime of watches before you're through.

But you have seen the sea; calm and smooth as the wardroom deck, and snarling and rough so that you're scared. You've seen the porpoises cartwheel, racing the ship, and you've watched with wonder the sparking of the gulf stream at night. Sailor, you have seen these things, and man's contribution; the circus of lights in Halifax's harbor, brilliantly lit British ship's in Jamaica's bay. You've passed the Statue of Liberty early in the morning at flight deck parade, and felt that unashamed chill of pride go up your spine. You've seen the flag go up countless mornings at quarters, and heard the band play the national anthem. Sailor, you've seen and heard these things; you know then, why you are here.

Someday, sooner than you think, perhaps, you will go down the brow for the last time, with your sea bag and your separation papers. You will be happy, but we bet the salute you throw to the ensign will be the snappiest you've ever rendered. You will walk down the pier for the last time, and we bet you will look back for a long time, at the home you are leaving. You won't see the long lines, the crowded living spaces, the small pay; you will see men, your friends, already gone and still remaining; you will see all the memories you have, and you will realize that it hasn't been so long after all.

Perhaps, in many years to come, when the last aircraft carrier has gone out of commission, when the "floating islands" are replaced with something we cannot yet visualize, you will tell your grandchildren of your home at sea. You will show them the pictures of your two years, three years or four; you will tell them: "Yes, this is where I lived, where I worked. She was my home and I was proud of her. She's gone now, but she was the best.

SHIP'S POST OFFICE SERVES CREW

"Mail call" at sea is as welcomed as liberty call in port. This is a generalization most sailors will agree to, and the motto *Lake Champlain's* high-rated post office operates by.

"When we get mail," Andy Wilson, PC2 stated, "it is sorted and handed out immediately. If a load of mail comes in at midnight, we would be ready for mail call soon after."

Lake Champlain's Post Office, getting a mark of 93.5 in the last Admin Inspection, would be rated as a "first class" post office in civilian terms, based on the amount of business it does. At-sea pay days bring in an average of $15,000 for money orders alone, while $500 is spent by the crew for stamps.

More money is always spent at sea on money orders than in port. "When we're in, the money goes right home to the wife," one of the postal clerks explained. "We, the 'middle-men,' are eliminated." Only two or three thousand dollars are spent on money orders on in-port pay days.

But, of course, mail is the, most important 'product of the Post Office. An average mail load coming aboard for just the *Champ* and her squadrons is 1,000 pounds.

"We are not trying to make the crew feel guilty about their writing habits," Wilson said jokingly, "but the outgoing mail is about one-fifth of what we take in." He then added that much in-coming mail is heavy with parcel post.

Wilson then explained how the ship gets its mail. The Fleet Post Office is informed by the Captain's Office as to where we will be during a given period. The mail is sent to the nearest naval facility, in this case, Bermuda, and from there, ship's planes or VRC-40s carry it to the task group.

The *Champ* receives its destroyer's mail too, and it is high-lined, flown by helicopter, or brought by small boat to them.

The Post Office, like any unit aboard ship, has its problems. The greatest headache of the clerks is mail not properly addressed.

"We really wish the men would tell their mothers, aunts, grandmothers and girl friends how to send their letters," Phil Nazak, PC3 said. "What can we do with a letter addressed to 'Smith, USS Lake Champlain,' or 'Bobby, USS Lake Champlain?' We have letters come in that we don't know who to deliver to, and the letter could be important."

Not all the problems involve wrongly addressed letters, however, Bob Allor, PCSN, remembers last Christmas when a box came in marked "live alligator," addressed to a man in E Division.

"The box was empty," Allor said "but when I looked in the mail bag, a 10-inch lizard jumped out at my nose. The man's girlfriend had sent him his gift."

"And the guy was on the beach when we got the lizard," Allor added. "Don't you think we didn't have a time!"

SICK BAY CHANTS

The sickbay is currently staffed by two doctors and 23 corpsmen. When the air group is embarked two additional flight surgeons and three hospital corpsmen join this staff. The Senior Medical Officer CDR N.V. White, states: "When we are operating at sea, our medical facilities closely parallel the capabilities of most small station hospitals. We have a bed capacity of 44."

"Every branch of surgery and medicine encompassed in the every day life is to be found in our sickbay. We treat 50 to 100 cases daily in addition to physical examinations, eye refraction ship-board first-aid training, sanitation, and other miscellaneous para-medicine requirements."

Dr. Gerritsen, a graduate of New York Medical College, reported to Lake Champlain in July for his first tour of duty. Although his specialty is surgery, he comments, "It has been a wonderful experience to do the type of general medicine required at sick call on a carrier. Naturally, I would like to see more surgical cases, but my only problem at present is finding the time to perform all the various tasks demanded by this billet."

Chaplain's Corner

by J.M. Danielson, Chaplain, USN

Not to know the facts of any given situation leaves the individual at the mercy of every rumor. Witness the rumors on the Champ these days about schedules.

In matters of faith and religious belief, not to know the scriptural teachings leaves the individual equally at the mercy of every passing teaching which carries the label of being religious.

Participation in the Daily Bible Study period in the chapel, habits of personal prayer and Bible reading, and regular attendance at chapel services will all increase your understanding and knowledge of the Bible.

"All scripture is inspired by God and profitable for teaching, for reproof, for correction, and for training in righteousness, that the man of God may be complete, equipped for every good work."

Cuban Missile Crisis

October 1962

by James A. Chappell (YN3, USNR)

"A Personal Remembrance"

Knowing how to use a typewriter accurately was a vital skill aboard any ship in the United States Navy. Everyone understood that the Navy floated on six carbon copes and tied up mired in coffee grounds. I came aboard the *Champ* during the summer of 1962 assigned to the Captain's Office. Lucky for me it was located just underneath the flight deck about 15 paces from the catwalk's routine starboard side action. This office was cooled, barely, with a piece of 8" air-duct rigged off the Captain's in-port cabin. The only other refrigeration on board was reserved for food.

The *Champ* was different. The only active straight deck CV remaining from World War II and always tied up stern first alongside its shared CV pier. Ready for action. Quonset Point NAS lay to port close enough for me to soon watch the *Honey Fitz* tie up to a short pier as Air Force One landed with President Kennedy aboard. He came to view the yacht races off Newport.

In a few weeks he would address the nation regarding a grave crisis in Cuba which offered the possibility of nuclear war. I had recently turned 26 with a pregnant wife bearing 249° over a thousand miles distant. My enthusiasm for a war was not the reason I entered the Navy.

Our Captain addressed the crew immediately and said… "we would NOT participate in the quarantine, but continue our routine ASW patrols in the North Atlantic sea lanes between Europe and Cuba." So, I joined one of the two lines extending from the end of the pier where the public telephones remained in constant use for hours. My three minutes were consumed comforting my wife with "the word." Then off to my rack, second from the top in "X" Division's space two levels below the hangar deck.

Sometime in the wee hours after midnight and well before reveille, I awoke. Unusual noise and activity just above our hole was the cause. Resting on my elbows, it dawned on me that the air group was coming aboard and my Navy had lied. Daylight arrived as the lines were drawn aboard. The *Champ* eased away from our pier without the time consuming assistance of tugs. I stood on the port side aft of a nearly empty flight deck and wistfully gazed at the vacant pier disappear in the dawn's early light. En route our Destroyers from Newport fell in behind. Soon the *Champ* was breaking Atlantic waves. She had set the transatlantic speed record bringing home the troops. It became apparent listening to groans, pops and creaks, that she might break another one heading south. No mail would go home until further notice. I wondered about widowhood.

We stored our-wool sweaters as flying fish began breaking the surface of an ocean changing into the colors of tropical latitudes. Airplanes, helicopters, the remainder of the crew, along with the assigned Destroyers caught up as we assumed our rectangle station in the shipping lanes near the Quarantine Line. The trained teams commenced looking for Soviet submarines. Our Division Officer explained that if a shot across the bow of any Soviet freighter approaching the line failed to stop it, we would be in a shooting war. His demeanor was not optimistic.

Awash in a somber mood, I went back to my typewriter, fixed athwart ship, and began banging out routine words as the keel held steady. On my very first at-sea, I had installed a simple inclinometer on the filing cabinet to my left with marks in half-degrees. A roll of a few degrees would stop my carriage in mid-key stroke and goodbye six copies. These waters were considerably smoother than those in the Atlantic when September marked a new winter's arrival north of 40° latitude.

Days of tension were broken by boredom. I took slides of aircraft launching and recovering, Destroyers coming alongside to refuel, performing my job in ignorance of events over the horizon hanging the world on the brink.

One routine afternoon the *Chaplain* excitedly entered finding only me. He had to tell someone. We had just forced a Soviet submarine to the surface. Unknown to the world until 2002, Captain Valentin Savisky had loaded one tube with a nuclear tipped torpedo and then had second thoughts. His diesel powered B-59 submarine surfaced.

The Soviets finally blinked at the line. Nobody trusted anybody. We remained on station. One evening near dusk, I stood on a quiet flight deck and watched a well lighted Soviet freighter steaming toward Europe. Close behind, one of our Destroyers followed in its wake. It was a breath of restored life for me and the world.

Departing our station, the *Champ* soon dropped anchor at Charlotte Amalie in the Virgin Islands. Cheap booze and rigid restrictions regarding access to women resulted in our weighing anchor before the third duty section could share liberty. At least the mail was moving toward home. My family would know why my letters had temporarily stopped. Better than a telegram. I didn't know how my Navy notified its widows. No officer had time to explain that procedure. My family thought we were in the shipping lanes of the North Atlantic and I safe. Ha!

We came, saw little, did our duty successfully and finally went home to Quonset Point. Easing into our slot at the pier, the lines were secured. Long ago empty gun tubs resting above a bow pointing toward the Atlantic Ocean.

On my birthday in October 2001, I returned to that pier and again felt the biting Narragansett winds sweep across an empty once upon a time home slot. Memories vivid. A reminder of what was - 40 years ago.

My First Day

by Jay E. Fuller, AT-2, CVS-39

It was my first day at sea on the *"Champ"* (my only ship) six years in the Navy behind me and the fire alarm goes off. The PA was frantically giving Deck, Frame, Fire party etc. With some concern, I looked at the guy who was showing me around and asked what should we do. He said unless it was burning in the same compartment you are in forget it. He said the ship was on fire when he came aboard two years ago and had been burning day and night since. In the next 18 months, I found a lot of truth in his statement. It was an event that has stayed with me.

THE FOLLOWING ARTICLE COMES FROM A JACKSONVILLE, FL, PAPER DATED OCTOBER 30, 1964:

WAR TEST CLAIMS FOUR MORE MEN

NAVY AIRMEN PERISH AS PLANE FALLS OFF SPANISH COAST

Madrid, Oct. 29 (UPI): Four U.S. Navy airmen were killed last Tuesday when a submarine-tracking plane crashed in the Atlantic Ocean during Operation Steel Pike 1, a Navy spokesman announced today.

The accident happened the day after two U.S. Navy helicopters collided in the air during the big amphibious maneuvers, killing nine American Marines.

The helicopter collision was announced Tuesday but details of the plane crash were not released until today. There was no explanation for the delay in the Navy's reporting it.

MESSAGE FROM ADMIRAL

"I was just informed of the crash myself in a message from ADM McCain," – Navy spokesman said. VADM John S. McCain is director of Steel Pike I and commander of U.S. amphibious forces assigned to the Atlantic Fleet.

The spokesman said the four Navy airmen were flying a Grumman S2 tracker plane taking part in an antisubmarine exercise.

The men were attached to Antisubmarine Squadron 32, based at Quonset Point, RI.

The four were identified as LT Charles W. Hall of North Kingstown, RI, pilot; LTJG John M. Fultz III of Wynnewood, PA, co-pilot; and two crewmen, PO3/c Robert L. McCreary of Skellytown, TX and Airman John R. Bates of Seely, CA.

Crashes Into Sea

Officials said the propeller driven plane was entering a landing pattern to return to the ship when it crashed into the sea.
The plane was operating from the aircraft carrier *Lake Champlain*.
It crashed off the southern coast of Spain, the spokesman said.
The two accidents cast a pall over the exercises, biggest peacetime amphibious operation in history.

All In A Days Work
by Harry J. Glass, CE1, USN, Ret

A harrowing experience aboard the *Lake Champlain* occurred one night during a major winter storm in Norfolk, VA.

I was returning from Shore Patrol duty, via the whaleboat, to the ship which was anchored in Chesapeake Bay. The seas beyond the breakwater were immense and continually tossed the struggling boat, which at times was nearly vertical. I took refuge under the bow to stay dry from the cascading waves. After considerable time, the coxswain repeatedly yelled to the boat officer that the boat was in imminent danger of capsizing, then turned the boat around (belatedly getting permission). The coxswain's decisiveness and superb seamanship undoubtedly saved the occupants from certain death! Cries of relief and anger rang out from the wet, half frozen, frightened, sick liberty party as the boat finally re-entered the calmer waters within the breakwater on the return to the base.

The next day (the storm slightly abated), the difficult return trip to the ship was accomplished. Because the high seas caused the carrier and whaleboat to alternately rise and fall to the other, repeated attempts to hook the Jacobs Ladder was only partially completed. Exiting the descending whaleboat to the ascending ladder (and attached carrier) was gained by each individual jumping when the two were briefly nearing alignment with each other!

Cold War Warming?
Harry J. Glass CE1, USN, Ret

During the Cuban Missile Crisis of 1962, an event occurred on the *Lake Champlain* which shows the humor, ingenuity and "sacrifices" required of men going to sea in harms way.

I was on duty in the radio shack when a pilot brought in a photograph to show our communication officer, LCDR Ellis.

Photographs were taken of foreign ships, especially those carrying outgoing missiles, but this particular photo - taken on a diving run with telescopic lens and uncanny aim, captured an image much more important than mere missiles. Among Russian crew members giving friendly greetings to the pilot with the international one finger salute was a female leaning on the life line - amply endowed in a very brief bikini! Could it be a malfunctioning camera, trick photography or was her top departing south?

Later, my twin brother Larry, a member of HS-5, showed me "verification." The squadron had enlarged the middle torso of the girl into a poster size photo! Although slightly fuzzy, it clearly revealed…errrr showed that an upward adjustment of her top had been necessary, but thankfully ignored!

Pranks And Practical Jokes
by Harry J. Glass, CE1, USN, Ret

The quantity and variation of pranks and jokes, executed by sailors in daily life at sea, are too numerous to be inclusive; however, some are worth mentioning:

•During the midshipman cruise of 1961, the air-dales set up the 'rare sea bat' trap for them on the hanger bay. Several air-dales surrounded a cardboard box, peeking into the 'air holes' while two or three men with brooms innocently swept nearby. As passing midshipmen inquired as to the box's contents and bent over to get a look at the sea bat, the waiting brooms moved into position and made contact with their posteriors!

• One night, I was having coffee with my twin brother Larry in the line shack of HS-5. Soon a game developed of dropping a nickel from an individual's forehead (eyes closed, head tilted back) into a paper funnel tucked into his front pants. Several waited their turn for this game of skill. (My brother alerted me that they were setting up a new guy). Soon he was asked if he wanted to try? He readily agreed, pleased to be accepted by his new friends. They gave him a couple of chances (near misses) and on the 3rd try as his head tilted back with eyes closed, a cup of water was poured into the funnel! He laughed as hard as the rest of us as he left to change his pants.

• One day a new member of the radio gang was introduced after morning muster and was immediately given the important responsibility of 'mail buoy watch' at the forward port radio space. He was instructed to call Radio One when the plane dropped the ships mail with a marker buoy so as to be picked up. The whole ship's morale depended upon his vigilance! (I've always wondered why someone didn't remind us that we had a perfectly good flight deck for this purpose.)

We all assumed our daily routine and later that evening, my watch section had duty. I was puzzled when the little used sound powered telephone rang; it was our mail buoy watchstander inquiring about a relief! (Everyone had forgotten him.) He had missed lunch and dinner and didn't know the way back to Radio One. I dispatched a guide and in about an hour, got him some chow at mid-rats. His dedication to duty surprised everyone.

LAKE CHAMPLAIN - DEPARTING!

by Harry J. Glass, CE1, USN, Ret

I had duty and was asleep aboard the *Lake Champlain* when she broke free from the pier at Quonset Point, RI, approximately 1962-63.

General Quarters sounded around 4:30 a.m. with the chilling words, "This is not a drill, this is not a drill!" Aware that we were drifting, I ran to Radio One and commenced my duties.

The enclosed article from *All Hands* magazine details this event:

HEAVY WEATHER

A CVS was moored starboard side to the north side of the carrier pier at Naval Air Station, Quonset Point, Rhode Island, with the bow of the ship extending approximately 125 feet beyond the seaward end of the pier. In anticipation of heavy weather, the ship was moored with standard mooring lines less a bowline, plus four additional wire breasts to the dutch bollards, and one additional wire breast forward. Four camels approximately 5-feet in width were in use; the port anchor was laid out underfoot; and the starboard anchor was ready for letting go. Weather and wind conditions became progressively worse until approximately 0419, when all lines except #5 and #6 parted almost simultaneously. The CVS commenced drifting toward the shoal water to port. Chain was immediately veered to the port anchor and the starboard anchor let go. The ship's movement was stopped with the ship riding to both anchors and #6 line. The #5 line did not part but pulled the cleat bodily out of its mounting on the pier.

During the day preceding the incident various advisories had been received on board, warning of winds up to 28 knots, with possible gusts to 35 knots. Small craft warnings had been issued in the Quonset Point area and remained in effect until after the incident. The Command Duty Officer cancelled the afternoon boat trip to Newport as a precautionary measure and instructed the quarterdeck not to dispatch additional boats without his express permission. The Commanding Officer was on authorized leave and the Executive Officer was unable to board the ship until after the incident occurred. The lines had been repeatedly checked and all appeared to be taking an even strain. At approximately 0340 the CDO was called and informed that the forward brow was dangerously close to falling from the pier platform. The wind, which had increased to approximately 20 knots from the south, was holding the ship off the pier and causing this dangerous situation. A crane for removing the brow could not be immediately obtained; therefore, the forward brow was secured, and shortly thereafter it crashed to the pier. The OOD had contacted the base weather facility and had been informed that no increasingly adverse weather conditions were expected throughout the night. At this point the decision was made to hoist one boat aboard, to move additional boats to the ship's lee, and to run out additional mooring lines in anticipation of a possible increase in the 20-knot winds. The engine-room was called and ordered to put power on all deck machinery. It began to rain heavily, and an increase in the wind force caused the ship to roll to port with each gust. The ship's boatswain was on the forecastle at approximately 0410 and noted increasing difficulty in moving about due to the wind force. The General Alarm was sounded when the lines parted, and the Boatswain immediately commenced veering chain to the port anchor to increase its holding power. When it appeared that further veering would allow the bow to swing onto the shoal area, the starboard anchor was lowered and held at approximately 15 fathoms on deck. It was estimated that 3 minutes elapsed between the sounding of the General Alarm and the holding of the starboard chain.

The word was passed to man the sea and anchor detail, and the OOD shifted his watch to the bridge. At the time of his arrival on the bridge, wind force as indicated on the anemometer was observed to be 50 knots. Emergency lighting off procedures were initiated, and port control was requested to send tugs and pilot.

Meanwhile, the holding of anchors and #6 line had stopped the swing of the ship, and soundings by leadline were ordered and taken from the catwalks. Soundings taken on the port side indicated depths of from 4 to 4-1/2 fathoms. At approximately 0506 main control reported ready to answer bells. The motion of the ship in the wind and sea contradicted the soundings and indicated that she was not aground; however, the engines were not used due to the possibility of fouling the screws. A bowline forward and two additional lines aft were put over with the assistance of shotlines and small boats. Two hours later 6 tugs and a pilot arrived from Newport. The wind force abated to approximately 18 knots by 0700, and shortly thereafter the ship was eased back to the pier and re-moored.

The investigation of the incident resulted in the following findings of fact and opinion:

•Observations by the Pilot and inspection of the underwater hull, propellers, struts and rudder by qualified divers indicated that the ship did not ground.

•The ship was adequately moored within the limitations of the facilities at this pier.

•All reasonable precautions had been taken. The weather which caused the incident was considerably more severe than had been predicted.

•The ship's instructions regarding heavy weather procedures were entirely adequate.

•The narrow camels in use caused the mooring lines to have too much vertical component.

•The incident was caused by a combination of high-wind and sea and marginal mooring facilities accentuated by extremely high gusts of wind.

"THE CHAMP"

THE STRAIGHTEST AND THE GREATEST

by Peter Kilduff with LT Pete Clayton, USN

Editor's note: To the men who go to sea in ships there are those ships which, for indefinable reasons, have a certain aura of pride and character. Others are less fortunate, have lesser reputations, and generate little pride in their crews. These attitudes prevail in the development of the character of a ship across its lifetime. There are some vessels which unaccountably are "winners;" special ships, which are always spotless, well maintained, and reflect the pervasive pride of their crew year after year, so much so that fierce loyalties to these "ladies" are developed. Not a great number of ships are blessed with this asset, but one of these special ships was USS Lake Champlain. There was something "extra" about her from the beginning and something special about serving on a ship with a straight deck that did the same job as her modernized sisters with their angled decks. Perhaps this was a manifestation of the not uncommon American custom of making a champion of the underdog. Whatever it was that made her special, the editors of THE HOOK admit to an unusual affinity for this great old ship, and perhaps the fact that two of them served aboard "The Champ," influenced the following tribute to this grand old lady.

During World War II the United States enjoyed the distinction of being the only major participant whose homeland was never under serious attack by enemy forces. Among other advantages, this allowed the United States to develop the largest shipbuilding program in history. A vital part of that program was the construction of the largest number of aircraft carriers of one class ever built by any nation, the 24 sisters of the Essex class.

The keel of the 15th Essex-class ship, USS *Lake Champlain* (CV-39), was laid down on 15 March 1943 at the Norfolk Navy Yard, constructed entirely in a drydock, she was named in honor of the American naval victory at the Battle of *Lake Champlain* during the War of 1812. She was the second vessel to bear that name, the first was a 4,300 ton mine carrier that served in World War I.

The aircraft carrier Lake Champlain was built with funds contributed by the people of New York state, which borders on Lake Champlain. The ship was subsequently "adopted" by New York and took the state's motto, Excelsior, for her own. At launching ceremonies on 2 November 1944, the ship was christened by Mrs. Warren R. Austin, wife of the U.S. Senator from Vermont, the other state that borders on Lake Champlain. The 33,000 ton (full load) *Lake Champlain* was commissioned on 3 June 1945.

Commanded by CAPT Logan C. Ramsey, *Lake Champlain* made her shakedown cruise in the Caribbean during July with Air Group 150 aboard, carrying out simulated attacks against Culebra Island, near Roosevelt Roads, Puerto Rico. But that training was not put to use, as the war in the Pacific had ended by the time *Lake Champlain* returned to her homeport at Norfolk for overseas assignment.

Consequently, CAG 150 left Lake Champlain, which was then altered for a unique non-flight mission. The new carrier became part of the Magic Carpet fleet assigned to bring American servicemen home from postwar Europe. Her sheer size and large hangar facilities made Lake Champlain an ideal troop transport.

In October 1945, Lake Champlain brought home over 3,700 Americans. The following month she brought home 5,000 troops, averaging 32.048 knots during the 3,960 nautical mile journey from Gibraltar to Norfolk. The elapsed time of four days, eight hours and 51 minutes was a transatlantic speed record that stood until the Summer of 1952, when it was broken by the ocean liner SS United States. The carrier's nickname, *The Champ,* was well deserved.

With the completion of the Magic Carpet cruises, *Lake Champlain* was decommissioned on 17 February 1947 at Norfolk. The U.S. Navy, possessor of the world's largest aircraft carrier fleet, simply could not afford to maintain all of its ships in an operational capacity and yet was unwilling to scrap large numbers of vessels. Hence, the process of ships and aircraft with weather and corrosion-resistant materials was developed. Naval shipyards around the country became the silent repositories of the instruments of America's excess military power.

By the time these instruments were reawakened in the early 1950s, the "cold war" between the western powers and the Communist bloc had gotten considerably hotter and the state of the art of military technology had become much more sophisticated. The World War II vintage aircraft carriers that had remained in service had been altered to accommodate the special requirements of the newly emerging jet-powered aircraft. Hence, most aircraft carriers brought out of mothballs to reinforce the United States effort in Korea had to first be modernized to provide capabilities for the operation of jet aircraft and to incorporate safety features in the postwar completion of USS *Oriskany* (CV-34) *(The Hook,* Spring 1978).

In addition to a redesigned island structure of shorter length, the Project 27A modernization included numerous changes to enable the ships to operate large numbers of heavier jet aircraft. Major alternations included the installation of H-8 hydraulic catapults, jet blast deflectors, Mk V arresting gear, increased aviation fuel capacity, hangar deck sub-division fire doors, enlarged bomb elevators, special weapons capability, and increased aircraft elevator capacity.

Her five-inch mounts were removed from the flight deck (four single mounts were installed on the starboard side to partially offset this) and fourteen 3-inch 50 cal. mounts replaced her 40mm battery.

Taking advantage of hard lessons learned in World War II, the squadron ready rooms were relocated from the 02 level to the second deck, requiring the installation of an escalator on the starboard side to move equipment laden pilots to the flight deck. The increased displacement (40,800 tons full load) brought by these improvements necessitated the addition of blister voids, which widened her hull by eight feet to provide increased buoyancy. Eventually a total of nine Essex class carriers received the 27A modernization, *Essex, Yorktown, Hornet, Randolph, Wasp, Bennington* and *Kearsarge* in addition to *Oriskany* and *Lake Champlain*.

Again ready for her role as an active duty carrier, *Lake Champlain* was recommissioned on 19 September 1952. After a one-month shakedown cruise in the Caribbean late in the year, the ship went to her new homeport of Mayport, Florida, where preparations were begun for her first combat cruise.

On 26 April 1953 *Lake Champlain* departed for Korea, where United Nations forces were engaged in a bitter struggle to keep North Korean and Chinese Communist troops from taking over the entire peninsula. As in the Vietnam conflict of a decade or so later, American and allied military commanders were hampered in their efforts to achieve a decisive military victory by the imposition of restrictions resulting from political considerations. In this case, United Nations control of the coast and air space did not halt enemy air activity, as Chinese and North Korean air units operated form Manchurian bases that U.S. airmen were forbidden to attack. All aerial combat had to be broken off just south of the Yalu River separating North Korea from Manchuria, a part of the People's Republic of China.

Lake Champlain's 20,000 mile voyage to Korea ended on 9 June 1953, when she arrived at Yokosuka, Japan. *The Champ* departed two days later as the flagship of Task Force 77 commanded by RADM Apollo Soucek, a pioneer naval aviator who had set three world altitude records for heavier-than-air aircraft in 1929 and 1930, making significant contributions in the development of engines, oxygen equipment, and flying equipment for high altitudes.

USS *Lake Champlain* (CVA-39) arrived in the Sea of Japan on 14 June with Carrier Air Group 4, led by CDR John Sweeney. She joined *Boxer* (CVA-21) with ATG-1 aboard, *Princeton* (CVA-37) with CVG-15, and *Philippine Sea* (CVA-47) with CVG-9. VADM J.J. "Jocko" Clark, ComSeventhFlt and a celebrated veteran of World War II carrier operations, chose that day to order an all-out assault on enemy forces taking advantage of bad weather to move supplies and reinforcements.

During *Lake Champlain's* first day on the line, components of her air group F2H-2 Banshees of the Cavaliers of VF-22 and the Gladiators of VF-62, escorted Air Force B-50 bombers over North Korea. At the same time, F4U-4 Corsairs of the Hornets of VF-44, AD-413 Skyraiders of the Blackbirds of VA-45, and a mixed bag of AD-4W, AD-4N and F2H-2P aircraft of VC-12, VC-33 and VC-62 carried out strikes against enemy ground targets. This was in keeping with VADM Clark's concept of Cherokee Strikes, named in honor of his American Indian heritage and to distinguish them from normal close air support operations. Cherokee Strikes consisted of heavy bombing of both the front lines, and enemy rear areas 20 or more miles behind the bomb line. By including the normally "safe" rear areas, they had the effect of hitting enemy forces twice at the same time.

One of the participants in those raids was now retired VADM William D. Houser, former DCNO (Air Warfare). At the time he was a lieutenant commander and the new CO of VF-44.

VADM Houser recalls an incident during *Lake Champlain's* first day on the line that could have put the ship out of action. "About sunset, we were recovering aircraft from the last launch of the day. An F2H Banshee came in and, either the pilot forgot to set the safety switch on his machine guns or they discharged of their own accord, but as soon as the plane touched the flight deck, the guns went off and fired into the pack of aircraft parked on the forward part of the flight deck. A fire instantly broke out and the flames rose quite high. A potential disaster was avoided by the quick action of the flight deck crewmen, who extinguished the blaze and minimized the damage. We lost at least two VF-62 Banshees. That was our baptism for the period we spent on the line in Korean waters."

While *Lake Champlain* operated off Korea, preliminary negotiations leading to an armistice were in progress. In anticipation of the coming cease fire, both sides stepped up their ground operations in order to hold the best possible positions when the truce line was established. Consequently, VADM Houser remembers, *Lake Champlain* aircraft were called on to fly one or two daily missions of two to three hours duration.

"We did not encounter any hostile aircraft," he says, "as we were operating principally on the east coast and along the border all the way over to Seoul. The hostile aircraft were by and large in the northwestern corner of Korea, near Sinanju. They did not come as far south as we were, nor did we go up as far north as they were. Our principal role was to assist the forces on the ground, as well as to interdict shipping and hit trains, trucks or other vehicular traffic that might be bringing supplies down to Communist frontline troops."

The different complexion of the Korean conflict dictated a change a VF-44's normal mission, VADM Houser notes: "Almost all the Navy aircraft there were used in the attack role. We performed close air support for our frontline troops, as well as deep interdiction and road reconnaissance. We also hit targets that were not associated with the battlefield; airfields, truck compounds and other facilities that were not necessarily close to the fighting.

"Most of our missions were visual strikes, carried out in reasonably good weather. Because of that and the overwhelming superiority of U.S. and allied air power over the North Korean skies, there was very little that moved during the daytime. It was more advantageous for the North Korean and Chinese forces to move at night, because at that time we had only a few airplanes that operated at night."

"In fact, it was our experience in the Korean conflict more than anything else that led to the development of the Grumman A-6 Intruder."

Despite the advent of jet-powered aircraft, there was still a place for propeller-driven aircraft in Korea. VADM Houser remarked that VF-44's Corsairs could operate with less fuel and carry greater payloads than the jet aircraft assigned to *Lake Champlain*. The instant power provided by the F4U-4's piston engine also gave the World War II vintage fighters another advantage over the jets, which could be launched only by catapult.

VADM Houser recalls an instance of that advantage: "*Lake Champlain* had a new H-8 hydraulic catapult that was very good. It was designed to launch the heavier jets at higher speed, but on occasion, it malfunctioned. Consequently, on some occasions the prop airplanes were the only ones that could carry the war to North Korea, because the jets could not get off the deck."

The Admiral recalls that deck launching a Corsair was a memorable experience, with take-off being achieved within 350 feet of the starting point.

"You would start out just abeam of the island and rev the engine to as many RPM as you could hold. You were practically standing on the brakes to keep the airplane from moving forward and, at that, you usually couldn't hold the tail down. You would try to hold it at about three-quarters power and, as soon as the flagman waved you down the deck, you released the brakes and added full power, and went shooting off the deck."

"We generally left the flight deck with enough excess airspeed so that it was just a question of rotating off the bow and getting up the landing gear as soon as possible," VADM Houser recalls.

As part of her Project 27A modifications, *Lake Champlain* received increased aviation fuel storage capacity. Since such facilities were particularly desirable for jet operations, ComSeventhFlt swapped VF-44 to USS *Boxer* for ATG-1's fuel-hungry F9F-5 Panthers of VF-111's Sundowners.

During the Korean deployment, Lake *Champlain* also had a distinguished civilian guest aboard. Author James A. Michener spent a considerable time aboard the carrier, gathering material for his novel *The Bridges at Toko-ri*. As might be expected, some of the fictional characters were based on members of CVG-4 whom the famed author met during his guest cruise.

One such character is the colorful helicopter pilot Mike Forney, who was faithfully recreated in the film version by Mickey Rooney. The character's rough and tumble ways and colorful dress (a green silk hat and a long white scarf) were drawn from two *Lake Champlain* people: a Marine for the rough and tumble characteristics, and an AD-4B pilot from VA-45 for the colorful dress. The Skyraider pilot was LTJG G.E.R. "Gus" Kinnear, II - now a Vice Admiral and ComNavAirLant Although VADM Kinnear is a foot or so taller than movie actor Mickey Rooney, it is apparent why James Michener chose the former Skyraider driver to make the Forney character interesting.

VADM Kinnear, one of the designers of VA-45's present squadron insignia, also brought that emblem to life. While on liberty in Genoa, Italy, he acquired the squadron derby hat from a horse-drawn cab driver. The hat was painted green (the color assigned the fifth squadron of a carrier air group, which was then a VA unit) and attached to his helmet. The cigar was added to indicate maturity. As for the boxing gloves, here's how VADM Kinnear accounts for that part of the emblem: "When we flew aboard the carrier for deployment I also wore a set of big boxing gloves with the centers cut out. I had the gloves hiked up and out of the way on my sleeves. Then, after I landed and was being directed down the flight deck, I'd have a cigar in my mouth and put my hands up on the side of the cockpit with the boxing gloves on, of course. We had an excitable Air Boss and he thought I had actually flown aboard wearing the boxing gloves. He got pretty excited about that until we showed him that the gloves could be pushed up and out of the way and I had really used my bare hands on the stick and the throttle."

In addition to such light-hearted episodes, it should be noted that VADM Kinnear's experiences operating from *Lake Champlain* involved some hard, and often hairy work. During his Korean tour with VA-45, VADM Kinnear received the

Air Medal and a Gold Star in lieu of a second award. The citations for the latter award reflects one of the tougher aspects of combat flight ops. It reads in part:

"...finding himself thrown into a steep diving turn by jammed aileron controls, he succeeded in completing a recovery at an altitude of less than a hundred feet above the terrain, and effected a climb to a safe parachuting altitude ... (where) ... he elected to save the aircraft and, by sustained physical force and the lashing of the control stick with his flight scarf to the side of the cockpit, proceeded over 100 miles to an emergency air strip ... With the stick still lashed as securely as possible against the locked controls, (he) executed a successful wheels down landing with no damage to the aircraft, on an extremely narrow landing strip ..."

Lake Champlain's aircraft made a total of 2,244 combat sorties over Korea and continued to pound Communist targets until the truce agreement was signed on 27 July 1953. On 11 October, she was relieved by USS *Oriskany* (CVA-34) and took a long westerly cruise back to her east coast homeport.

The spirit and indefinable quality of excellence among *Lake Champlain's* aircrews- and, for that matter, all carrier based aircrews-is no doubt best described on the final page of Michener's *Bridges at Toko-ri* when the fictional Flag Officer ponders the question: "Why is America lucky enough to have such men? They leave this tiny ship and fly against the enemy. Then they must seek the ship, lost somewhere on the sea. And when they find it, they have to land upon its pitching deck. Where did we get such men?"

With the winding down of hostilities in Asia, *Lake Champlain* joined the regular rotation of east coast based CVAs on station in the Mediterranean.

On 22 September 1954, *Lake Champlain* left Mayport en route for the Mediterranean and her first tour of duty with the Sixth Fleet. Onboard was CVG-8, which combined Panthers (VF-84), Cougars (VF-61), with Banshees of VF-82 VC-4 and VC-62 on the same deck. There were three variants of Skyraiders in the air group, AD-6s (VA-85), AD4Ws (VC-12) and AD-4Ns (VC-33). For strategic weapons delivery VC-5 was attached, flying AJ-1 Savages. *Champlain* returned from this near seven month deployment on 22 April 1955.

After just over four months in the states, *The Champ* was back on station in the Mediterranean, deploying on 9 September, having exchanged CVG-8 for CVG-6. There were just two fighter squadrons on this cruise, VF-74 (Cougars) and VF-33 (Furys), however, instead of the single AD squadron usually found in CVA air groups at this time there were two, VA-25 and a Marine attack squadron, VMA-324. The normal detachments rounded out the deck load. She completed her second Mediterranean cruise of nearly seven months on 31 March 1956, which combined with her 1955 cruise, won her a battle efficiency "E." Following a fleet training cruise to Gitmo in October, the *Champ* joined *Forrestal* and 21 other ships off the Azores during the Suez crisis until 10 December.

Lake Champlain's third Mediterranean cruise, and her final deployment as a CVA was with Air Task Group 182.

She left Mayport 21 January 1957 for a six-month cruise as an attack carrier, despite the fact that *Forrestal* class carriers were coming into service and many of her sister ships were leaving the shipyards with such alterations as steam catapults, angled flight decks, and hurricane bows. In fact, it was because *Lake Champlain* could operate modern aircraft that these ships could be spared from the operating schedules for the length of time required to modernize them. With these ships returning to service to operate in the CVA role, *Lake Champlain,* on 1 August 1957, became the tenth Essex-class carrier to be redesignated an anti-submarine warfare support aircraft carrier (CVS), interestingly enough, well after the modernized angled deck *Wasp* was reclassified CVS on 1 November 1956.

Tragedy struck *Lake Champlain* 3 July, 1957 while she was anchored at Marseille, France. A fire started on the starboard side aft, where a barge carrying three automobiles was moored alongside. The ensuing fire destroyed the vehicles and damaged several spaces in the ship, killing five crewman and several civilians. A saddened *Lake Champlain* returned to Mayport on 27 July.

The *Champ* wasn't content to leave the ranks of the CVA's just yet, however, as she was to make one last effort as an attack carrier, even though all her paperwork said "CVS-39."

Loading aboard Marine Air Group 26 (MAG-26) she departed for the Mediterranean on 5 September 1957, only five weeks after having returned from deployment.

MAG-26 was made up of three fixed wing squadrons, VMF-312 (FJ-3s), VMA-324 (AD-6s) and VMA-533 (F2H-4s), and three helicopter squadrons, HMR(L)261 (HUS-1s), HMR(L)262 (HRS-3s) and HMRM-461 (HR2S-1s). The purpose of the quick return trip was to participate in NATO Exercise Deepwater, supporting amphibious landings on the Turkish coast. Following the exercise she performed in a humanitarian role providing flood relief to residents of Valencia, Spain on 16 October. She then returned to the United States, arriving on 31 October, and shortly began a three month yard period at Portsmouth, Virginia.

The *Champ,* returned to Mayport early in the year and began training as the center of an ASW task group. On 9 June 1958 she left Norfolk en route to Europe with her first complement of ASW aircraft. These were Grumman S2F-1 and 2 Trackers of VS-27 along with Sikorsky HSS-1 Seabats of HS-3. Also onboard for this Midshipmen cruise were HUP-2's from HU-2 and FASRON 3 Det Bravo which was formed specially to provide COD support with TF-1 Traders for LantFlex 1-58.

Returning to Norfolk 7 August 1958, the carrier entered New York Navy Yard on 8 December to begin a four month regular overhaul, completing this availability at the Bayonne Annex on 4 April. She was then underway for Mayport and on to Guantanamo for a Caribbean shakedown cruise prior to overseas deployment. On 5 June 1959 she departed for the Mediterranean with VS-30, HS-1 and detachments of VAW-12 and HU-2 aboard.

As part of the redistribution of carrier-based ASW forces, however, *Lake Champlain* did not return to her Florida base. Instead, at the conclusion of the 1959 Mediterranean cruise, she steamed for her new homeport, NAS Quonset Point, Rhode Island, arriving 3 September. There, she acquired a new complement of squadrons and got into a routine of two and three week cruises up and down the east coast. She alternated at-sea periods with two other ASW carriers, the Quonset Point based USS *Essex* (CVS-9) and the Boston-based USS *Wasp* (CVS-18).

Life aboard *Lake Champlain* at this time was considered good duty. There was no shooting war going on and the brief at-sea periods were quite bearable. The ship always managed to conduct flight ops in cool climates during the summer and warm areas during winter.

Extended summer cruises ended up in Canada; Halifax in 1960 and Quebec in 1961, to provide the midshipmen aboard for the summer an opportunity to pull some "foreign" liberty. Since *Lake Champlain* was then the last of the straight-deck, open-bow carriers, groups of middies found their "mail buoy watches" augmented by muster lists for working parties to rig and unrig the non-existent hurricane bow and angle deck.

For all that, *Lake Champlain* did fill a vital role in America's ASW network. And, as ASW methodology and technology became more sophisticated, the carrier-based ASW groups were upgraded accordingly. Aboard *Lake Champlain*, for example, the S2F squadron VS-32 was split in two, with the newer half being designated VS-22 and both portions being ultimately brought up to full squadron strength.

On 18 May 1960, Anti-Submarine Carrier Air Group 54 (CVSG-54) was formed at NAS Quonset Point. CDR Robert W. Raddatz, CO of HS-5, assumed command of the air group as well. Also at this time HS-5 became the first east coast helo squadron to be fully equipped with the new Sikorsky HSS-1N helicopters equipped with Doppler navigation equipment to facilitate nighttime operations in working with other elements of CVSG-54 in locating and tracking submarines with the retractable sonar equipment.

In 1961 *Lake Champlain* played a prominent role in America's manned spaceflight program. On 5 May, she was the primary recovery ship for the suborbital flight of LCDR (now RADM) Alan B. Shepard Jr. Following the launch from Cape Canaveral, Florida, Shepard's Freedom 7 Project Mercury space capsule proceeded downrange in the Caribbean to a point where *Champlain* was stationed with three newly-arrived U.S. Marine Corps HUS-1 helicopters from MAG-26.

The three USMC helos were joined by two HSS-1Ns from HS-5. As LCDR Shepard's capsule approached the splashdown area, LTs Wayne Koons and George Cox in a MAG-26 helo were on hand and secured a line to the vehicle while retrieving the first American astronaut. Hovering nearby all the while were LTJGs Dan Manningham and Richebourg Gaillard, III of HS-5.

America's first space triumph was marked by a thunderous reception for the astronaut by crewmen of The *Champ*. Naval aviator Shepard was welcomed aboard by the ship's skipper, CAPT (later VADM) Ralph Weymouth, a Navy Cross winning veteran of World War II.

After that moment in the international spotlight, *Lake Champlain* resumed her normal routine of ASW exercises. During the summer of 1961, a brief glimpse was provided of the future of ASW helicopters when the new turbine powered Sikorsky HSS-2 *Sea King* carried out carrier suitability trials aboard the ASW carrier.

When American intelligence specialists discovered Soviet built guided missiles stationed in Cuba in 1962, President John F. Kennedy imposed a naval blockade of that island to force the Russians to remove the weapons. *Lake Champlain* was one of the first military vessels assigned to the blockade and, with her air group, was able to provide coverage over a broad area of the Caribbean.

Normal ASW training operations with CVSG-54 continued through 1963 and into 1964. Early in the morning of 6 May 1964, the destroyer *Decatur* (DD-936) collided with *Lake Champlain*, as the destroyer was breaking away after completing alongside refueling operations. Decatur lost steering control before she cleared the carrier and slid underneath the overhang of the flight deck at the starboard bow. The flight deck of the *Champ* sheared away everything above the level of the bridge of the destroyer, including the mast and forward stack. An S-2 spotted on the flight deck was damaged, as were the starboard cat walks and bow gun tubs. The latter subsequently were removed as a result of the collision. Decatur, though severely damaged, made Norfolk under her own power.

Less than one month later, on 3 June 1964, while proceeding up the Chesapeake Bay in dense early morning fog en route to Annapolis, *Lake Champlain* was overtaken and rammed by the 15,895 ton Norwegian freighter *Skauvagg*. Extensive damage was done to the starboard side amidships above and below the waterline. Stubborn acetylene fires broke out in the hangar deck catwalk and heavily damaged that area and the adjacent battery locker and jet engine shop. Fortunately, no personnel casualties were sustained. Annapolis and NROTC midshipmen were embarked at Annapolis the next day and were transferred to USS *Essex* at Norfolk on 5 June for completion of LantMidTraron '64 cruise to northern Europe. *Lake Champlain* spent the next 20 days in the yards to repair her damage.

The *Champ* got underway on 8 October 1964 to participate in exercise Steelpike I the largest amphibious exercise held since World War II. The *Lake Champlain* task group provided ASW protection for the amphibious task group on the

Atlantic transit to the Bay of Cadiz and following assault on the Spanish beaches near Huelva. From 10 to 30 October, CVSG-54 conducted continuous round the clock flight operations compiling 3,446 flight hours in just 20 days. *This cruise was Lake* Champlain's last overseas employment. She returned to Quonset Point on 25 November.

The *Champ* was again involved in the space program when she launched a Navy helicopter on 29 August 1965 to retrieve Gemini 5 astronauts LTCOL L. Gordon Cooper, USAF, and LCDR Charles "Pete" Conrad, USN, who had just completed eight days in orbit. This event was a reunion of sorts for LDCR Conrad, who made his first carrier landing in 1954, aboard *Lake Champlain*.

By this time, *Lake Champlain* was beginning to show her age. Moreover, the distinction of being the last straight-deck carrier was beginning to work against her despite a fierce pride by the ship's company and air group, which fondly called her "the straightest and the greatest." But even that pride couldn't ward off the cutting jabs directed at "Building 39," an unkind appellation the ship acquired when her in-port periods became longer and longer and she became more of a fixture at NAS Quonset Point.

On 2 May 1966, after 65,000 arrested landings, the long and honorable life of *Lake Champlain* came to an end. Her commissioning pennant was hauled down for the last time and she was placed "out of commission—special" at the Philadelphia Navy Yard. This special status was unusual for a decommissioned ship and was intended to allow time for the consideration of alternative uses of *Lake Champlain*. She was seriously considered for use as a dedicated spacecraft recovery vessel or as a training carrier, the latter was to have included the removal of the angle deck from *Antietam* (CVS-36) and installing it on *Lake Champlain*. The *Champ* was not initially mothballed and only after considerable delay was her hull sealed and dehumidified in 1967 when other plans were all rejected for cost and manning reasons.

In August 1972, what was left of the old carrier, following the removal of serviceable equipment, was sold for scrap to the Union Minerals and Alloys Corporation. But even at the end, the *Champ* was a fighter. As she was being towed up a narrow channel to a maritime salvage yard in Kearny, New Jersey, the big ship, almost with a will of her own, suddenly swung across the channel and jammed into an open drawbridge.

It took several tug boats more than five hours to rectify the last defiant act of the U.S. Navy's last open-bow, straight-deck aircraft carrier. A champ to the end, she went out fighting. *Above article from the Winter 1978 Hook and submitted by Dwight E. Lubich.*

PADDLE LANDINGS TOOK SKILL

All Hands Article, January 1967, submitted by Dwight L. Lubich

For nearly six decades, Navy pilots have progressed through various stages of carrier landings ranging from the seat-of-the-pants methods to the fully automatic landings now becoming operational.

Antisubmarine Squadron 22 claims for herself (and other units of her air group) the distinction of being the last group of Navy fliers to make paddle landings—a skill which became archaic when USS *Lake Champlain* (CVS-39), the last of the straight-deck carriers, was decommissioned.

The paddle method of landing has played an important role in aviation history, and the squadron's pride in the skill it required is indeed justified.

Paddle landings under the guidance of the Landing Signal Officer—patron saint of all naval aviators—were characteristic of straight-deck carriers. Aircraft landing aboard them touched down on the aftermost part of the flight deck and headed straight down the ship's centerline.

During landing operations, other aircraft were parked on the forward end of the flight deck. The two areas were separated by barriers of large steel cables, hopefully strong enough to catch any aircraft not stopped by the arresting wires. Should a plane hit the barrier, it sometimes meant minor damage to the plane, but this was, at least, the lessor of two evils.

Since the deck space forward of the landing area was occupied with parked aircraft, pilots were committed to a full-stop landing earlier in the approach. There was no opportunity for a touch-and-go. No margin for error of any kind. Precision flying, honed by constant practice, was essential.

The landing signal officer with his paddles signaled an incoming aircraft whether it was too high, too low, or just right. Some LSOs could judge within a knot or so the speed of the approaching plans.

To present-day viewers of World War II movies, the LSO, with his paddles held in outstretched hands, appears to be merely picturesque. Quaint. To present-day aviators, it seems almost incredible that all our carrier-based aircraft were recovered in this manner during World War II.

Now, of course, newer angled-deck carriers use mechanical/optical systems to give their pilots needed assistance. The LSO is still there to monitor the approach, but rarely uses paddles to give signals.

Although carrier flying still requires an immense amount of skill and still has its thrills, modern techniques have largely eliminated the type of cliff-hanging carrier landings favored by scenario writers but which were by no means fictitious.

A Holiday Present

by Dwight E. Lubich

Out in the L'antic, one bleak, gloomy night,
came a loud call, wrought with great fright.
"LSO to the platform," thus my accord,
radar had something wanting aboard.
I picked up my paddles and peered thru the night,
only an apparition with pulsing red light.
Into my dance I went, but to no avail,
for this one was trouble by the tail.

The wave-off a sure thing to bet,
it came in high, low, fast and slow, so no choice
but dive in the net.
Another try for this carrier, with cut but no hook,
this strange craft succumbed to the barrier.

Over on it's back with raindeers all tangled,
another mortal pilot would have been mangled.
The crew quick with the rescue,
retrieved red suit and helmet askew.

"Ho, Ho, Ho!" his laugh-filled glee,
presents for all,
and glasses for me!

Memorable Experiences While On The "Champ"

by Charles W. Monaghan

On the morning of May 5, 1961, the USS *Lake Champlain* (CVS-39) recovered our first astronaut, CDR Alan B. Shepard, in the Atlantic Ocean about 302 miles downrange from Cape Canaveral, FL including his Project Mercury spacecraft, "Freedom 7."

I had the 04-08 bridge watch (OOD) and was relieved by the navigator early to get in the correct position (Hell, our navigator never could find the proper chart!). Went to the wardroom for breakfast and than positioned myself one deck above the bridge level to observe this historical moment. All the good viewing areas were filled by the Champ's Officers and men plus many reporters.

We heard Freedom Seven break the sound barrier before we saw it. We had two hellos in the splash down area specially equipped to bring the spacecraft (and Shepard) back to our flight deck. Also there were a couple of destroyers to render assistance if needed.

The sky was clear blue with small white clouds and then we saw something. It was a very strange looking sight with a shiny can hanging from a parachute. As soon as it splashed down our helos were right on top of it but we were too far away to see the details.

We had a large pile of mattresses by the deck edge elevator to lower his shiny spacecraft on. We were briefed before hand to maintain silence since they weren't sure-whether it would be Shepard or a monkey! So there was a deadly silence on the ship when our two helos return, one with Freedom 7. The capsule was lowered to the mattress and once secured by our riggers the other helo landed just forward. Of course there was a large sign saying, "Welcome Aboard the *Lake Champlain* (CVS-39)."

With Freedom Seven and the other helo on our flight deck there was still a very strange silence.

We didn't know where the hell Shepard was - is he still in the helo or still in the capsule? Than the starboard hatch of the helo slide back and we saw two legs encased in a shinning space suit. The hair on the back of our necks stood straight up.

Then Shepard was helped out of the helo in his silver space suit and just stood there staring at us as we stared at him! It was still dead quiet and Shepard looked somewhat confused because of the silence so he waved at us and the crew came alive with the loudest roaring sound that never ended - Alan Shepard smiled and gave us the OK sign (thumb up) and that caused a near riot.

During this event one reporter on the deck above was talking into his reel tape recorder and I suddenly heard cussing and his tape appeared in front of me as it streamed down to the flight deck causing much laughter among the crew and other reporters. Think he was from CBS.

Of course there were many other memorable experiences serving on the *"Champ."* Will never forget the "fun nights" on every Wednesday at the Officer's Club when the local fair young ladies came to meet and drink with the daring naval officers. Than there was the "Kingston Inn" where I was introduced to great sea food and prime ribs with a warm piano bar on Friday and Saturdays. Skiing in Vermont and New Hampshire in the winter, hiking in the white/green mountains in the fall, spending weekends in either the great city of Boston or New York.

Two Experiences As Second Division Officer

by Charles W. Monaghan

• As the "Champ" was refueling from a naval oiler (AO) one of the ships lost steering control. My station was the aft fueling rig and we were taking on fuel (NSFO) by the old span-wire method. As the distance between the two ships increased we were ordered to do an emergency breakaway but couldn't trip the span-wire due to the tension. The riggers (my men) were ordered to take cover and/or clear the weather deck. The six inch fuel hose was the first to part with oil spraying over all, then the span-wire snapped, sounding like a five inch gun with a bright white flash spraying pieces of the wire into the ship's side. Fortunately none of the crew was injured. Usually an operation at sea is very boring but there are times when it becomes sheer panic (and the crew had better know what to do and fast).

Being in charge of the aft refueling rig I always noticed that my BMs took great pride in throwing the "monkey fist" to the ships (DDs) coming alongside for fuel. Both ships blew their whistles telling all to take cover while the mighty BM threw the "monkey fist" to them to haul in the line which eventually got larger until the fueling hose was dragged across using the "close-in" method of rigging. It really took great skill throwing that line having it land right at their feet. Finally after about eight months the green Ensign said "I want to throw the 'monkey fist,'" and since I was in charge got my way (if the leading BM approved). Than it was my turn and a beautiful new Forest Sherman destroyer came alongside - I remember that I took off my hat, stepped into the empty gun turret and started swinging the "monkey fist" around my head - the bridge and refueling crews started laughing when they saw what this Ensign was about to do - the whistle blew with a returning whistle from the DD and I let fly. It was a near perfect throw except that the "monkey fist" went straight down into the DD's aft stack which prompted a roar of laugher from both ships - the line was pulled from the stack before it burned and all was well once again on the mighty "Champ," except the green Ensign had a beet red face!

• It was a dark stormy night and we were underway off the East Coast trying to find the damn Russie subs. I had the 00-04 bridge watch as OOD and was trying to get some zzzzs when one of my men stormed into my cabin screaming about the mid-rats. In his hand was a green slimy piece of meat which was unfit for human, or any consumption. He was pissed and so was I since I was now awake.

It was about 2000 and I proceeded to the XO's cabin. His Marine guard informed me that the XO was taking eight o'clock reports and since all Marines hate Ensigns ordered me to wait. The Private First Class then asked me what the problem was and I held up this slimy piece of green meat & inform him this was mid-rats. He immediately knocked on the XO's door and went into the room, dragging the Ensign (me) with him, stating to the XO that a major problem had developed - and I explained the situation holding up this slime green thing, in front of all the ships's department heads. The XO (CDR Rutledge) exploded and screamed at our supply department head (another CDR) to "go down to the mess deck, correct the damn problem, kick some ass and report back to me!"

I ran into the XO the next day and he thanked me for bringing the problem to his attention and stated "we just may make a naval officer out of you yet!" He was a damn good XO who always put the men first and after that incident the ship's security detachment (USMCs) always gave me a smart salute which prompted the other Ensigns to ask why I was the only Ensign that got a Marine salute.

A few months after the green meat incident we were docked at the Boston Navy Shipyard and around midnight the same Supply Officer and the Ship's Chef Boatswain Mate (CWO4) were returning across the officer's gangway and were burned to death. After the investigation it was discovered that welder's torch (across the pier) had ignited some fuel vapors that had gathered under the pier. It was a horrible accident which the crew would always remember since both of these officers were loved deeply by the crew. (60 or 61)

Reporting For Duty

by John Robben

The USS *Lake Champlain,* a 27,000 ton aircraft carrier, was anchored in the harbor of Norfolk, Virginia when I first reported aboard for duty on February 24, 1953. She had just returned from a shakedown cruise to Cuba, and I had just graduated from three months of boot camp at Bainbridge, Maryland. It was a chilly, breezy night when the liberty boat I was riding in pulled up alongside what to me looked like a terrifyingly huge shape in the dark. I stepped out of the liberty boat onto a bobbing platform attached at water level to the ship. A narrow ladder angled up the side of the ship to the hanger bay where, 90 feet above me, an Officer was waiting to welcome me aboard.

I hoisted my heavy canvas sea bag over my left shoulder and held it in place with one hand as I'd been taught to do in boot camp, and with my free hand I gripped the ladder railing and started pulling myself up. It was not easy balancing the heavy sea bag over my shoulder, and I had the feeling each time I let go of the railing that if I lost my balance I'd tumble backwards into the dark, oily, swirling water below me. The higher I climbed the more uneasy I became.

In the distance I could see the lights on shore, and all around me were other ships, some anchored like mine, others moving slowly through the harbor. Norfolk was a very busy port during the Korean War, with warships, freighters and other vessels constantly coming and going, all day. and all night long. The ships underway were steadily sounding their horns, sending forth a mournful chorus. The liberty boat that had delivered me to my ship had already pulled away and I could see it scuttling across the choppy water to another ship at anchor.

Not only were there all these noises, and lighted ships gliding around like spooks in the dark, but there was also the smell of the harbor, fishy, oily and damp. And here I was, nervously climbing a steep ladder with my heavy sea bag, fearful of falling into the water, and uncertain of what my new Navy home was going to be like.

"Hurry it up, sailor!" the Officer at the top of the ladder shouted down at me.

I'd stopped halfway up the ladder to catch my breath, and to readjust the bag over my shoulder. I don't know how long I'd stopped to do this but it was long enough for the Officer to grow impatient. There was a fleeting instant when I thought I might freeze on that ladder, not from cold but from fright, and that someone would have to come down to help me get to the top. But when the Officer shouted down at me it got me started again, and I managed to complete the trip. Standing at the top of the ladder at the entrance to the ship I could feel the night at my back, the open harbor behind me, the wind and the danger it held if you ever fell overboard and into all that dark water.

I quickly saluted the Officer, requested permission to come aboard, and moved into the lighted hanger bay, a gigantic open arena through which hundreds of sailors were walking, running, carrying things and knowing what to do. I stood there in utter amazement, bewildered, still recovering from my climb up the ladder and wondering how was I ever going to cope with all this?

I was now aboard a Navy aircraft carrier, one of the biggest of its kind at that time, 900 feet long, something like seven stories high, housing thousands of men and Officers. Her cooks would serve 9,000 meals a day, movies would be shown every night, and specially-trained pilots would fly off and land on her deck in planes that could travel nearly at the speed of sound and drop bombs powerful enough to influence the outcome of battles. Just the number of rolls of toilet paper such a vessel had to carry was staggering. As was the number of potatoes, hamburgers, plates, cups and beds. No wonder ships like this were called "floating cities."

In time I learned to feel "at home" aboard the *Lake Champlain,* and over the next few months as the ship prepared for her Korean duty, even to enjoy myself. Not that I didn't miss my girl, my real home and my civilian life, which I was happy to return to 17 months later, but I discovered something very important about myself. I learned I could do it. I could do the Navy's work. I could eat the Navy's food and put in a good night's sleep and then I could start all over again the next day. I became a member of ship's company, a ship large enough to shelter, feed and employ 3,000 men.

I'd been a team-member before in my life when playing sports, but it was nothing like this. Now I'd become part of something huge, and not just part of a ship, however large she was, but of something even bigger. I'd become part of the U.S. Navy itself!

MARSEILLE FIRE

by Kenneth Theodore Schweda

I was a nozzleman in Repair 3 and was one of the first hoses that went into the fire in Hangar Bay 3. I was also the first hose directed on the starboard boat pocket so we could cool that area in order to cut the burning barge loose. I just got released from mess cooking after we secured from Sea Detail and reported back to the Power Shop on the 3rd deck when the explosion occurred. If memory serves me, I think I still had my Tee shirt and white pants on from working in the galley. If anyone has any pictures of the Hangar Bay 3 and starboard boat area, I'd appreciate some copies. The last duty I had, after the fire was out, was to bring oxygen bottles down to Sick Bay. I'll never forget the badly burned shipmates I saw down there. In closing, on 3 July 1957, I was a month from my first year anniversary in the Navy and also a month from my 17th birthday. A boy in a man's world grew up very fast that day.

HISTORY OF A CHAMPION

Submitted by Frank Talarico

Endowed with the victorious fighting spirit of Commodore MacDonough's naval triumph on *Lake Champlain* in the War of 1812 and equipped with some of the most modern weapons for naval warfare, the USS *Lake Champlain* has served as an ever-ready, powerful guardian of American principles for almost 20 years.

Marseille Fire

Commissioned an Essex-type attack carrier (CVA) on June 3, 1945, in Norfolk, VA, the USS *Lake Champlain* joined the Atlantic Fleet in the latter part of World War II. Shortly after the armistice, she became part of the troop- transporting "Magic Carpet." During this good-will operation, the USS *Lake Champlain* set an Atlantic crossing speed record by whisking 5,000 GIs from Gibraltar to Virginia in 87 hours, maintaining an average speed of 32 knots over the 3,960 mile course. The "Champ," as she was now called, held the coveted speed record for seven years.

The USS *Lake Champlain* was reclassified an antisubmarine warfare carrier (CVS) on August 1, 1957. Since that time, she has strenuously engaged in NATO exercises and antisubmarine maneuvers throughout the Atlantic. Liberty ports in the. Mediterranean, Northern Europe, the British Isles, Canada, and the Caribbean have played host to the Champmen.

On May 5, 1961, the USS *Lake Champlain,* as primary recovery ship in the Project Mercury space program, gained worldwide fame when America's first astronaut, Navy Commander Alan B. Shepard, was brought aboard immediately after his dazzling flight through outer space.

In 1962, the *Lake Champlain* has continued her assignment as part of the antisubmarine warfare force. With her embarked Air Group, and escorted by destroyers, she has regularly departed her homeport of Quonset Point for duty in the North Atlantic Ocean.

The Battle Efficiency "E" was awarded the USS *Lake Champlain* on August 15, 1962, designating her the outstanding antisubmarine carrier in the Atlantic Fleet for the second consecutive year. In addition, the Operations and Gunnery Departments won individual "E's."

As she completes 10 years of active duty in the fleet, the Champ has earned a total of three "Big E's" and 17 departmental "E's," a record of which we are proud.

The City Of The Champion

Submitted by Frank Talarico

In population and complexity, the USS *Lake Champlain* is a veritable "city at sea." Her chain of command can be compared to that of a municipal government with the Commanding Officer as the "Mayor," the Executive Officer as the "City Manager," and the Chief Master-at-Arms as the "Chief of Police."

With a gross displacement of 40,000 tons and a 30 foot draft, the massive *"Champ"* (896 feet in length with a 101 foot beam) can be driven through the water at speed in excess of 35 mph with 150,000 shaft horsepower transferred to her four giant 14 ton screws. She is the only "straight deck" carrier presently in the U.S. fleet.

Working on, above, and below her 862 foot flight deck are more than 2,000 men who comprise the ship's ten departments (Administration, Air, Communications, Dental, Engineering, Gunnery, Medical, Navigation, Operations and Supply). She operates with an embarked air group of over 40 antisubmarine aircraft.

Included in the scores of crewmen aboard the *"Champ"* are expert cooks, cobblers, tailors, barters, laundrymen, printers and storekeepers. Ship's Servicemen operate the ship's two variety stores, the soda fountain, and tobacco shop which tend to the "civilian" needs of her men. Recreational facilities include a well-stocked athletic gear locker, a weight lifting room, a ship's library, a crew's lounge, a reception lounge for the crew and their guests, and numerous TV sets. Movies are shown nightly in the wardroom and in the hangar bay which is also the scene of basketball and volley-ball games and boxing smokers, recruiting local talent. The *"Champ"* also has varsity basketball, boxing, and softball teams which actively participate in many all-Navy tournaments. A case full of trophies attests to their successes. At sea, the *"Champ"* publishes a daily newspaper, the *Nighthawk Express,* and operates radio station WVLC, devoted to shipboard news and popular music.

There is a fully-equipped, non-denominational Chapel aboard the "Champ" which has been the scene of Navy weddings and christenings in addition to a full program of religious services.

Almost 200,000 meals are served monthly aboard the "Champ." Her monthly payroll tops the $500,000 mark. With more than 90,000 gallons of fresh water produced daily at sea, water ration days are rarely required.

All her attributes and conveniences only serve to make the USS *Lake Champlain* a more efficient deadly weapon against enemy submarines. She's a "city at sea" to protect those on land.

A Tale from the Korean War

by Robert E. Womack

It was not "a dark and stormy night," but it was dark and a fog had settled over the Sea of Japan that made our lookouts next to useless. We were cruising very near the eastern coast of Korea, near enough that Captain Southerland, having just assumed command of the ship from Captain Mundorff a short time before, was justifiably nervous when the radar repeater on the bridge showing our position off the Korean coast suddenly went blank. LORAN, our back-up navigation system was next to useless in that part of the world. Radar was our most dependable navigation tool. The captain ordered the Officer of the Day to report the outage to the electronics shop and expedite repair, fearing that we could run aground without the radar display to guide us.

The electronics repair crew was severely undermanned, and we often had to trouble-shoot and repair devices when we had little or no training as to their inner workings. Thus, during off-hours we maintained a skeleton crew, and assigned whomever was available at the time to make emergency repairs, calling in the specialist on that gear only when absolutely necessary.

Among our men was Bill Dunn, who had been a radio station engineer at WSM, as I recall, in Nashville, TN before his recall to active duty and assignment to our crew. Bill was an affable, capable, likeable fellow, and completed his assignments, but left no doubt that he would have preferred to be in Nashville rather than on our ship. As fate would have it, he took the call to examine the repeater on the bridge, did so promptly, and reported to the captain that the trouble was not with the repeater, but with our Model SG-6 precision surface search radar which fed position information to the bridge repeater.

"How long will it take to fix it?" asked the captain. Dunn replied, "About 30 minutes." "Then get at it! We need this radar to see where we are!"

"Aye, aye, sir!" said Dunn and exited to the radar equipment compartment to begin his post mortem of this unfamiliar (to him) piece of equipment. Time passed, and the captain grew more uneasy as we cut our way through the fog. "Find out how that repair is progressing," he ordered. Dunn was up to his elbows in equipment instruction books, circuit boards and test instruments when the phone rang. "How long is it going to take to fix that thing?", he was asked. "About 30 minutes, sir!" replied Dunn, unhappy about having his work disrupted.

More time passed. The phone rang again, and the story I heard was of the following conversation:

OOD: How long is it going to take to fix that radar?

Dunn: About 30 minutes!

OOD: You told me that over an hour ago. Now, how long will it take to fix it?

Dunn: About 30 minutes after I find out what's wrong with the damned thing!.

I didn't actually hear this conversation, so I cannot swear that it happened, but I do know the next time we were in port at Yokosuka, Bill Dunn did not go ashore.

Banshees over the Champ - Summer 1953

An F9F Panther taxis forward after successful trap 1954

GORDON E. ALMY JR., born Sept. 29, 1932 in Troy, NY. He entered the USN Oct. 1, 1952 and went to boot camp at Bainbridge, MD.

He served in the USS *Salerno Bay* (CVE-110), 3rd Div. BM from 1953-54 and in the USS *Lake Champlain* (CVA-39), 7th Div. GM from 1954-55. He loved every bit of his service time.

After his discharge he worked several different jobs, then as a shipper for General Electric in Schenectady, NY, where he retired 30 years later.

Gordon and his wife Shirley married in 1961 and they have one daughter Terri. They live in Mayfield, NY where he enjoys fishing and making things out of wood. He belongs to VFW Post 8690 and American Legion Post 0337 in Broadalbin, NY.

RICHARD AWL, born March 19, 1933 in Canton, IL and was drafted in the service Nov. 23, 1955. His assignments include RTC, USNTC,

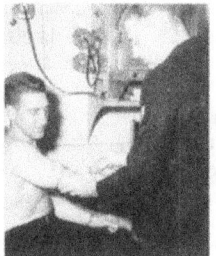

Great Lakes, IL; Hospital Corps School, Bainbridge, MD; USS *Lake Champlain* (CVA-39/CVS-39), June 24, 1956-Aug. 30, 1957; Mediterranean Cruise (6th Fleet).

A memorable experience was a fire on the USS *Lake Champlain* in Marseilles, France on July 3, 1957; also, tours for US sailors in Paris, Barcelona, Rome, Athens, Istanbul, Pompeii, etc.

Discharged from active duty Aug. 30, 1957 with the rate HM3 and later attained the rate HM2 in USNR.

He married Charlotte Pate in 1962 and has three children: Deborah, David and Stephen. He was an organic research chemist at USDA "Ag Lab" in Peoria, IL and retired after 33 years.

HERMAN C. BAINDER, born May 21, 1916, Baltimore, MD. He entered the service in November 1942 with boot camp at Parris Island where he earned a Sharpshooter Medal. He remained at Parris Island and was a drill instructor, 1943-44. Other assignments include: 1944, pre-OCS, New River, NC; 1944, OCS, Quantico, VA; 1945-46, CV-39, 2nd lieutenant gunnery officer; 1946, 2nd lieutenant, Marines, "Oregon City, antiair cruiser.

Participated in anti-sub duty in Atlantic Ocean, Caribbean, Mediterranean Sea and English Channel. Memorable experiences were the two shakedown cruises to Guantanamo, Cuba; serving on CV-39 in Naples with ship converted to troop carrier for 5,000 men (from Naples to New York); visiting ancient Pompeii while in Naples in 1946.

Discharged in May 1946 from Washington, DC as second lieutenant. He obtained first lieutenant status in Volunteer Reserve (until 1950s).

He was a school teacher in Baltimore City Public schools before enlistment and after WWII until his retirement. He also served in the summer of 1950 (just before Korean War) at Quantico in Public Relations.

WILLIAM BAUMHOLSER, born Nov. 6, 1926, Evansville, IN. He entered the USN Aug. 27, 1944 with assignments at Great Lakes, Newport, RI and USS *Lake Chaplain* (was a plankowner).

A memorable experience was when they crossed the Atlantic hauling troops when two roller curtains blew in during a storm at night and the

R Div. carpenter had to repair it. Also, memorable was beating the *Queen Mary's* record crossing the Atlantic.

Discharged Aug. 16, 1946 with the rate DCW3. He was called back during the Korean War and served from 1950-52.

William and Eileen have been married 50 years and have four children: Donald, Jennie, Barbara and Diana. Grandchildren are Ben, Holly, Mary Jo, Katie, John and Jessica. There is also one grandchild, Matty. A truck driver for 37 years, William retired in 1990. He also worked as a carpenter.

TUNNEY BAYLES, born April 18, 1931, Downsville, LA and graduated Ouachita Parish High in 1949. He attended Amarillo, TX, Col-

lege, 1949-50 and was a member of boxing and baseball teams. From 1950-51 he went to Marion Military Institute, making Varsity football and baseball teams.

He joined the USN in late 1951 and went through boot camp at San Diego; Airman and Electronic schools in Florida and Tennessee, then assigned to Norfolk, VA, in 1952. He made the 1952 Norfolk Navy Tars Football Team as a "2 way" guard and linebacker. After football he went aboard *Lake Champlain* to make the Korean Cruise. Upon returning to Florida, he was transferred to USS *Midway* for World Cruise in 1954-55.

Discharged as airman first class in 1955, he became a steeple jack, sandblasting and painting water towers, bridges, radio and TV towers nation-wide. In late 1956 he enlisted in the USAF and became an air traffic control tower operator. He resumed boxing, winning several tournaments including the Mid-South Golden Gloves Middleweight Championship in Memphis, TN in 1958.

When assigned to Carswell AFB in Fort Worth, TX, he was introduced to the sport of judo in 1959. He was fascinated and enthralled so completely by this "new sport" that with dedication and winning several tournaments, worked his way up to 1st degree Black Belt in three years. He was discharged in 1960 and went back to climbing water towers and entering judo tournaments.

Married Merry McDowell in 1962 and had a beautiful daughter, Melody, born in 1963, then his world collapsed. He fell from a tower in New Orleans and spent the next several months in hospitals in a body cast, traction and eventually crutches.

Of course that ended his sports career and almost his life. He went back to school and was a car salesman. Miraculously, he recovered enough to resume blasting and painting in paper mills and eventually returned to climbing water towers in 1968 until his retirement in 1998.

RICHARD ROBERT BELISLE, born Jan. 3, 1941 in Woonsocket, RI. He enlisted in the USN July 12, 1960, completing his boot camp training at Great Lakes, IL, September 1960.

Assignments were the USS *Lake Champlain,* homeport NAS Quonset Point, RI, 1960 to mid-1962. He then transferred to the newly recent commissioned USS *Constellation* (CVA-64) soon to be homeported in San Diego, CA. He began his ships naval duty as a boatswain's mate for a few months, then qualified for transfer to G Div. where he spent the remaining time in the service of the Navy as a gunner's mate.

Memorable experiences include when his ship was called upon, amongst other US ships, to bring about a blockade of the Russian ships, attempting to transport missiles on to Cuban soil, resistance powerfully shown by our government and US ships and planes, forcing them to turn back – that was something to behold!

Another memorable experience was when their ship was called upon to retrieve CMDR Alan Shepherd, USN, Astronaut, and his space capsule upon landing out at sea after his historical first manned (and only man) space flight. Other memories include sailing around South America, crossing the might of Cape Horn, the magnitude and strength of the sea, crossing the Equator, stopping at different ports and meeting people of the world over.

A sad experience was the assassination and ultimate loss of President John F. Kennedy – to most all in the military, in the US and around the world, we lost not just a president, but also a friend.

His final two years in the Navy as a gunner's mate were quite busy. He was discharged around mid-1964 from ship at sea. Richard is single. He has a younger brother Roger and a sister Claudette who has two children. Richard has worked 16-1/2 years with the USPS, Providence, RI, as a mail-handler.

CHARLES E. BEYER, born June 30, 1926, Bloomfield, NJ and joined the USN in September 1943. Boot camp was at Newport, RI and Gunnery School in Virginia. He transferred to Armed Guard in New York and sailed on tanker SS *Great Meadows* as Navy gunner for 14 months.

Re-assigned to Navy Pier 92 on the Hudson River; transferred to carrier training in Newport, RI; transferred to USS *Lake Champlain* in 1945 and assigned to 3rd Div. with duty on twin five 38-inch guns aft of island. He was part of the world record run from the Rock of Gibraltar to Newport News, VA in four days, eight hours and 51 minutes. He's also a plankowner.

Unforgettable memories include watching Navy and Marine pilots take off and land on the carrier and his association with a superb group of shipmates.

Discharged in November 1947 with the rate GM3/c. His awards include the European Victory Medal. After discharge he returned home and worked for the Board of Education in Bloomfield, NJ in building maintenance for 41 years.

Married 52 years to the former Joan A. Walsh and has a son, daughter and three grandchildren. Now retired, he lives in South Carolina.

HARVEY BLANKENSHIP, born Aug. 16, 1924, Jasper, TX and served in the Navy, E Division. Boot camp was at San Diego Training Station. He went aboard the USS *Sepulga*, a Navy oil tanker. He spent 22 months in the South Pacific fueling the fleet going into battle and had some scary times.

Memorable Experiences: On shakedown run to Cuba they lost 13 of their crew, pilot included. On one of their runs they broke a world record. Once, while changing fuel to the boiler, his shipmate didn't open the valve to second pump before closing valve on first pump and the fires went out in both boilers. He yelled at him to open the valve and the oil came in, united off of the hot fire wall inside the boiler and blew Harvey's cap off his head. It made a loud bang and rattled the fireroom.

Transferred back to the States and went to school at Newport to train for the USS *Lake Champlain*. He put it in commission and is a plankowner.

Discharged in February 1946, he worked for Texaco Oil Refinery for 37 years. He lives in Nederland, TX and enjoys fishing, hunting and traveling. Married since 1949 and has three sons: Harvey, Dick and Mark.

RICHARD E. "DICK" BOGDEN, born in October 1937, Great Falls, MT. He enlisted in the USN, Aviation, V-6 Div. in April 1955. Assignments include boot camp at San Diego; schools at Norman, OK and Memphis; USS *Lake Champlain* (CVA-39); VF-22 NAS Jax; shore duty at NAS Pensacola.

He participated in blocking the Straits of Gibraltar during the Suez Canal crisis in 1956. Discharged in October 1958 as AD2. He received the Good Conduct and is proud to have been part of the US Navy.

Married the former Betty Jo Hudgins in 1958 and they have three children: Richard II, Randall and Rebecca. A farmer, rancher and owner of a slaughter house and distributing company in Montana, he is now retired.

JOHN MITCHELL BOWLING, born May 22, 1929, Yonkers, NY. He joined the USNR and went to OCS at Newport, RI, March-July 1952, Ensign 1105; fleet activities, Sasebo, Japan, July 1952-December 1953; USS *Lake Champlain* (CVA-39), asst. communications officer, December 1953-July 1955.

He participated in the Korean War and European Occupation (CVA-39 Mediterranean Cruise). Separated July 26, 1955, LTjg, active duty and CAPT, JAGC, Reserves. His awards include the National Defense Service Medal, Korean Service Medal, UN Service Medal, Navy Occupation w/European Clasp.

His wife Mary-Margaret is deceased. John has a son J. Mitchell Jr. John is semi-retired from his law practice and business.

ROBERT T. BREGLIA, born Dec. 15, 1931 in Brooklyn, NY and is a graduate of Brooklyn Automotive High School. Employed as pipefitter apprentice at Brooklyn Navy Yard prior to joining USN on Jan. 2, 1952.

After boot camp at Bainbridge NTC, he attended Class A Pipefitter School, NS, Norfolk. Assigned to Ships Company Re-commissioning

Crew for *Lake Champlain,* he was summarily relegated to three months of mess cooking (galley slave). He later graduated to compartment cleaner, instilling in him a meticulous sense of cleanliness and high regard for people in the janitorial services. While assigned to Engineering "R" (Repair) Division Pipe and Metal Shop, he was able to do what he liked best, work with tools.

After shakedown at GITMO and service on the line off Korea, he made two cruises to the Mediterranean. In early 1955 in the port of Naples, Italy, he and shipmate Angelo Cirillo were granted four days leave to visit relatives. Traveling by rail to Fardella Potenza, they visited with Robert's relatives and Angelo took movies of Bob with them. After dinner and a night's stay, they bussed east to Bari, to visit Angelo's relatives and were treated formidably by Angelo's uncle the judge. On leaving Bari, the judge assigned a bodyguard to protect the two sailors traveling by rail to Naples. The movies were converted to video and recently given to Bob's relatives who are now US citizens.

Separated January 1956 with the rate FP1 (E-6). Final discharge from inactive reserves in 1960 with rate converted to HT1 (Hull Tech). His medals include Good Conduct, European Occupation Service (Navy) National Defense, Korean Service w/Battle Star, UN Service Medal, Korean PUC and Korean Service Medal (issued by ROK).

He resumed work at the Brooklyn Yard and in early 1956-the "Champ" arrived for repairs. He boarded CVA-39 this time as a yard pipefitter assigned to replace defective piping and make required alterations and to fraternize with shipmates.

He fabricated and installed a gamut of shipboard piping in the super carriers, *Saratoga* (CVA-60), *Independence* (CVA-62), and *Constellation* (CVA-64) during their construction. At close of the shipyard in 1965, he took a position as steamfitter with New York City School Facilities. Retired in 1993 after 28-1/2 years of service (14 years as supervisor and six as general supervisor of steamfitters with citywide control).

He married the lovely Josephine Pulvirenti in 1957 and has four children: twin boys, Thomas and Joseph; two girls, Monica and Teresa; and five grandchildren.

ALFRED P. BREITBACH JR., born May 19, 1925, Cascade, IA. Navy service started Oct. 12, 1943 with boot camp at NTS, Farragut, ID; Aviation Machinist School NATTC, Norman, OK; Catapult School RS, Navy Yard, Philadelphia, PA; USS Lake Champlain Detail, Navy Yard, Portsmouth, VA; with about 140 others (temp. duty) on USS *Randolph* (CV-15) shakedown cruise; CASU 21, FFT *Lake Champlain*; *Lake Champlain* (CV-39) flight deck Catapult Crew, also the "magic carpet" trips; early in 1946, USS *Mindoro* (CVE-120) qualifying pilots off the east coast. Separated from active duty, May 3, 1946, with rating of ABM (CP)3/c.

Received BA degree from Loras College, Dubuque, IA; MA degree from State University of Iowa, Iowa City, IA. He was employed at Iowa State Employment Service when "recalled" to active duty May 1951. He served aboard USS *Wasp* (CV-18), until August 1952 in Aviation Gasoline Division "after" pumproom control.

Employed at Iowa State Employment Service until September 1956, then at Iowa Power and Light Company (later known as Mid-American Energy) until retirement Oct. 1, 1985.

Married Rita Kutsch, Dubuque, IA, April 14, 1951, and has six children: Alecia, Jerome, Christine, Connie, Dennis and Paul. There are 17 grandchildren (including triplet boys born June 30, 2000) and five great-grandchildren.

FRANCIS J. BRENGARTH, born in Boonville, MO, enlisted in the Marines (seagoing) on Nov. 11, 1944 and served aboard the USS *Champlain*. Memorable experience was shipboard burial. Discharged July 6, 1946 as CIP, he received the European Theater Medal.

Married S. Odom on Sept. 27, 1948 and has four sons: John, Frank, Steve, Jim; one daughter Lisa; and 10 grandchildren. A farmer, cattleman and pork producer, he lives in Wooldridge, MO where he still helps his son farm. He's a wonderful friend, spouse, father, grandfather and most of all a great person.

JAMES R. BROWN, born May 5, 1933 in San Francisco CA, but grew up in San Diego. On June 16, 1952, he enlisted in the USN. Boot camp was in San Diego, then sent to Norfolk, VA where they were transported by troop ship to Guantanamo Bay to board and serve on the USS *Lake Champlain* (CVA-39).

In January 1953 they left for Korea via the Atlantic through the Mediterranean to Athens, Greece where they saw the Parthenon. They went on through the Suez Canal, which was quite an experience. After that, Ceylon, India, where they toured Candy (the capital) and had lunch. Soon after they crossed the International Date Line and he became a shellback. They headed through Manilla and Yokosuka, Japan, reaching the coast of Korea during wartime. The only sign of action was a Chinese plane dropping foil. Their compliment of planes launched quicker than any other carrier. In August 1953 the Armistice was signed and they returned to the US via the same route they came.

Upon returning to the States he went to Dental Tech School in Bainbridge, MD. He had been a dental striker aboard ship. After finishing school, he reported to the Dental Clinic in Charleston Naval Shipyard. He was there from 1954 to 1956 (six months was spent at Charleston Naval Hospital).

While stationed in Charleston he was manager of a Little Boys Baseball team (Piggly Wiggly #13). They came in second and were one of the teams whose game was on TV.

His medals include the Good Conduct, European Occupation, National Defense, Korean Service w/Battle Star, UN Service Medal and Syngman Rhee Medal.

After retirement from US Federal Civil Service, he pursued his interest in the Civil War as a re-enactor. He is part of the 4th Artillery Battery B, Cannoneers Live Fire. He was also in the film North and South II and an episode of Quantum Leap as a re-enactor. He is also a volunteer at Old Town San Diego. He is involved in Living History where he portrays a soldier from 1846-60, complete with authentic uniform and firearms.

On June 26, 1965, he married Donna Small and they have a daughter Marie, son-in-law Troy and a son James Lowell.

CARROLL L. BUMGARNER, born May 7, 1937, Waynesville, NC. He enlisted in the USN July 4, 1954 with boot camp and Class A Radio School in San Diego, CA. Other assignments include US Submarine Base in New London, CT; USS *Ticonderoga* (CVA-14); and USS *Lake Champlain* (CVS-39).

A memorable experience was joining elements of the fleet in a high-speed run to the scene of tension in the Middle East; helping fight the ship fire on the *Champ* in Marseilles, France; playing guitar with other shipmates for the chief's quarters and receiving a bottle of Canadian Club!

He is proud of his radio Speed-Key license (being one of the selected few to have one in the Atlantic Fleet) and Good Conduct Medal. He was discharged April 4, 1958 as Radioman 3, OR DIV, on both ships.

After his discharge he worked for Charles Pfizer Pharmaceutical Co. in Groton, CT. Married, he has six children and several grandchildren. He is now retired and playing bluegrass music with his family band, The Rose City Bluegrass Band, consisting of himself; his wife Maryann; daughters, Cathy and Cheryl; and son-in-law, Jim. He enjoys fishing, gardening and spending time with his grandchildren.

ROBERT E. BURGER, born Aug. 14, 1936 in Lexington, KY and joined the Naval Reserve Unit while in high school. He volunteered for active duty in May 1957. During his reserve training in electronics, annual obligations included basic at Great Lakes and seamanship basics aboard the USS *Roberts* (DE-749).

After spending six weeks at the transient barracks in Norfolk, VA, his first assignment was to report to duty aboard the USS *Lake Champlain* in Mayport, FL, just recently redesignated to CVS.

Other than the short-lived conflict in July 1958 when Marines were deployed to Beirut and resulted in the fleet to be battle prepared, things were reasonably quiet during his active status.

His most memorable experience was simply to be a part of a diversified and impressive crew commanded by a respected captain. Included was the challenging and often uptempo work to keep communications equipment up and running.

After his discharge in May 1959 with the rate ETN3, he joined IBM in Lexington as a technician and later transferred to Austin, TX. He retired in 1997 as a staff engineer after 30 plus years.

Now residing in Cedar Park, TX and enjoying the company of his family of four children, six grandchildren and one great-grandchild.

ROBERT HENRY BURNSIDE, born May 20, 1933 in Columbia, SC. He enlisted in the Navy in January 1952 and served as Navy Aviation Ordnanceman, Attack Squadron 45.

Locations included Bainbridge, MD; Jacksonville NAS, FL; and USS *Lake Champlain* for Korean cruise in 1953. Discharged in 1953 as AO.

Married, he has three children and nine grandchildren. He's an attorney and retired state judge and lives in Columbia, SC with his wife. They enjoy traveling and spending time with family.

GORDON T. CALDWELL, born Jan. 6, 1927, Bridgeport, CT. He attained the rank PFC in the USMC and LtCol in the USAF. With the USMC he served at Parris Island, SC; Camp Lejeune, NC; Sea School, San Diego, CA; USS *Lake Chaplain;* Norfolk Naval Yard, VA, Quantico, VA. USAF locations were at Texas, Louisiana, Guam, Washington, Iceland, Germany, France, Kansas, Alabama, Massachusetts, Guam and Okinawa.

After WWII ended they visited Boston, New York City, Philadelphia with CV-39 to show to the public. Memorable Experiences: 1945-46, Magic Carpet, moving troops from Southampton, England and Naples, Italy to New York's Staten Island. Also memorable was being squadron commander in Vietnam, 1970-71.

He spent three years in the USMC and retired from the USAF April 1, 1974 after 26 years of service. He completed 59 combat missions in Korea (B-29) and 106 combat missions in Vietnam (C-7). His awards include the Distinguished Flying Cross and Air Medal w/8 OLCs.

Married Oct. 8, 1949 to Elizabeth Karen Hanghoj and they live in Cummington, MA, where he is owner/manager of 176 acre farm, beef cattle and forest products. He has a BS degree from the University of Massachusetts. Gordon and Elizabeth have four children: Carol Lyn, Gordon Thompson, James Michael and Richard Douglas and nine grandchildren. He is proud to be an American and having served his country.

CHARLES CALHOUN, born Feb. 12, 1926 in Langdale, AL. He enlisted in the USN June 4, 1943 and went to boot camp at NAS Pensacola, FL. After boot camp he transferred to Whiting Field, Milton, FL, then to Norfolk, VA and worked on sea and land planes. He was on the USS *Charger* and USS *Randolph*. He then returned to NAS Norfolk, VA and Edenton, NC. He was a crew member on *Lake Champlain* with the VIT Flight Deck Division.

In 1944 he went to Trinidad on USS *Randolph* on a shakedown cruise. Most memorable experience was sleeping on the same mattress cover for six weeks. He was discharged Dec. 18, 1945 at Millington, TN as SF1/c.

He married Agnes Teel and has four children: Susan, Charles, James and Elizabeth. He worked with Lafayette Light and Water for 19 years and Montgomery Water Works for 24 years as plant supervisor. He is currently retired and living in Wetumpka, AL.

JOSEPH M. CAMPION, born Aug. 21, 1940 in Buffalo, NY, and enlisted in November 1959. Duty assignments were at NAS Jacksonville, FL, O&G Div; USS *Lake Champlain* (CVS-39), G Div., Quonset Pt., RI. Discharged in November 1963 with the rate AO3.

Two memories: while on the Cuban Blockade they passed within a few thousand yards of what looked like a Russian cruise ship. Sailors were leaning on the rail staring at the ship. The ships photographer posted a photo in the Mess Deck of a bunch of Russians in bathing suits leaning on the rail, staring at us. Our compartment was on the 03 level, just aft of the forecastle, under the catapults. Once, returning from the Caribbean they spent four days riding out a hurricane off Cape Hatteras. When seas calmed both forward flight deck catwalks were folded up against the deck edge. What a ride!

He has been married for 41 years, has three children and two grandchildren. He's employed by the town of Orchard Park, NY as supervising building inspector.

JOHN R. CARROLL JR., born Oct. 27, 1937, Baltimore, MD and enlisted in the USNR at Baltimore, MD on Nov. 7, 1955 and assigned to Division 5-5. Attended boot camp at Bainbridge NTC, MD.

Ordered to active duty Sept. 9, 1957 and attended Electrician's Mates, Class "A" School at the USNTC Great Lakes, IL, then assigned aboard the USS *Lake Champlain* (CVS-39). Released from active duty Sept. 9, 1960 at Quonset Point, RI. He was discharged from the USNR on Nov. 25, 1960 as EM2 (E-5).

Employed by Black and Decker, Maryland Drydock and Shipbuilding, RCA Service Co., Westinghouse Electric Co. and Northrop Grumman Corp. He attended night classes at York College of Pennsylvania earning a BS in management.

Married Margaret Stroud April 8, 1957 and they live in Shrewsbury, PA. They have three children: John III, Charles and Bonny.

He has been retired for five years from Northrop Grumman. He and his wife enjoy their grandchildren, traveling in their RV and snowmobiling. Twice a year he serves on the local election board. He is a member and past master of Shrewsburg Lodge No. 423 of Free and Accepted Masons where he served as a trustee and on the committee of instruction and examination. Also, a member of the Scottish Rite, Valley of Harrisburg, PA.

WILLIAM L. "BILL" CARWARDINE, born Aug. 8, 1927 in Cleveland, OH. He enlisted in the USN Sept. 1, 1944 at the age of 16, went to Great Lakes USNT then to USNTS Newport, RI.

He served a short time on the USS *Duluth* and was next on the *Lake Champlain* at its christening and is a plankowner. He served in the European, South African and SE Pacific Theaters. Bill was injured and spent some time at Bremerton Naval Hospital. He was discharged June 19, 1946 with the rate WT3/c. His awards include the Victory Medal, American Ribbon, European-African ME Ribbon and SE Pacific Theater.

Employed at Fisher Body Plant (now General Motors). In 1955 he joined Janesville Fire Dept and retired as captain/fire inspector in 1982. Married Bernice Mullen in 1954 and had two sons, Kurt and Bernie. He fought a four year battle with cancer and passed away Nov. 5, 2000. He was very proud of his Navy time aboard "the Champ."

MICHAEL PAUL CAYLEY SR., born Nov. 12, 1938, Detroit, MI. In 1956 he enlisted in the USN, Div. N and served aboard the USS *Lake Champlain.*

Most memorable experience was the fall of 1958 while operating off the coast of Cape Hatteras, they went through a hurricane. He can't recall the name, but the winds were over 110 mph. They steamed into the eye of the storm and it was very eerie, but getting into and out of the eye was really scary. The ship was listing from port to starboard more than 28 degrees. He was discharged May 27, 1959 with the rate QM3.

He started Midaco Corp. as a job shop in 1969 and today they are a manufacturer of manual and automatic pallet changers for the machine tool industry sold world-wide. His son Michael Jr. is in the business with him. He also has a daughter Kerry Scinta. Grandchildren are Michael III and Ross Cayley; Samuel and Anthony Scinta. He lives in Elk Grove Village, IL.

RALPH S. CHAMPNEY, born July 4, 1933 in Watertown, NY. He entered the USN, Communications, June 15, 1950. Assignments include PC 1233, Great Lakes and Communication School at Norfolk, VA; Pvt. Thomas at Cuba and USS *Lake Champlain* (CVA-39).

He took part in the last two months of the Korean War aboard the *Champlain.* Memorable experiences include recovery for space mission Gemini V; service with Korea; around the world cruises, covering 52 ports in two years; being second in communication class of 26; and USN lightweight boxing champ for two years.

Discharged in June 1959 as PO1/c. His awards include the Korean Service Medal, UN Service Medal, Honor Grad at Communication School, three Good Conduct medals, European Occupation USN Service and National Defense.

Married June Farmer in 1955 and has three children: Cyndi, Steven and Carolyn; five granddaughters and one grandson. Employed 32 years, Blue Cross-Blue Shield, chief financial officer and corp. treasurer. Retired from corp. life and for the past 12 years has been president of his own consulting firm.

JAMES A. CHAPPELL, born Oct. 6, 1936 in Houston, TX. Joined the USNR in February 1962 and eventually reported to the USS *Lake Champlain* (CVS-39) at Quonset Point, NAS. Assigned to the captain's office as YN3 with a "Secret" clearance and was responsible for the captain's in-coming/out-going mail correspondence. The location of the captain's office and a flexible schedule while at sea provided opportunities for many at sea photographs.

While serving on the *"Champ,"* he experienced exciting adventures underway and in a variety of ports. The most memorable was coming to love the sea while experiencing its constantly changing emotions. He participated in the Cuban Missile Crisis; in February 1963 New York City and the "Mona Lisa;" shore duty in Port-a-Prince; Haiti for relief caused by Hurricane "Jane;" and returning from Bermuda when President Kennedy was assassinated.

Discharged from active duty in February 1964 and returned to Texas. He and Penny reared two daughters and are enjoying two granddaughters.

A teacher of US History, he retired from the Houston Community College in June 2002. Currently spends many hours each week as an author, having published in five genre.

LEON R. CLAYPOOL, born Aug. 2, 1933. He enlisted in the Navy, R Division, on July 6, 1952. He served in the USS *Salerno Bay* (CVE-110) and USS *Lake Champlain*, Mayport. Served with 6th Fleet in Mediterranean.

Memorable was getting underway for a Mediterranean Cruise and a tug boat put a hole in the bow. He was discharged July 15, 1956 as FP-2.

Worked as iron worker and welder for Allegheny Ludlum Steel and is now retired and lives in Leechburg, PA. He is married and has one daughter and two grandchildren.

VAN H. COLES, born Oct. 30, 1927, Nashville, TN. He enlisted Aug. 7, 1944 in the USN at age 16. Assignments included boot camp at Great Lakes; New Port, RI; and USS *Lake Champlain*, where he was a plankowner and served aboard until his discharge.

He participated in Magic Carpet runs bringing troops back from Europe. Memorable was visiting England, North Africa, the great storm in the North Atlantic, Cuba on shakedown, loss of *Corsair* due *Saratoga* and decommission at Norfolk.

Discharged June 6, 1946 as F2/c. His awards include the European Theater of Operations and Blue Ribbon for fastest ocean crossing.

He and Margaret have been married 51 years and live in Houston, TX. They have two daughters and four grandchildren. He was employed 33 years at Broghill Farm Ind. as mfg. rep. and is now retired.

GEORGE R. CRABB, born Oct. 6, 1933 in Mt. Morris, NY and joined the Navy on July 10, 1952. He served aboard the USS *Lake Champlain* (CVA-39) from April 15, 1953 until July 1, 1956. Took boot camp at Bainbridge, MD from July to September 1952, Class A Electrical School at Montgomery Jr. College, Takoma Park, MD.

Most memorable experience was the 40 days on the line sending planes in to attack North Korea and the signing of the armistice aboard the *Champ*.

Left the *Champ* on July 1, 1956 to be discharged on July 5 as an EM2. His medals include Navy Good Conduct, Korean Service, National Defense Service, Navy Occupation Service (Europe), UN Service,

Republic of Korea Presidential Unit Citation (Foreign) and Republic of Korea War Service (Foreign).

After leaving the Navy he worked 37 years at Rochester Gas and Electric Corp. and retired Nov. 30, 1993. Married Betty Smith in 1954 and has three children: David, Daniel and Diane. They also have nine grandchildren.

ROBERT W. CRAIG, born Aug. 3, 1938 in Detroit, MI. He enlisted in the UCMCR on Aug. 12, 1955 as a cannoneer at the 2nd 155 Gun Battalion in Miami, FL. He enlisted in the USMC in February 1957 at PIRD, Platoon 68 where he qualified as high sharpshooter with the M-1 rifle.

Robert was assigned to the Marine Detachment aboard CVA\CVS-39, USS

Lake Champlain from September 1957 to March 1959 and while aboard the *"Champ"* his duties consisted of securities for SASS Posts 1 and 2, guard duty for the brig, orderly at court-martials and responsibility for transporting military prisoners. During his assignment on the *"Champ,"* he took a Mediterranean cruise in 1957 and a North Atlantic cruise in 1958, during which time Lebanon occurred and the ship was put on high alert.

After his tour of duty on the *"Champ,"* he was reassigned to Camp Lejeune in March 1959 to a line company in "D" Company, 2nd Battalion, 8th Marine Regiment, 2nd Marine Division. During his last year in the Corps he was reassigned back to his original MOS as a cannoneer in "I" Battery, 10th Marines, 2nd Marine Division.

After discharge from the Corps he enlisted in the US Army Reserves from 1974-77 and was assigned as the driver for the commanding general of the 76th Division, retaining his E4 status.

He married Sylvia Sawyer on Feb. 5, 1961 and has two sons, Robert Jr. and Richard. He retired from Motorola after 17 years and still enjoys being at sea on the *SS Sawyer*. He currently resides in Boynton Beach, FL.

ARNOLD L. CRAWFORD, born April 5, 1935 in Kittanning, PA. He enlisted in the USN in February 1955 and went to boot camp at Bainbridge, MD; AP School at Norman, OK; Aviation Electrician School, NATTC, Jacksonville, FL; VA-16 Squadron, Oceana, VA, 1956-58.

He went aboard the *Lake Champlain* for shakedown cruise to Cuba, then Mediterranean Cruise (1956-57) shore duty O&R North Island, San Diego, CA; Radar School, Imperial Beach, CA.

His memorable experience was a fire aboard the Champ in Marseilles; flying test hops in jets, props and helicopters for O&R test line.

Discharged in February 1959 as AE2 and stayed in the UNNR until February 1963. He received the Good Conduct Medal.
After discharge he was a lineman for West Penn Power Co., 1959 to retirement in 1996. He married Phyllis Stennett April 28, 1956 and they live in Kittanning, PA. They have three children: Mindy, David, Beth and six grandchildren. He enjoys golfing, woodworking and traveling.

EMERSON E. DEALE JR., born Oct. 3, 1930, Annapolis, MD. He joined the USNR in 1948 and was called into active service July 9, 1952 at the Naval Yard PRNC Washington, DC.

Transferred to Norfolk, VA for duty aboard the USS *Lake Champlain* for its recommissioning in July 1952. Assigned to B Division and participated in Korean Conflict.

Discharged in May 1954 as FN. His awards include the UN Service Medal, Korean Service Medal and National Defense Service Medal.

After discharge he worked 39 years for Nationwide Ins. Co. with 34 years as an insurance agent. He married Mary Tastet Oct. 23, 1954 and they live in Annapolis, MD. They have six children: Donna, Mary, Carol, Charles, Margaret and Aliene, and 14 grandchildren.

ROYAL B. DELAND, born May 4, 1919, Magna, UT. He enlisted in USN Sept. 24, 1940 with boot camp at San Diego, CA; Aviation Machinist School, North Island; Aviation Machinist School, Chicago, IL; Aviation Fuel System, Philadelphia, PA. Correspondent courses include Military Justice, Navy Regulations and Naval leadership. Education and Training, Part 1-2; Practical Damage Control, Theoretical Damage Control Radiological Defense, Security of Classified Matter, Aviation Specialist, Aircraft Electrical Systems, Airplane Power plants and Jet Aircraft Engines.

Assignments at Rodd Field, Corpus Christi, TX, 1941-44; Casu 48, Saipan Marinas, 1944-46; Commander Fleet Air Alameda, 1947-50; Attack Squadron 195; Korean Theater, 1950-53; USS *Princeton;* Commander Fleet Air Alameda, 1953-56; Patrol Squadron 9, 1956-57; commissioned warrant officer; USS *Lake Champlain,* 1957-59 aviation fuels officer, aircraft maintenance officer; NAS Alameda, 1959.
Retired in March 1961. His medals and commendations include the Good Conduct Medal (4 awards), American Defense, American Area, Asiatic-Pacific Area, WWII Victory Medal, Korean Service, United Nations, Presidential Unit Citation, Navy Commendation, USS *Princeton*, Commendation for Meritorious Service, Attack Squadron 195 and Commendation Commanding Officer USS *Lake Chaplain* J.R. Penland.

Following Navy service, he was owner/operator of Health Food and Sporting Goods Store and director, Rogue River Senior Club, 1980-94. Now retired and lives in Grants Pass.

Married Erma Weinberg in 1943, and she passed in 1993. He married Neoma McCoy in 1996. He has three children: Royal, Donald and Darilyn.

JAMES O. DERSHAM JR., born May 17, 1930, Duncannon, PA. He enlisted in the USN Feb. 13, 1952 and went to boot camp at Bainbridge, MD. For duty he was attached to NATTC Jacksonville, Light Photo Sqdn. 62, NAS Jacksonville, VR-1 Patuxent River, MD, Helicopter Sqdn. 5, NAS Quonset Point, RI.

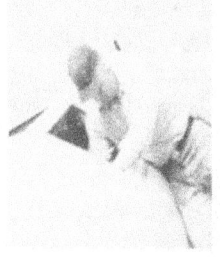

He served in the following ships: USS *Coral Sea, Lake Champlain* and *Forrestall.* Shore duty assignments include VR-1 NAS Patuxent River, MD, where he qualified as a plane captain and flew regularly. His most memorable incident was the fire on the *Champ* while entering port in Marseilles, France.
Left the Navy in October 1961 while stationed at HS-5, Quonset Point. At the required time, he passed the exams for advancement and came out as AE-1. Awards include the Good Conduct, European Occupation and National Defense Service Medal.

Coming back to civilian life, he went to work at New Cumberland Army Depot in aircraft maintenance. Later he moved to Mechanicsburg Naval Supply Depot where he became a general supply officer. Next he went into the hydraulic repair business and bought a small business which he operated for 10 years, then sold it. He went to work for USPS and eventually served as postmaster until retirement in 1985.
Married Jane Emert and they live in Duncannon, PA. They have four children, nine grandchildren and two great-grandchildren.

JOSEPH M. DI ANGELIS, born Aug. 15, 1935 in Weirton, WV. He joined the USN in 1952 and went to boot camp in Bainbridge, MD. He went to RPT and then to Co. 104, 42nd Bn., 4th Regt. Honor Company. First Class Gunner's Mate Blue was their company commander.

First assigned to the USS *Hornet* (CVA-12), 7th Div. then went to the *Lake*

Champlain (CVA-39), 7th Div. and mess cook, followed by the USS *Alsteda.* He was a boxer and Bainbridge Champ, Mediterranean Champ and Air Landt Champ. While on the *Champ* he was nick-named the Ohio Whirlwind.

After his discharge in 1960, he reared a family and joined the USAR, from which he retired in 1994. He received the Navy Good Conduct Medal, National Defense Service Medal w/Korean and Desert Storm Clusters, Army Achievement Medal, Army Reserve Component Medal, Army of Occupation Medal, Army Forces Reserve Medal, NCO Professional Development Medal and Armed Service Medal.
He and his wife Donna have been married 43 years and live in Weirton, WV. They have five children and 12 grandchildren. He is retired from

Weirton Steel Co. with 35 years service. A Fourth Degree Knight of Columbus, he enjoys volunteering at his church, playing bocci, gardening, movies and playing with his grandchildren.

STANLEY R. DONNELL, born Dec. 25, 1939 in Shickshinny, PA. He enlisted in the USN Sept. 27, 1957 and went to basic training at San Diego Naval Training Center; TDA: China Lake Naval Ordinance Test Station (NOTS), China Lake, CA; Electrician Class A School, San Diego.

Shore duty was at Philadelphia Naval Base and sea duty in the USS *Lake Champlain* (CVS-39). Memorable experiences include MoJave Desert sand storms at China Lake and riding the ship's bus back from the SeAir Club in Quonset Point to the ship and the many heavy discussions between the "Air-dales" and the ships company and trying to look squared away when going up the gangway to salute the OOD (dress whites don't look to good after one of those discussions).

Discharged Sept. 26, 1963 as EM2. He received a Good Conduct Medal.

He married Amy Doris Creutzburg in 1962 and they live in Stone Mountain, GA. They have two sons, Paul and David. Son Paul produced two exceptional grandchildren, Lilly and Mark.

After a short stint at the Philadelphia Naval Base, going to the Universities of Temple and Drexel in Philadelphia, PA, he has spent 37 years working for Siemens Energy & Automation (previously ITE Circuit Breaker Co.) where he is currently a market manager in the international marketing group.

GLENN W. DYE, born Aug. 21, 1921, Wildwood, NJ. He enlisted Aug. 10, 1942 in the USNR as FN3/c at NRS, Philadelphia, PA; Aug. 27, 1942, transferred to SecBase, Cape May, NJ aboard USS *Flamingo*; Oct. 16, 1943, USS YR-30, Norfolk, VA; Dec. 4, 1943, RecSta, Nyd, Philadelphia, PA.

Promoted to FN2/c Jan. 1, 1944 and sent to USS YMS-11, replacing the *Flamingo* in sweeping German mines in Atlantic; July 10, 1944, RecSta, Norfolk, VA; Sept. 19, 1944, NavSta, Arzew, Algeria; Oct. 12, 1944, AATB, Bizerte, FFA; Oct. 18, 1944, USS LCI(L)-552; Dec. 14, 1944, USS LCI(L)-36; made FN1/c; July 29, 1945, NavPhibBase, Little Creek, VA; Oct. 30, 1945, RecSta, Norfolk, VA; Nov. 6, 1945, USS *Lake Champlain;* Jan. 17, 1946, PSC, Bainbridge, MD.

Discharged Jan. 26, 1946. His medals include Occupation Bar, Victory Medal and Cold War Medal.

After discharge he worked as a claims manager for GM then parts manager for Packard dealer. He lives in Buckeye Lake, OH.

STEPHEN EBBENGA, born Jan. 15, 1939, Rapid City, SD. He enlisted in the USN Dec. 4, 1957, machinist mate, M Division, #1 Engine Room. Boot camp was at San Diego, December 1957-February 1958; Machinist Mate School, March-May 1958, Mayport, FL; Quonset Point, RI then to USS *Lake Champlain* from 1958-61.

Memorable experiences include Mediterranean Cruise in 1959; move to Quonset Point, RI; picking up first astronaut in 1961; and taken off liberty in Norfolk, VA to blockade Cuba in 1961. Discharged Dec. 4, 1961 as MM3/c. He received the Good Conduct Medal.

After discharge he worked at US Steel and in the Post Office. He married Ruth Marvin on June 30, 1962 and they live in Tonopah, NV. They have two sons, Grant and Gregory.

JOHN D. ECKBERT, born Dec. 4, 1939, Denver, CO and enlisted in June 1958 in the USNR. Assignments include VAW-12 Det 1 and Det 34; NAS Norfolk, VA; and NAS Quonset Point, RI.

Memorable was participating in Cuban Missile Crisis; Air Crew VAW-12 flying in AD5W Guppies; and night cat shots with the hyd catapults was always a thrill. He was discharged in August 1972 as ADJ-1.

He lives with his wife Margaret in Los Angeles, CA. They have two daughters, Jennifer and Amy, and two granddaughters.

Employed with America West Airlines and works in Operation Engineering Dept.

GEORGE ESSEY, born June 24, 1935, Monessen, PA. He enlisted April 13, 1954 in the USN, Medical Department (H-Div.). Boot camp and Hospital Corps School was at Bainbridge, MD; Hospital Command and Med School Command, Bethesda, MD; and USS *Lake Champlain* (CVA/S-39), Mayport, FL.

Memorable experience was 1957 Mediterranean Cruise and the fire at Marseilles, France.

He married Doreen Stofka in 1955 and has three children: Chip, Lori and Susan, eight grandchildren and one great-granddaughter.

George retired as postmaster of the Monessen, PA, Post Office after 33 years of USPS service. He retired as secretary of BPO Elks #773 after 26 years of service. Works part-time as assistant treasurer of the local Postal Federal Union and active as choir director, cantor and treasurer of St. Michael Antiochian Orthodox Church, Monessen, PA.

JOHN A. FARROW, born March 27, 1935, Boston, MA. He enlisted June 27, 1952 in the USNR, AE, V2E at Bainbridge, MD; Norman, OK; Jacksonville, FL; Massachusetts; and USS *Lake Champlain.*

A memorable experience was Mediterranean Cruise; being

flight deck electrician, ships motor pool (driver). He was discharged April 30, 1955 as aviation electrician mate. His awards include the Navy Occupation w/European Clasp and National Defense Service Medal.

His wife Mary is deceased. He has four children: John Jr., Brian, Theresa and Stephen. A retired electrician, he lives in Weymouth, MA, and enjoys traveling.

JAY E. FULLER, born July 28, 1938, Pensacola FL. He served in the NC NG 30th Inf., 1955-57, then joined USN in 1957. He went to boot camp at San Diego, CA and "AT" School, Memphis, TN, 1957.

Other assignments include VW4/AEWBARRONPAC, Barbers Point, Hawaii, 1958-61; NAF LaJes Azores, 1961-62; VS-32/USS *Lake Champlain* (CVS-39), Quonset Pt, RI, 1962-64; VA-44, Cecil Field, FL, 1964-65.

He joined USAF in 1965 with duty in Tampa, FL; Eglin, FL; Topeka, KA; two tours in Thailand, 1967-68 and 74-75. He retired at Myrtle Beach AFB, SC in 1978.

His memorable experience was as electronic technician, Aircrew VS-32 on S2F Aircraft; aboard USS *Lake Champlain* (CVS-39) from 1962-63.

Retired in 1978 as Master Sergeant, USAF. His awards and medals include American Spirit Honor Medal, Boot Camp USN, Air Crew Wings USN, Good Conducts and Vietnam Service.

Following retirement, he owned a video store in Henderson, NC for 14 years. Some say he participated in the last gold rush of the 20th century.

Married Patricia Mulhearn in 1970 and has two children, Kim Ann and Michael Jay. They also have two grandchildren.

JOSEPH R. GENZANTO, born Aug. 20, 1930 and enlisted Jan. 25, 1951 in the USN, Airman, V3G, Av. Gas. Div. Boot camp was at Newport, RI, followed by NAS Quonset Point; NAS Brunswick, ME; USS *Lake Champlain;* and Atlantic Reserve Fleet, Bayonne.

He participated in the Korean Conflict. Memorable experience was crossing the Equator. He was discharged in January 1955. His awards include the National Defense, UN, and Korean Service Medal.

After discharge he worked in the field of data processing and is now retired. He married Mamie in 1959 and they live in Freehold, NJ. They have three daughters and two grandchildren.

CLIFFORD L. GIEBLER, born Dec. 21, 1921 in New York City. He entered the USN as an aviation cadet in July 1942. After two years at the University of Alabama, he received his wings and commission as Ensign, USNR in October 1943.

He joined VC-97 as a fighter pilot for its commissioning in Seattle, WA, March 8, 1944, VC-97 served aboard USS

Makassar Strait (CVE-91) during the Iwo Jima and Okinawa Campaigns in 1945.

Some assignments include VF-62, May 1948-June 1950; instructor, basic flight training, Pensacola, FL, July 1950 to August 1952; assistant CIC and OI Division Officer, USS *Lake Champlain,* March 1953-September 1954. Also served in VF-43 and attended Navy Line School, Monterey, CA. He was an air control instructor at NAS Glynco, GA and staff electronic warfare officer, Carrier Division Six, July 1958 to July 1960.

Retired as LCDR, USN in July 1964 and was recalled to active duty, November 1966 to June 1971. His medals include the Distinguished Flying Cross, three Air Medals, Asiatic-Pacific Campaign Medal w/2 stars and Korean Service Medal w/star.

Married Fern Holmquest July 3, 1948 and they have five children: Karen, Lauren, Bruce, Frederick and Clifford.

HARRY J. GLASS, born Jan. 9, 1936 in Syracuse, NY. Joined the Navy in July 1954, completing basic training at NTC Bainbridge, MD. Attended Communication Technician Class A School at Imperial Beach, CA. Served at communication stations (message and crypto centers, security group and post office) in NAS Sangley Point, Philippines and San Diego, CA. Separated in June 1958 as teleman second class.

He re-enlisted in October 1960 serving three years on USS *Lake Champlain,* NAS Quonset Point, RI; and NavCommSta Long Beach, CA. Attaining rank of radioman second, he was discharged in October 1964.

His memorable experience was the blockade of Cuba in 1962 while aboard the *Lake Champlain*.

In 1982-84, he served two years as a sergeant in the Army Reserve Combat Engineers with the 3rd and 479th Engineer Battalions, 98th Division. He graduated from the Primary NCO School for Combat Arms, conducted by the Massachusetts Military Academy.

He enlisted in the reserve Seabees in June 1984 serving in NMCB 13, 21 and 27 as an construction electrician first class. Duty stations: NAS Brunswick, ME (2); Westover AFB, MA; Fort Jackson, SC; NCBC Gulfport, MS (3); Fort Benning, GA; NCBC Davisville, RI; MCB Camp Lejuene, NC; NCHB Cheatham Annex, NOB Norfolk and NAB Little Creek, VA. Glass retired from the Navy Jan. 9, 1996 at age 60.

He was awarded three National Defense Medals for service during the Korean, Vietnam and Gulf Wars. For participation in the Cuban Missile Crisis, he was awarded the Armed Forces Expeditionary Medal. His other awards include Good Conduct, Navy E, Navy Reserve Meritorious Service w/star, Armed Forces Reserve Medal, Navy Sharpshooter Rifleman and Pistol Shot, NCO Professional Development, Overseas Service, Marksman Rifleman Badge and New York State Service (Naval Militia - 10 years).

Employed as a civilian in the architectural/engineering field for 30 years, he was an electrical design engineer of building systems for commercial, industrial and institutional projects, including a nuclear power plant. He also worked as a journeyman electrician on industrial projects.

He's a life member of American Legion, American Gulf War Vets, Fleet Reserve Assoc., Korean War Vets, Korean War Vets International, Naval Cryptologic Vets, Navy Enlisted Reserve Assoc., Navy Radioman Assoc., Navy Seabee Vets of America, Navy Mail Service Vets, NTG

Bainbridge Assoc., USS Lake Champlain Assoc., VFW, and Vietnam Vets of America.

Married JoAnn Rhoades in 1961 and they have five children: Cheri, Harry, David, John and Joannah. They also have seven grandchildren.

After moving to Tidioute, PA, he worked for the Borough Maintenance Department for two years and six years for a general contractor. He retired in 2000 to continue renovating their over 100-year-old home. He also does construction and electrical work for family and friends. Among his many hobbies is compiling his family genealogical record, some of which has been published.

ROBERT E. GLASSFORD JR., born July 28, 1946, Boston, MA and enlisted in the USNR in July 1963. Assignments include NAS So. Weymouth, July 1963 to July 1964 and USS *Lake Champlain*, July 1964 to July 1966. After his discharge in July 1966 with the rank A2-3, he became a law enforcement officer. He lives in Ossipee, NH.

EMIL W. GLOW, born Jan. 31, 1934, East Otto, NY and served in the NYNG, 106th FA, 1951-53. He joined the Navy Nov. 21, 1953, FP2, R Div. Boot camp was at Bainbridge, MD, 1953-54; Pipe Fitters School, Norfolk, VA, February to June 1954.

Other assignments include USS *Lake Champlain* (CVA-39), June 1954 to November 1957; USS *Tarawa* (CVS-40), 1958-59; USS *Randolph* (CVS-15), 1960-62; USS *Constellation*, 1962-64; USS *Klondike*, 1964-68; NAS El Centro, CA, 1968-70; Naval Station Chu Lai and Da Nang as naval advisor, 1970-71; USS *Dixon* (AS-37), 1972-74.

Retired March 18, 1974 as HTC. His awards include the European Occupation, National Defense w/star, four Good Conduct, four Vietnam Service and four Naval Reserve.

Married Virginia Streck Sept. 4, 1998 and they live in Hennessey, OK. He worked as water plant operator in El Centro, CA for 17 years. He enjoys fishing, hunting and RV traveling.

CHARLES B. GREER, born Jan. 4, 1940, Winnsboro, SC. He joined the USN with assignments at USN Training Center, San Diego, CA and USS *Lake Champlain* (CVS-39), 1958-61.

His memorable experience was making new friends and seeing new places. He was discharged in June 1964 as FN and received the Good Conduct Medal.

Single, he lives in Lizella, GA. He worked at Robins AFB for 38 years and currently is an integrated electronics system mechanic.

JAMES A. HAGY, born April 21, 1932. Enlisted USN in September 1950 and went to boot camp at Great Lakes NTC; 1950-51; Airman School, Memphis, 1951-52, Base Operations, Quonset Point NAS; 1952-53, VA-45 based at Jacksonville NAS; 1953, VA-45 aboard USS *Lake Champlain*; 1953-54, VA-45 at JAX NAS.

Memorable experiences include fire at sea episode in June 1953 during operations off Korea; the ritualistic and diverting ceremony of crossing the Equator; an enlightening exposure to other, fascinating cultures during stops in Japan, Hong Kong, Singapore, Columbo, etc.

Discharged in June 1954 with rank of AD3. Medals include the Korean Service Medal w/star, UN Service w/Korean Clasp, National Defense, China Service, European Occupation and Good Conduct.

After discharge he attended University of Maryland, College Park, MD for BA in English, 1959 and American University in Washington, DC for master's in 1961. Worked as an English/journalism teacher (now retired) and writer/editor for Union Teachers Press Associations and local teachers unions.

In 1965 he married Sharon Lee Myers and they live in Poolesville, a quaint small town in Montgomery County, MD. They have four daughters and nine grandchildren.

DAVID L. HALL, born Aug. 17, 1926, Little Rock, AR. He volunteered in the Navy Aug. 16, 1944 to keep from being drafted in the Army. Assignments include NTC Great Lakes; training at Newport, RI; USS *Lake Champlain*, Norfolk, VA, and is a plankowner.

He participated in shakedown cruise; Guantanamo, Cuba; Magic Carpet to Naples, Italy; Southampton, England; open house New York; Philadelphia and Boston.

His memorable experience was making world record for fastest crossing of Atlantic; storm in North Atlantic (written up in *Stars & Stripes*); cold winter in Rhode Island; celebration of V-J Day; Capt. Ramsey asking for volunteer that could type (resulting in transfer from Gunnery Div. to Personnel Office).

Discharged Aug. 1, 1946 as Y3/c. He received the European-African-Mediterranean Campaign, WWII Victory Medal, Cold War Medal and Good Conduct.

Married in 1946 and attended one year college. He worked 35 years as FHA Real Estate Appraiser and five years as mortgage loan officer for S&L Assoc. He lives in Little Rock, AR and has three children: Jay, Jon and Jana and eight grandchildren. He's retired and enjoys golfing, fishing and hunting. He belongs to DAV and American Legion.

RAYMOND E. HALL, a native a Milwaukee, WI, died Aug. 29, 2002. He was preceded in death by his parents, Frederick and Hillevi Hall and his brothers, Kenneth and Deane Hall.

Raymond served in the US Navy for four years aboard the USS *Bennington* and the USS *Lake Champlain*. He was very proud to have served in the Navy. He was a former composing room machinist for the *Daily News* and *Washington Post*. He was the past president of the Columbia Typographical Union #101, Washington, DC and a retired commissioner of Federal Meditation in Evansville, IN, Richmond, VA and Jacksonville, FL.

Raymond is survived by his wife, Marie Syvertsen Hall; one son, Steven; two daughters and their spouses, Susan and Terry Brueser, Karen and Tom Bertlett; his grandchildren Carlee, Tommy and Madison; two brothers, Glenn Hall, Keith Hall and his wife Catherine; four sisters: Eunice Nielson, Jacqueline Pizzo and her husband Tom, Beverly Lind and Hillevi Blucher; three sister-in-laws: Evelyn Syvertsen, Betty and Ruth Hall.

Ray Hall, an avid gardener, would have wanted expressions of sympathy to take the form of a living plant to be planted in his garden or a garden of your choice.

He was a special father and a friend to many. He will be missed very much.

WILLIE J. HALL, born Aug. 17, 1942 and entered the USN in July 1960. Assignments include 9th Fleet, mothball ships, Stockton, CA and aboard the USS *Lake Champlain.* He participated in the Cuban Missile Crisis, Cuban Blockade, Guantanamo Bay, Cuba.

A memorable experience was playing football, basketball team, riding out the hurricane at sea and his time aboard the *Champlain*.

Discharged in November 1966 as fireman third class. He received awards for the missile crisis.

Married to Eula Gates for 23 years (she died in 1985), no children. He's worked 27 years for A.M. General Corp., distributor of auto polish and glaze.

SAMUEL BLAIR HARDY, born Aug. 1, 1915 and entered the USN Jan. 10, 1945. Assignments include NTC Sampson, NY; NTSCH Gulfport, MS; USS *Lake Champlain*.

His memorable experience was making highest speed of any ocean crossing average 32.048 knots between Gibraltar and Norfolk in November 1945. Discharged Feb. 24, 1946 as F1/c. He received the Victory Medal and EAME Medal.

Married and has son and daughter. He was employed at a paper mill and is now retired and lives in Flemington, PA.

JAMES A. HARPER, born June 26, 1924, New York City. Enlisted as apprentice seaman, Nov. 23, 1942 in Harvard NROTC program. Commissioned Ensign, USNR, Oct. 20, 1944 and assigned to USS *Lake Champlain* (CV-39) pre-commissioning detail at NTC, Newport, RI. He participated in the christening and commissioning of "The Great Lake" and became a plankowner.

Served on board as junior division officer, then division officer, 3rd Division, Gunnery Department. Participated in the shakedown cruise to Guantanamo Bay, Cuba and two out of three Magic Carpet Trans-Atlantic crossings. Also Victory Bond cruises to Philadelphia, New York and Boston. He stood watches in CIC and JOOD (OOD in port). Released to inactive duty June 18, 1946.

After graduate studies at Harvard he went into banking in New York City but kept up Naval Reserve activities by drilling with Organized Surface Division 3-81, later 3-79, on the training ship USS *Prairie State* (formerly the battleship *Illinois*). Served as training officer, later, XO. In 1962, he joined the all-officer Naval Reserve Advanced Base Lion Division 3-1 drilling in the Brooklyn Navy Yard, also as training officer and XO.

In 1967 voluntarily transferred to the Retired Reserve with the rank of Commander, USNR. Decorations are American and European-African Theater ribbons, WWII Victory, Occupation, Naval Reserve and Armed Forces Reserve medals.

EDWARD J. HASSING JR., born July 6, 1932, Cleveland, OH and entered the USNA Air, VIF Division, Dec. 26, 1951. Assignments include boot camp at Grosse Isle, MI; Akron AB, Fire Division; USS *Lake Champlain* (CVA-39), Norfolk, VA.

He participated in operation off Korea with Commander Task Force 77 during Korean hostilities, April 26 to Dec. 4, 1953.

His memorable experience was night refueling, Typhoon Judy, fighting fires on the deck, being called to battle stations on July 27, 1953 and seeing a squadron of Korean fighters ready to attack the ship – then they just flew away, as the cease fire became effective at 2200.

Discharged from USNR in April 1959. His awards include the National Defense Service Medal, Navy Occupation, Korean Service Medal w/star and the UN Service Medal.

Married Alice M. Mertens May 15, 1954 and they live in Brook Park, OH. They have four children: Edward III, Kathleen, Mary Pat and Timothy, and 10 grandchildren. He retired as supervisor from Cleveland Plain Dealer Newspaper.

WILLIAM F. HEMSEL, born Oct. 19, 1935 in Elizabeth, NJ and joined the USN in January 1954. Duty assignments: January-April 1954, recruit training; April 1954-April 1955, Service School, Class A, Fire Control Tech., both at USNTC, Bainbridge, MD; Ship's Company, Fox Div. USS *Lake Champlain* (CVA-39), Mayport, FL, May 1955-June 1956; and USS *Hissem* (DER-400), Newport, RI, June 1956-November 1957. Released to inactive duty as FTG-3, Nov. 18, 1957 and honorably discharged Jan. 11, 1962.

Attended Rutgers Univ. School of Engineering, 1958-60. Civilian employment included Bell Telephone Labs, Mitronics, Gulton Industries and Precision Circuits all in New Jersey. Relocated to the West Coast and was employed by Bourns Inc. in Riverside, CA, from September 1969 and Logan, UT, from June 1990-June 1997. Retired as a certified and licensed professional manufacturing engineer after 28 years service with Bourns Inc.

In retirement, he relocated from Utah to Eugene, OR. Post retirement part-time employment has been with LaVelle Vineyards, Elmira, OR as tasting room host and office assistant.

Married Olga Benda, RN, in 1961 and has two children, William and Kathryn. Now blessed with two grandchildren, Kelsey and Baily by Kathryn.

JOHN G. HERBEIN, born April 13, 1938, Macedon, NY and entered the USN in June 1956. Assignments include USS *Abbot* (DD-

629), South American Cruise as midshipman; USS *Lake Champlain* (CVS-39), Mediterranean Cruise in 1959 as midshipman; USS *Beatty* (DD-756), 1st lieutenant; USS *Purdy* (DD-734), weapons officer; USS *Moale* (DD-693), engineer officer and won Engineer E; USS *Gainard* (DD-706), Destroyer School Cruise ship as engineer.

Left the service in June 1998 as CAPT, USNR. His awards include the Navy Achievement Medal and US Navy Expeditionary Medal.

Married Angela on Oct. 29, 1983 and they live in Johnstown, PA. They have four children: Mike, Chris, Jeffrey and Steve. Retired, he spends his time competing in 45/22 pistol and power lifting.

ROBERT W. "BOBBY" HOAGLAND, born April 28, 1937, Charlotte, NC and enlisted USN June 12, 1956. Boot camp was at Great Lakes NTC, IL. Stationed aboard the Great Lady September 1956 and assigned to V-1 Division. Working in Repair 8, he operated the Aviation Crash Crane "Tilly," and spent some very nervous time in the "Hot Suit."

In November 1957 he transferred to FASRON 102 NAS Norfolk and was assigned to Admiral Jerauld Wright's service crew.

He was discharged June 20, 1960 as ABUAN. His most memorable experience was the fire aboard the USS *Lake Champlain* in port at Marseilles in 1957. Being blessed by our Lord to serve in peace time his only medal was the Good Conduct.

Married Virginia Davis in 1960 and has two children, Joel and Joni. He joined the police force in Charlotte, NC in 1961 and retired in 1987. He now lives in Lincoln County, NC and enjoys power lifting and entertaining local seniors singing traditional country music.

RAYMOND W. HOPE, born Aug. 11, 1928 in Hartford, CT and joined the USN in January 1947. Duty assignments include NTC, Bainbridge, MD; NAS, Guantanamo Bay, Cuba; NATTU, Pensacola, FL; NAS, Guantanamo Bay, Cuba; NPC, NAS, Anacostia, DC; USS *Lake Champlain* (CV-39); US Naval Intelligence School, Washington, DC.

He was discharged on Dec. 28, 1956, with the rank of photographers mate first class. His medals included the National Defense Medal, UN Medal, Korean Medal w/star, Syngman Rhee's Presidential Unit Citation, Good Conduct Medal and Bronze Star.

His most memorable experience was crossing the Equator. He enjoys attending the reunions of the *Lake Champlain* and renewing acquaintances.

He retired as a partner from Meyers Studio, Hartford, CT and joined Continental Airlines as a flight attendant and is completing 10 years of service with the Airlines (June 2, 2002).

Married Carmella in 1951 and has three children: Patricia Velez, Stephen Hope and Diane Peckham. He also has six grandchildren.

WILLIAM JOHN HOPMAN, born Jan. 2, 1933, Waukegan, IL and entered the USN, 3rd Div. on May 23, 1952. Assignments include Great Lakes, IL; Norfolk, VA; Cuba; Korea; and Green Cove Springs, FL. His memorable experience was crossing the Equator. Released from duty May 22, 1956 and discharged May 22, 1960. His awards include the United Nations, Korean Service, National Defense, Good Conduct, Navy Occupation Medal, European Clasp.

After his release he worked as a crane operator and a store room clerk for three years. He then started working in an oil refinery as a laborer, working his way up to fire chief, which was his position for many years until retirement. For about 20 years he also served as a volunteer firefighter for his home town, working his way through the ranks to fire chief. Though he is retired he keeps himself busy working as a porter at a local car dealership and he loves to golf.

Married Ethel R. Harness on March 13, 1954 and they live in Tinley Park, IL. They have two daughters, two sons, four grandsons and four granddaughters.

RICHARD D. HORINKA, born Dec. 20, 1933, Schenectady, NY. He entered the USN, Airman, VF-62, CAG4. Boot camp was at NTC Great Lakes, IL, Cecil Field, JAX, FL, NAS, JAX, FL, USS *Wasp*, USS *Coral Sea*, USS *Lake Champlain*, FASRON6, JAX.

Participated in the Korean Conflict, April through December 1953 on the "Champ." Most memorable experience was helping his buddy Leo Le Clerk (plane captain) on flight deck when his Banshee 204 was on fire and removed the pilot from cock pit. Richard's nickname was Hinks the Jinx.

Discharged Oct. 19, 1954 as airman. He received the Korean Service Medal, Navy Occupation Medal w/European Clasp and UN Service Medal.

Married Dorothy Smith Dec. 5, 1953 and they have three children: Richard, Ronald and Lynda. A telephone installer/repairman, he retired in 1994 and now lives in Ormond Beach, FL.

CHESTER E. IHINGER, born Aug. 27, 1929, Topeka, KS and on June 15, 1950 entered the USN, AK2, S-1. Assignments include USNTC San Diego, Airman School, Aviation Store Keepers School, Memphis, NAS Jacksonville, USS *Lake Champlain* and Task Force 77 in Korea.

His memorable experience was all the friendships made (he still corresponds with six of his shipmates).

Discharged April 7, 1953 as Av. Storekeeper 2/c. His awards include the UN Service Medal, Navy Occupation Service Medal, Good Conduct Medal, National Defense Service Medal and Korean Service Medal w/star.

He and his wife Jo Ann live in Junction City, CA, and have two children, Jo Ellen and Aaron. He was a teacher and counselor for 32 years and is now enjoying retirement, family and travel.

LUMIR F. JANSKY, born Aug. 18, 1933, and served in NENG, 34th Field Artillery, 1951 to November 1953. He enlisted in the USN in November 1953 and went to boot camp at NTC San Diego, CA, then to Pipe Fitter School at Norfolk, VA from March 1954 to August 1954.

He went aboard the *Lake Champlain* (CVA-39) at Guantanamo Bay, Cuba. On the Champ he made several six month trips to the Mediterranean, and spent six months in the Brooklyn Navy Yard for ship repair in drydock.

Most memorable experience was the Rome tour in Italy and hearing the Pope say mass. Discharged in November 1957 and served in the reserves until 1959. His medals are the American Defense and Good Conduct Medals.

He has been operating a grain and livestock farm and was a supervisor at IPSCO Steel Inc. at Geneva, NE, for a number of years. Married Mary Cruess of Queens, NY, Aug. 19, 1956 and they have one son William, daughter-in-law Ann and two grandsons, Brent and Darin.

ROBERT WALTER JOHNSON, born July 16, 1918, Milwaukee, WI and entered the USN, WT3/c, Engineering. Assignments include USNTC Farragut, ID; USNTSCH Great Lakes, IL; USNTS Newport, RI; and USS *Lake Champlain*.

Participated in Magic Carpet, bringing American soldiers home from Europe at war's end. He was a member of *Lake Champlain's* crew breaking record for crossing the Atlantic from Gibraltar to Norfolk, VA (fastest crossing to date). He received a medal for this achievement.

Discharged on the point system March 18, 1946 as watertender 3/c, USNR. Awards include the Victory Ribbon, American Area Ribbon and EAME Ribbon.

After discharge he worked for Allis-Chalmers Mfg. Co., Milwaukee, WI. He passed away June 7, 1973. Survived by his wife, the former Lorraine Roedel, and three children.

ALFRED D. JOSEPHSEN, born May 25, 1926, Union City, NJ and enlisted May 23, 1944. Boot camp was at Samspon, NY; Hospital Corps School at San Diego, CA; US Naval Hospital, Charleston, SC; USS *Rescue* (AH-18); USS *Lake Champlain* (CV-39); Lido Beach, NY.

While aboard *Rescue* he was assigned to Adm. Halsey's 3rd Fleet operating in the Asiatic-Pacific Theater including the Okinawa Campaign at Naha Harbor, March-April 1945; screened, processed and repatriated approximately 6,000 POWs (Operation Ramps) at Hagushi Beach, Hamamatsu, Sendai, Kamaishi, Japan.

Most memorable experience occurred in September 1945 when their ship, *Rescue*, witnessed the surrender of the Japanese Empire aboard the USS *Missouri* with Gen. Douglas MacArthur presiding.

Duty on the *Lake Champlain* was in the Medical Dept. assigned to the dental officer of the Medical Division. In 1946 the basketball team of the Champ participated in the Navy, Army, Marine Service tournament sponsored by the Norfolk YMCA and brought home the Gold by not losing any games to their service opponents. Lt. Cmdr. Argy was the coach of that team and Josephsen was a member of that group. Discharged May 23, 1946 as PhM3/c(T). His awards include the Good Conduct, Asiatic-Pacific w/2 stars, WWII Victory Ribbon and American Area Service Ribbon.

Graduated from Seton Hall University, South Orange, NJ and worked as insurance agent and broker. Currently semi-retired and living in West Caldwell, NJ with his wife Joan. They have three children: Alfred, Craig and Joanne.

EDWARD HOWARD KALBER, born July 29, 1927 in Hartford, CT and joined the USN on Sept. 12, 1944 in New Haven, CT. He completed Navy Training Course for Seaman First Class on Dec. 1, 1945 (Recruit Training, Sampson, NY; Pre-commissioned, Newport, RI; Mark 63 Director, Dam Neck, VA).

He was a member of the original crew of CV-39, which was commissioned in June 1945 with Capt. L.C. Ramsey as commander. They went to Italy and England to bring home over 5,000 soldiers from the European Theater. He was a member of the crew that set the record for crossing the Atlantic at 32.048 knots (beating the *Queen Mary*) between Gibraltar and Norfolk, VA. The ship received a blue ribbon symbolic of record. A memorable experiences was witnessing a burial at sea.

He received the Victory Medal, American Theater Medal, European Medal and a Letter of Commendation. He was separated from the service at USN Personnel Separation Center, Lido Beach, LI, NY on June 19, 1946 as seaman first class.

Employed one year with the Hartford Fire Dept., Royal Typewriter, 27 years with Lord and Taylor, and 9-1/2 years with Sanford & Hawley Lumber Co. Retired, he now works part time as sexton of his church.

He married Ann W. Smith in 1951 and they reside in Cave Creek, AZ. They have three children: Ruth, Eileen and William, and six grandchildren.

PAUL R. KEEFE, born Nov. 19, 1934, Boston, MA and enlisted in July 1956 in the USN, AEM3, V-6 Division. Military stations include NAS Willow Grove, PA; USS *Lake Champlain* (CVS-39); and NAS Jacksonville FL. He made the Mediterranean Cruise in 1957.

Most memorable experience was working on the flight deck during flight quarters.

Drove a NC5 (mobile generator unit) and started the planes before launching. It was tough driving on the flight deck at night time with no head lights or moon. He apologize to anyone he might have bumped into accidentally. It sure was crazy and a dangerous place to be - when you made a decision you had better make sure it was the right one. He was working in Hanger Bay 2 when the aviation gas fire broke out in Marseilles, France and he thought they were all goners. A buddy of his was on one of the barges alongside and was killed.

Graduated from Boston University with a degree in aeronautical engineering. He worked for E G & G Corporation (20 years) and did a lot of work for the Atomic Energy Commission. They did all the nuclear testing in the Pacific in the 60s. He worked for Digital Equipment Corp. (26 years) and retired in 1992. Still working (part time) at the Steamship Authority at Woods Hole, MA. They run the passenger and auto ferry services from mainland to Nantucket and Martha's Vineyard.

Married to Grace, they have five children and all graduated from college.

CHARLES A. KEMP, born July 11, 1931, Oblong, IL and enlisted Nov. 23, 1948 in the USN. Assignments include USS *Preserver* (ARS-8); USNS San Juan, Puerto Rico; USNTC Great Lakes, IL; USS *Lake Champlain* (CVA-39); USNAS St. Louis, MO; USS *John Blish* (AGSC-8) Orange, TX; USS *Maury* (AGS-16); USS *Allegheny* (ATA-179); USS *Malabar* (AF-37).

His memorable experience was diving in Persian Gulf; feeding hurricane hunters, San Juan; making special cakes for record setting events; rescue salvage work in Persian Gulf; running bake shop on *Lake Champlain;* boxing, pitching soft ball and playing band in Navy; making friends; and traveling around the world.

Discharged Oct. 23, 1957 as CS1. His awards include the Good Conduct, Korean Conflict and Bronze Award.

He and his wife Beulah live in West Frankfort, IL. They have four children: Ted, Charlie, Laura, Chris, and 11 grandchildren. He owns a company, Energy Culvert Co., Inc., farms and raises and shows cutting horses.

KENNETH W. KIFER, born Dec. 27, 1920 in Kane, PA and enlisted in USNR June 22, 1942, DuBois, PA. Basic training was at Newport, RI.

Duty Assignments: Radio School, Bedford Springs, PA; Aviation Radio and Radar School, Millington NAS Millington, TN; Gunnery School, Hollywood, FL; CASU (Carrier Aircraft Service Unit) NAS Quonset Point, RI; NAS Moore Field, Ft. Devens, Ayer, MA; NAS Sanford, ME; NAS Squantum, Quincy, MA; NAS Quonset Point, RI; NAS Oceana, Virginia Beach, VA; CASD (Carrier Aircraft Service Detachment) USS *Lake Champlain* (CV-39), Shakedown; NAS Norfolk, VA.

He's a plankowner (CV-39) and received his 5" plank from USS *Lake Champlain* flight deck after decommissioning. Medals include Good Conduct, American Campaign, Asiatic-Pacific Campaign, and WWII Victory Medal. Discharged Jan. 23, 1946 in Sampson, NY Naval Base with rank aviation radioman second class PO.

Following discharge he spent 34 years as a production engineer for American Can Company Machine Shop, Fitchburg, MA, and retired in 1984.

Married to Rosalie Secino in Fitchburg, MA and they celebrated 55 years of marriage in 2002. They have three sons: Kenneth, John and Robert, six grandchildren, three step-grandchildren, one great-grandchild and four step great-grandchildren.

WILLARD THOMAS "TOM OR STORMY" KNIGHT, born May 31, 1919 in Green Cove Springs, Clay County, FL. He attended Public Schools in Green Cove Springs, Palatka and Orlando, FL. He later attended the University of Florida and Florida State University. He enlisted in the USN on July 8, 1937, and boot camp training was in (Platoon #36), Norfolk, VA. He retired from active duty in 1958.

Assignments included Diesel Engineering School, Advanced High Pressure Boilers and Turbines Laboratories School, Fire Fighting Schools and the "ABCD" (Atomic, Biological and Chemical Defense) School.

Other assignments included considerable experience with Military Police and the Office of Naval Intelligence; Material and Security Inspector, Civilian Shipyards, (Jacksonville, FL); USS *Nokomis* (one of the Navy's last coal-burning ships), USS *Bushnell*, USS *Omaha* (CL), USS *Trenton* (CL), USS *Jacob Jones* (DD), USS *Niagara* (AGP I & PG 52), USS *Callaghan* (DD-792), USS *Belle Isle* (AG-73), USS ARD-14, USS *Mosopelia* (ATF), USS *Catawba* (ATA), USS *Whidbey* (AG-141), USS *Lake Champlain* (CVA-39), (Engineering Department, July 1954 to January 1957), USS *Intrepid* (CV-41), and USN Fleet Activities (Ship Repair), Sasebo, Japan.

He received several meritorious medals for his services during WWII and the Korean War.

His worst experience occurred on May 23, 1943, when the Japanese sank his ship, the USS *Niagara* (PG-52).

His happiest experience was on Valentine's Day in 1968, when he ceased being a bachelor and married Miss Tadako ("Shim") Shimoishi in Sasebo, Japan. Tadako was employed at the USN Dental Clinic in Sasebo as a dental laboratory technician. Her father, Dr. Ichibe Shimoishi, was a well-known medical doctor and dentist in Japan.

After retirement from active military service in 1958, he was employed by the state of Florida for 23 years before he retired, again, in 1981. Since 1981 he has owned and operated a very successful Private Investigative Agency.

He would love to hear from previous shipmates. His E-mail address is willardtk@hotmail.com

GORDON K. KNOPF, born Aug. 2, 1933 in Madison, WI and enlisted in the USN, FP3, R Division. Assignments include basic training at Great Lakes, IL; USS *Bennington* (CVA-20), 1953-55; *Lake Champlain* (CVA-39), 1955-57. He participated in the Suez Canal crisis.

Most memorable experience was being on leave for his sister's wedding when catapult exploded on the *Bennington*. The newspaper carried headline "Luckiest Sailor Alive!" Also memorable was shore leave in the Mediterranean and maneuvers in the North Atlantic. Discharged Feb. 14, 1957 as FP3.

He and Carole have been married 47 years and live in Marshall, WI. They have three daughters: Kim, Jodi and Barri, and five grandchildren. He's owner of Bud's Plumbing Service and is now semi-retired from plumbing and farming. Enjoys fishing, hunting and traveling.

RONALD F. LA BRUYERE, born June 4, 1945, in New York, NY. He enlisted Sept. 22, 1963 in the USNR, AN, V-3. Assignments include USS *Lake Champlain,* Quonset, RI.

His memorable experience was Gemini recovery and freighter collision. He was discharged Sept. 22, 1965 as AN.

He's a computer tech and still working. He lives with his wife in Newburgh, NY. They have three daughters.

JAMES A. LAGAN, born Nov. 21, 1935 and enlisted March 15, 1956 in the USNR, SR, Division S1. Assignments include boot camp at Bainbridge, MD; sub base, New London, CT; USS *Lake Champlain* at Brooklyn Navy Yards, NY.

Memorable experiences include Shakedown Cruise to Guantanamo Bay, Cuba; peace keeping exercises in Cyprus in 1957; NATO exercises in Turkey; two peacetime cruises to the Mediterranean with liberty in six countries, touring ports in France, Italy, Spain, Turkey, Greece and the Rock of Gibraltar. A memorable event was when they had a fire and explosion aboard the Champ in Marseilles, France. Discharged Dec. 21, 1957 as SN.

Married Nancy Ryan in 1956 and they have three wonderful children: Shari, Tom and Rick; as well as three wonderful in-laws: John, Lori and Dawn, who have given them six fabulous grandchildren: Katie, Michael, Andrew, Nicole, Kari and Sean. Employed 32 years for A&P Tea Co.; Pier I Imports. Still actively employed part-time and enjoying family, all of whom live locally. They enjoy traveling within the US, Canada and have also been to Ireland, where they plan to visit again in the future.

JOHN D. LEOPOLD, born Oct. 2, 1925, Bucklin, MO. He entered the USN on July 15, 1943. Assignments include USS *Attu* (CVE-102), USS *Burleigh* (APA-95), USS *Amphion* (AR-13), Philadelphia Reserve Fleet, USS *Gilbert Islands* (CVE-107), USS *Lake Champlain* (CVA-39), NTS Farragut, NTC Great Lakes FT School and NTC Washington DC FT School.

He participated in action at Okinawa, Saipan, Tinian and Korea. Memorable was making chief on the *Lake Champlain* and also the first time being transferred to a destroyer by high line and returned by helicopter.

Discharged July 27, 1957 as FTC. His awards include Good Conduct (3), American Campaign, Asiatic-Pacific w/2 stars, WWII Victory Medal, National Defense, Korean Service Medal w/star, Vietnam Service Medal and ROK Service Medal.

Married Marjorie Hedrick in 1949 and they have five children: Harry (Navy vet), Denise, Lynnette, Douglas and Paul (Navy vet). They also have six grandchildren and two great-grandchildren. Worked as a heating, air condition and electrical contractor for 35 years, also as antique dealer and military collector for 40 years. He lives in Marceline, MO, and does a lot of volunteer work.

RONALD H. LIPPOLD, born March 5, 1935, Oshkosh, WI and joined the USN Jan. 4, 1955. In April 1955 he went aboard the *Lake Champlain* (CVA-39) in Norfolk, VA, and spent his whole enlistment aboard her. He spent the first two years in A Division, working in hydraulics on elevators and the next two years in M Division as a throttleman on main control in Forward Engine Room.

He made two cruises to the Mediterranean, 1956-57, a shakedown cruise to Cuba, and a North Atlantic Cruise in 1958. Most memorable experience was the big fire in Marseilles, France in July 1957, where they lost some good men. Capt. James Flatley from Green Bay, WI was his favorite skipper, 1955-56. They received the E Award in 1956 for being best carrier in 6th Fleet.

Discharged in Brooklyn, NY, in December 1958 as machinist mate third class. His ribbons include National Defense, European Occupation (Navy), and Good Conduct.

Married Marie Fischer in 1959 and they have two children, Brenda and Paul. He worked as a pipefitter for 15 years then went in business for himself as a gunsmith and gun shop owner, which he is still working at. He still lives in Oshkosh, WI.

ROBERT LIVZEY, born Sept. 15, 1935 and enlisted in the USN Aug. 4, 1953, R Division. Assignments include Bainbridge, Norfolk, Mayport and aboard *Lake Champlain* April 1954 to September 1956.

Discharged Sept. 14, 1956 as FP3/c. His awards include the Good Conduct, European Occupation and National Defense.

Retired from the profession of construction, pipefitting and welding. Married with two daughters, he lives in Middletown, OH.

DWIGHT E. LUBICH, born March 21, 1936 in San Francisco, CA, and joined the Naval Air Reserve at NAS Oakland in 1953. He became an ADR3/Aircrewman in VS-875, graduated from San Jose State University in 1959, followed by flight training at

Pensacola with completion at NAAS New Iberia, LA in 1961. He reported to RAG training with VS-30 at NAS Key West and subsequently to VS-22 aboard the *Champ* by mid-1961.

After four years as an ASW Plane Commander and LSO (Landing Signal Officer), he departed VS-22 in 1965 for two years of shore duty at the David W. Taylor (Model Basin) Naval Research and Development Center at Carderock, MD as Aerodynamics Program Officer. In 1967 he resigned his regular commission and joined VS-82 in the Naval Air Reserve at NAS Alameda. While serving as Executive Officer, the squadron was decommissioned in 1974. He then drilled with a Tactical Support Unit at NAS Moffett until retiring in 1966 as a commander. Medals include National Defense Service, Armed Forces Expeditionary and Armed Forces Reserve.

In civilian life he was a pilot for United Airlines at San Francisco, retiring as captain in 1966. He is a volunteer docent aboard the Hornet Museum at (now) Point Alameda and is the Director of the Champ Association Room in Hornet. Also in retirement, he occasionally flies passengers around the bay area, sightseeing with a carrier approach to *Hornet*!

Married Elaine Shearer in 1973 and has two sons, Dana and Derek.

ALBERT R. MAAS, born May 11, 1937, Pittsburgh, PA and enlisted in the USN Feb. 14, 1956 as damage controlman with R Division.

Served in USS *Lake Champlain* (CVA-39) and made Mediterranean Cruise in 1957. Memorable experience was fire aboard ship at Marseilles, France. Discharged Dec. 6, 1957 as DC3.

Worked as instrument tech in a coal fired electrical generating station and is now retired and lives in Sewickley, PA.

LLOYD R. MADER, born Aug. 3, 1933 and entered the USN Nov. 26, 1952, 2nd Div., Ships Company. Assignments include training at Great Lakes, IL, USS *Lake Champlain* (CVA-39), Port Lyautey, French Morocco, USN Air Facilities, Air Navigation Office; North Africa and USS *Tarawa* (CVS-40).

Participated in the Korean War with Task Force 77. A memorable experience was in 1953, age 19, sailing through the Suez Canal and standing on the centerline of the flight deck of the *Lake Champlain,* looking to port and starboard and seeing only land. It felt like he was riding on the roof of a large bus instead of a sea going aircraft carrier, a caravan of Arabs and camels on one side and the other with British soldiers manning a machine gun post.

Discharged Nov. 20, 1956 as GM2/c. His awards include the Korean Service, Navy Good Conduct Medal, National Defense Service Medal w/star, UN Service Medal, ROK PUC and Honorable Discharge Button.

Worked as construction electrician for 27 years and owned business as electrical contractor for 10 years. He retired in November 1993 and lives in Lynnfield, MA. Married Helene Murphy in 1958 and they have four children: Sharon, Dianne, Steven and Brian, and 11 grandchildren.

WILLIAM L. "BILL/BOOMER" MAGNUSON, born May 28, 1933, and reared in the small, northern Illinois town of Harvard. He graduated from high school in spring of 1951 and enlisted in the USN in March 1952. Boot camp was at Great Lakes NTC (Co. 138 and member of Blue Jackets Choir), followed by Airman "P" School at Norman, OK, followed by Aerographer's Mate School at NAS Lakehurst, NJ (Class 5245).

He reported aboard the USS *Lake Champlain* (CVA-39) as a member of ship's company in March 1953 at Portsmouth Naval Ship Yard, VA. Shortly thereafter, the ship sailed for Korean duty by way of the Mediterranean, Suez Canal, Indian Ocean, Philippines, and up to Japan. Crossed the Equator just south of Singapore on May 30, 1953 and morphed from a Pollywog to a Shellback after paying tribute to King Neptune and his court. After a seven month Korean deployment, the ship returned to USA and home port of Mayport, FL by same reverse route in November 1953.

Minor short sea tests and refittings/dry dock were followed by a six month Mediterranean cruise with the Sixth Fleet from October 1954 through March 1955. He was transferred off ship in April 1955 to the U.S. Fleet Weather Central at the Marine Corps Air Station in Miami (Opalocka), FL, and subsequently discharged from active service at that facility in March 1956 with rank of first class petty officer (AG1). Medals include the Navy Good Conduct, Navy Occupation, National Defense, United Nations, Korean Service w/battle star (K-10), Syngman Rhee Presidential Citation, and Korean War Service. Released from inactive service in March 1960.

Many great friendships and rapport were established during two+ years aboard the *Champ* along with all the world traveling and visiting plus the dramatic experience that goes on board an operating aircraft carrier (especially during the two months of active Korean Conflict and subsequent patrol). The small town midwest farm boy matured very rapidly as part of a team on a ship in Task Force 77. From being chewed out by RADM Johnson for not knowing the dew point temperature in a weather briefing during a critical air operations "on the line" on a hazy day, to watching air ops from the forward 07 level and seeing a banshee's port tip tank drop off half way down the starboard catapult run with the fighter plane proceeding into a right bank power dive into the sea. Looking for but not seeing anything of plane or pilot (an ENS in VF-22) as the fantail swept portside to clear the impact site. As he walked back into the aerographer's office, a quantum leap in maturity and priorities had been made. Three days later, at 0300 hours Sunday morning, he was awakened by the gong of General Quarters being sounded as the voice on the ship's speaker was saying "this in not a drill." A sense of GQ alarm swept through him that remains active to this day no matter how benign the current situation may be.

Bill attended the University of Illinois (Champaign-Urbana) on the GI Bill from the fall of 1956 through January 1961 and graduated with a BS degree in petroleum engineering. He immediately joined Shell Oil Co. in their West Coast Region (west of the Rockies). Many short term training assignments/locations that first year were followed by assignment to the Ventura, CA office for the next five years. This was followed by a five year assignment to the Bellaire (Houston), TX research lab which in turn was followed by positions on various field projects in both Production and Exploration Departments while maintaining home in Houston. Projects/locations included west Texas, central Illinois, northern Michigan, north coast/Beaufort Sea, Alaska, European partnerships, Cameroon, Syria, Tunisia and Brazil. Frequent domestic and foreign business travel was associated with vacation travel whenever possible. He retired from Shell in 1989.

He married Virginia L. Lenss of Harvard, IL in 1959 and has four children: James (born in Champaign, IL), Kenneth (born in Ventura, CA and delivered by his father was unplanned), David (born in Ventura) and Barbra Ann (born in Houston, TX).

Retirement years (since 1989) have been spent working genealogy and traveling (domestic and foreign), woodworking, participating in many adult softball and basketball leagues, plus light workouts at YMCAs. Currently living in Houston, TX and single. He joined the USS Lake Champlain Association Inc. in 1992 and is a past trustee.

BILLY THOMAS MARSH, born June 17, 1933, Nectar, AL and entered the USN Jan. 15, 1951 with active duty from 1952-53. Assignments include VF-22, USS *Lake Champlain* (CVA-39); NTC Newport, RI; NTC Bainbridge, MD; NAAS Cecil Field; NAS JAX FL.
Memorable experience was when GQ sounded early with message "this is no drill, man your battle station;" also first day on the line in Korean water during Korean Conflict.

Discharged Dec. 15, 1953 as AKAN. His awards include the National Defense, Korean Service w/star, UN Medal, China Service and Korean PUC.

Attended Samford University, BS degree, 1957; University of Alabama, MA in 1962 and Ed.D in 1979, school administration and higher education. Retired from education after 39 years as teacher, coach, assistant superintendent, principal and Birmingham Board of Education. Currently an assistant professor, Miles College, Birmingham, AL. He's a member of numerous civic, fraternal and professional organizations.
Billy and his wife Joyce have two sons, Timothy and Matthew.

IRA MASSIE JR., born Sept. 6, 1931, Cinderella, WV and enlisted April 4, 1951 at Lynchburg, VA in the USN, Fox Division. Assignments include basic training at Bainbridge, MD; Ceremonial Guard, Washington, DC; *Lake Champlain* and made Korean and Mediterranean Cruises.

His memorable experience was returning from Korea and while in Singapore when he and a couple of buddies met a member of Richard Nixon's party (who were on a good will tour) and asked him for directions to a good place to eat. Well, he took them to the dining room of the hotel where he was staying and told the waiter to give them anything they wanted to eat and put it on his account.

Discharged March 23, 1955, Norfolk, VA. His medals include the Good Conduct, Korean Service, European Occupation and National Defense.

He was a millwright for 30+ years at Lynchburg Foundry Co. in Virginia. Today he lives in Monroe, VA and has a 180 acre farm and a few cattle. He married Barbara Bryant March 10, 1953 and they have four children: David Lee, Randall Wayne, Thomas Bryant and Deborah Lynn; also, two grandchildren and one great-grandchild.

J. CLAYTON MCCAIN, born Nov. 20, 1939, Corsicana, TX. He joined the USNR in March 1957 and went on active duty in December 1958. He went aboard the USS *Lake Champlain* in January 1959 and separated while still aboard at Quonset Point, RI in December 1960.

He was assigned to the 5th Div. doing maintenance and training of the 5" 38s mounted on the ship.

Most memorable experience was their Mediterranean Cruise and the great bunch of guys he served with. He separated from active duty as a GMM3 and completed his reserve commitment while attending college.

He and his wife Margie have two daughters, Denise and Terri; two sons-in-law, Mike Schnider and Mark Thompson; and one granddaughter, Jaycee Thompson. He worked 32 years with Austin Bridge and Road Co., then nine years with GSI Hwy. Prod. He and Marge are now retired and enjoy showing a custom 1963 Chev. pick-up on the show car circuit.

BERNARD MCGOUGH, born Oct. 8, 1930, Holyoke, MA and served in the MA State Guard as a private in 5th Co., 22nd Inf., 1945-46. He enlisted in the USN Nov. 20, 1950 and went to boot camp at Newport, RI.
Assignments include USS *Conewango* (YTB-388), 1951-52, Charleston, SC; recommissioned the *Lake Champlain* in 1952 and served

aboard her until his discharge at Jacksonville, FL Sept. 17, 1954.

Medals include the Navy Commendation, China Service Medal, Naval Occupation w/European Clasp, Korean Service Medal w/star, National Defense, UN and Good Conduct.

Memorable experience was rescuing dock workers from burning submarine aboard floating dry dock, Charleston, SC; making a flight to Cario in 1953 on Capt. Mundorff's personal aircraft. He served in the USAFR, 1955-65 attaining the rank of captain.

Following service he received a BA in history, MSLS from University of Rhode Island; MA, University of Connecticut and MED from Westfield State College. He taught high school 1959-64; from 1965-93 was associate professor and chairman of Dept. of Media and Communications, Worcester State College, MA. He's listed in *Who's Who...* and was awarded Professor Emeritus in 1993.
Since his retirement from teaching, he and his wife Mary own and operate the Juniper Hill Kennels and Stables in Millbury, MA. They have two daughters, Ann and Rachel.

GEORGE P. MCNAMARA, born Aug. 6, 1924, Worcester, MA, and enlisted Nov. 11, 1942 in the USN. Assignments include Newport, RI; USS *Core* (CVE-13), North Atlantic; USS *Lake Champlain*, Atlantic.
His memorable experience was becoming a plankowner of Champ; 36 days of combat while aboard Champ; making Atlantic record; bringing

home troops and the friendships made.

Discharged March 5, 1946. His awards include WWII Victory Medal, American Theater, European-African, Bronze Star, Good Conduct and still waiting for his Purple Heart.

A supervisor at the time of his retirement. He lives with his wife Stella in Clinton, MA. They have two sons, Brian and George.

HARLEY J. MCNATT, born 1934, Lansing, MI. He entered the service with boot camp at Great Lakes, IL. Other assignments include Mayport, FL; Norfolk, VA; Charleston, SC. He participated in the Korean Conflict.

A memorable experience was almost getting blown off the flight deck. He was discharged in October 1956 as SN. Awards include Navy Occupation Medal, Korean Service Medal, UN Medal and National Defense.

He worked at General Motors for 30 years and retired in 1991. He has a life-time membership at Fitness USA and uses it. Also, plays a baritone uke and entertains senior citizens more senior than him. He and his wife Donna have three daughters: Teresa, Julane and Michelle and nine grandchildren.

RONALD P. MCNAVICH, born Aug. 30, 1938 in Brooklyn, NY. He enlisted in the USN in December 1956 and served in the USS *Lake Champlain* (CVS-39), 1958-60 and in the Reserves until December 1962 when he was discharged with the rank of DK2.

His memorable experience was the Med cruise in the summer of 1957 with the midshipmen.

His civilian career is running his own CPA practice. He lives in Rockville Centre, NY with his wife Lynne. They have six children.

NOAH JOHN "JOE" MEDINE, born Dec. 27, 1931, White Castle, LA and enlisted in the USN April 26, 1951. Boot camp was at San Diego, CA, Class 11, Co. No. 462, April-August 1951; Hospital Corps School, Class 28-51 NTC Bainbridge, MD, August 1951 to January 1952, graduating 10th in a class of 60.

Next assignments were Naval Hospital, Memphis, TN; USNAAS Glynco, GA; and the *USS Lake Champlain* (CVA-39) in July 1954. Memorable was the size of the ship, cruise to Gitmo and Mediterranean Cruise of 1954-55.

Courses completed were UCMJ, NTC for HM2, GTC and Pharmacy and Materis Medica. Medals received were National Defense, Navy Occupation Service (E) and Good Conduct. He was discharged in April 1955 as HM3.

Following naval service he worked in the Petre-Chemical field until retiring in 1986. He married Christine Larsen of Brunswick, GA on June 18, 1954 and they have three children: Scott, Dawn and Kristina. He currently resides in Plaquemine, LA and is enjoying retirement, grandchildren, volunteer work at school and church, the casino's and some travel.

THOMAS C. MILLER, born Nov. 20, 1937 in McVeytown, PA and joined the USN, B Division, March 5, 1955. Duty stations include *Lake Champlain* (CVS-39), USS *Johnson*, USS *Dyss*, USS *Soley*, USS *McDonough* (DLG-8) and shore duty at Pensacola, FL and Keywest.

Memorable experience was when they were the recovery ship for space mission Gemini V and recovered the two astronauts, Conrad and Cooper. Retired June 25, 1975 as BT1 (E-6). He received five Good Conducts.

He and his wife Jean have four children: Clara Jane, Kenneth, Samuel, William; and nine grandchildren.

Civilian employment: Norwaric Furniture, health-care, handicap.

ROBERT F. MOHLMANN, born Sept. 1, 1926, Patchogue, NY and entered the USN in July 1944. Boot camp was at Sampson, NY, followed by Newport, RI for pre-commissioning USS *Lake Champlain* (CV-39). He participated in Magic Carpet.

Memorable experience was seeing the *Champlain* for the first time (didn't know anything that big could float) and getting underway the first time. Discharged in June 1946 as Cox. Awards include the American/European Theater and WWII Victory Medal.

Married 55 years to Alice and has four sons (the oldest is Army vet), eight grandchildren and two great-grandchildren. He retired from the Long Island Lighting Co. after 37 years of service and lives in Winchester, VA. He enjoys traveling, golfing and refinishing furniture.

CHARLES W. MONAGHAN, born in August 1937, Clinton, IA and graduated from the University of Iowa, June 1959. Attended OCS, Class 46C, Newport, RI, and commissioned Ensign in February 1960.

Reported to the USS *Lake Champlain* (CVS-39) in February 1960, served as 2nd Div. officer for 18 months, then assigned to the mighty "B" Div. for the remaining 18 months. Departed the *Champ* in February 1963.

Other assignments include USS *Gunston Hall* (LSD-5), based in San Diego as operations officer, completed two Westpac deployments, landing USMCs in Vietnam, plus one short cruise of three months to WestPac; USS *Halsey Powell* (DD-686), based in Long Beach as operations officer; NROTC Iowa State University as senior instructor; USS *Halsey* (DLG/CG-23), based in San Diego as operations officer and last four months as XO, one deployment to WestPac in the Sea of Japan and off northern Vietnam, and took the *Halsey* around South America to Bath, ME for update conversion; USS *Sarsfield* (DD-837) based in Mayport, FL as XO, made one deployment to WESTPAC serving on the gunline from the DMZ to the Gulf of Siam, and also made one Mediterranean deployment.

Assigned as Personnel Exchange Officer in the British Royal Navy on the staff of Flag Officer Carriers and Amphibious Ships (FOCAS) as assistant Operations Officer to the Amphibious Warfare (AW) staff. Served many NATO exercises in the Mediterranean and Northern Sea on their capital ships. Assigned as Commanding Officer, USS *Charles P. Cecil* (DD-835) based in Groton, CT. Assigned to the US Embassy in Islamabad, Pakistan, in the Office of Defense Representative to the Pakistan Armed Forces (Death Merchant). Tour was abruptly terminated after 20 months when the Embassy was attacked and destroyed by a mob of over 20,000 Pakistan, Nov. 21, 1979. Two Americans (Army and USMC) were killed, many injured and about six women from the Embassy were taken to the "hill villages," beaten and raped. Assigned to the Pentagon and after three months in the puzzle palace, put in his papers to retire on Nov. 1, 1981 as Commander, US Navy.

Personal awards include Defense Meritorious Service Medal, two Navy Commendation Medals (one with combat V), Combat Action Ribbon, plus numerous theater ribbons/medals.

He lives in Sabula, IA and raises chickens, guineas, ducks and geese.

THOMAS LEE MOORE JR., born July 20, 1923, Kenbridge, VA, moving to Alberta, VA and graduated from Alberta HS. Inducted in the USN June 29, 1943, with assignments at NTS Sampson, NY; NAS Willow Grove, PA; NAS Quonset Point, RI Ships Company; NATTC Jacksonville, FL; Norfolk Navy Yard, Portsmouth, VA; NAS Norfolk, VA (CV-39);  USS *Lake Champlain* (CV-39) Portsmouth, VA for duty.

When the war ended in Europe, the ship went to Philadelphia, New York and Boston, receiving visitors for tours at each port. They became part of the Magic Carpet program, returning service personnel from Europe. With aircraft removed, bunks five high on the hanger deck, 5,000 troops could be returned each trip. He made three trips to Southampton, England and one trip to Naples, Italy.

Most memorable experiences include being a plankowner; part of the Magic Carpet; making fastest Atlantic crossing; helping commission a carrier then ready it for the mothball fleet.

His medals include American Campaign, EAME Campaign, National Defense Service, WWII Victory and Honorable Service Button. He was discharged May 20, 1946 as AK2/c. He joined the Naval Reserve and served 11 months during the Korean War at NAS Patuxant River, MD.

He was employed by David M. Lea Co. Inc., Richmond, VA, as supervisor and sales engineer for 19 years and 14 years with General Box Co., Toledo, OH in the same capacity.

Married Rebecca Nolen Nov. 1, 1947 and they have two daughters, Constance and Donna; two sons-in-law, Bob and Ken; and three grandchildren: Jake, Shelby and Casey.

FRANCIS W. MORAN JR., born June 7, 1929, Island Falls, ME. Enlisted in the USN Sept. 15, 1947 and completed boot training in Great Lakes, IL.

His duty assignments were USS *Saipan* (CVL-48); FAAWTC, Dam Neck, VA; USS *Mindoro* (CVE-120); USS *Antietam* (CVS-36); USS *Lake Champlain* (CVA-39); USS *Terre Bonne Parish* (LST-1156); USS *Chilton* (APA-38); Naval Station, Guantanamo Bay, Cuba; Assault Craft Unit Two, USNAB, Little Creek, Norfolk, VA.

His awards include European Occupation, Korean Service, National Defense and Good Conduct Awards. His rate was ships service man second class (SH2). He retired Oct. 14, 1966.

Following his naval service, he worked as a barber, prison guard, deputy sheriff and retired as a park ranger for the city of Norfolk, VA in 1989. He is married to Betty and they have five children, 15 grandchildren and four great-grandchildren.

JOHN D. MORGAN, born 1942 in Louisville, KY and enlisted in March 1961 in USN, VS-32. Assignments include NAS Quonset Point, RI and NAS PaxRiver, MD.

Member of CTG 83/4 and CAG 54, he participated in surveillance of Cuba. Memorable experience was Jamaica independence. Discharged June 5, 1965 as PN3.

His wife Rita is also a Navy vet. They have two children, John Jr. and Sheri. Worked 33 years for Ford Motor Co. (still working, but planning on retiring soon). He lives in Mt. Washington, KY.

WILLIAM G. MURPHY, born Oct. 12, 1935, Greenwich Village, New York, NY. Enlisted May 27, 1954, USN, Dental Division.

Assignments include US Naval Base, Bainbridge, MD, boot camp and Dental Technician School, May 1954 to February 1955; Dental Clinic, US Marine Base, Quantico, VA, February 1955 to May 1956; USS *Lake Champlain* (CVA/CVS-39), May 1956 to May 1958.

Missions include two Mediterranean Cruises aboard the *"Champ"* as CVA-39 from January to July 1957 and as CVS-39 from September to November 1957.

Memorable experience was the fire aboard the ship on July 3, 1957 in the harbor of Marseilles, France when the ship nearly blew up - except for the heroism of its crew and ships like the USS *Johnston* (DD-821). He helped identify five char-burned bodies by examining their teeth. They were all Frenchmen attached to the barge that was off loading the ship's vehicles.

He received the Good Conduct Medal. Discharged May 6, 1958 as Dental Technician 2nd Class.

After he left the "Champ" in 1958, he enrolled in the University of Florida in Gainesville, FL receiving a BA degree in political science in 1962. Upon graduation, he joined the Peace Corps and served two years as a teacher and community development worker in Sacred Heart College in Bamenda, Cameroon as part of the project, CAMEROON ONE. When he returned from Africa, he then attended Law School at George Washington University graduating in 1967 while working in the Law Library of Congress in the District of Columbia. In February 1969 after passing the New York Bar, he worked for a Wall Street litigation firm, Leahey & Johnson, P.C., as a trial attorney and managing attorney for over 33 years. In June 1971, he married his lovely wife, Margaret Curcio Murphy, of Hoboken, NJ. He is now retired and living happily ever after at Staten Island, NY.

P. KENNETH NEWMAN, born May 27, 1932, Neptune, NJ. He entered the USN, H Division, Jan. 3, 1951. Assignments include Newport, RI; school at Portsmouth, VA; OR Tech School, USNH Philadelphia; USS *Lake Champlain* for pre-commission detail and regular duty.

Attended Bucknell Temple Medical School (Senior Med Student Program), USNH Jax, internship, USNH Philadelphia, residency in anesthesiology, USNH Jax, FL; USN MC, 1968, at Phu Bai, Vietnam

Discharged from USN in November 1954 as HM2 and from USN MC in June 1969 as LCDR. His awards include the Good Conduct, China Service, National Defense w/star, Korean Service w/Battle Star, Korean PUC, Korean Service Medal, Vietnam Service and Vietnam PUC.

Memorable experience was taking care of an airman who was struck by a propeller and helping to care for three Destroyer captains who were in an auto accident in Ceylon.

After discharge he practiced anesthesiology from 1969 to retirement in 1996. He and wife Audrey celebrated 50 years on June 14, 2002. They live in St. Augustine, FL and have one son P.K. Newman; two daughters, Linda Puente and Debborah Smith; and nine grandchildren.

JOSEPH P. NOLAN, born July 24, 1941 and enlisted in the Naval Reserve September 1958 while a junior in high school. Active duty was from July 1960-June 1962 with Carrier Antisubmarine Air Group Fifty Four, USS *Lake Champlain* (CVS-39). He went to boot camp at Great Lakes NTC, IL.

Remained in the USNR from 1960-68 when he was discharged. Re-enlisted in 1973 and joined the NJ National Guard, later transferring to the US Army Reserve. He spent 35 years in the military, retiring as a command sergeant major.

Awards include ARCOM w/4 OLCs, Army Achievement Medal, Armed Forces Reserve Medal, National Defense and Meritorious Service Medal.

Other assignments include Personnel Management Specialist; Training NCO HHD 3/311/1, 78th Div.; Senior Instructor, 78th Div.; CSM 1st Bn., 418th Regt. and CSM 1018th Reception Battalion.

Most memorable experiences occurred in 1961 when they picked up Alan Shepherd and his capsule and the day he graduated from the US Army Sergeants Major Academy (1988).

Upon his release from active duty in 1962 he went to work for Public Service Electric & Gas Company in Plainfield, NJ. He currently works as a procurement analyst and has 39 years with the company.

Married Emmy Jo in June 1962 and they have two children, Mary and Colleen with one grandchild, Abigail.

JAMES M. O'BRIEN, born Oct. 5, 1930, Flushing, NY. He served in the USNR, 1948 and active duty began in March 1952 in M Division. Assignments include Bainbridge, MD; Great Lakes MM School; Norfolk, VA and Mayport, FL.

Military Battles: "Task Force 77," eight months of "distant duty" in Korea. A memorable experience was visiting three continents and 10 foreign ports of call. He became Neptune's shellback in May 1953. During flight operations in Korea, the #3 shaft alley bearing overheated during his watch and he summoned help to prevent the possibility of the ship having to slow down, which could have shut down flight operations. He was able to see many parts of this big world we all live in and the experience was something he will never forget. Their captains made the *Champ* a floating city on which all of the crew worked and played as friends.

His medals include the Korean Service Medal w/Combat Star, UN Service Ribbon and the National Defense Service Ribbon. He was discharged Nov. 30, 1954 as MMFN.

He and Lorraine married in May 1952, and have five children, 13 grandchildren and two great-grandchildren. They celebrated their 50th anniversary in 2002.

From draftsman to machinist and spent 20 years in sales, (last 13 years selling lubrication equipment). He has lived 36 years in Clifton Park, NY and became a North Carolina resident in September 2002. Now retired, he plays golf, travels and visits his children. He loves to work with wood, designing and building things.

GERALD W. O'KEEFE, born Oct. 24, 1934 and entered the USN Jan. 27, 1955. Assignments include USS *Lake Champlain* (CVA-39); USN CIC School, NAS Glynco Brunswick, GA.

Discharged Jan. 27, 1959 with the rate AK3. His awards include the Navy Occupation Service Medal and Good Conduct Medal.

He lives in El Paso, TX and has one son Michael.

ANDREW G. OLSON, born Sept. 10, 1939, Boston, MA and entered the USN Nov. 14, 1957. Boot camp and Machinist Mate School were at Great Lakes Training Center, followed by Quonset Point, RI; USS *Tarawa* (CVS-40) and USS *Lake Champlain* (CVS-39), 1960-61.

A memorable experience was a cruise to South America aboard the *Tarawa*; a port visit to Rio de Janerio in August 1959; crossing the Equator aboard the *Tarawa*; and the recovery of Alan Shepard (first space man) in May 1961.

Discharged Nov. 3, 1961 as MM2 (E-5). He received the National Defense Medal.

Married Rita Urban in October 1960 and they have four children: Christine, Andrew, Adele and Katherine. He worked seven years for Crystal X Corp., Darby, PA (plastic bag manufacturer) and 30 years for Penn City Elev. Co., Philadelphia, PA. Now retired, he lives in Stockholm, ME, and is a member of the American Legion.

JOHN OSUCH, born June 19, 1934, Stupnica, Poland. He joined the USN, Flight Deck V1-F, Dec. 1, 1952. Boot camp was at Great Lakes, IL. Other assignments include USS *Lake Champlain* (CVA-39); USS *Wasp* (CVA-18); NATTC P School, Norman, OK; AK-A School Jacksonville, FL; Quonset Point, RI. He participated in Task Force 77 and 1953 Korean Conflict.

During his Navy Reserve career he served aboard the USS *Miller* (FF-1091) and USS *Iowa* (BB-61). During his two week activity duty at NAS Brunswick, ME; NAS South Weymouth, MA; NS Norfolk, VA; NS Colts Neck, Earl, NJ; MCAS Cherry Point, NC and the Navy Supply Officers School, Athens, GA.

Retired June 19, 1994 as SKC, USNR. His medals include the Navy Achievement Medal, Meritorious Unit Citation w/star, Navy Reserve Meritorious Medal (4) awards, Armed Forces Reserve Medal w/Hour Glass, National Defense Service Medal w/2 stars, Korean Service Medal w/star, UN Service Medal, China Service Medal, Armed Forces Expeditionary Medal, Combat Action Ribbon, Korean PUC, USAFR Meritorious Medal, USN Good Conduct Medal, USAF Longevity Service Award, Pistol and Rifle Marksman ribbons, Korean Service Medal, and Navy Occupation Medal w/European Clasp.

Married Arlene Zaiko Sept. 24, 1966 and they have two children, Timothy John and Melanie and one grandchild John Nicholas Osuch. He lives in Plainville, CT and is a contract administrator, Barlow Metal Stamping, Bristol, CT.

ALBERT W. PETER, born Oct. 13, 1937, Newark, NJ and joined the USN in October 1955. Duty assignments include recruit training at Bainbridge, MD; DK "A" School, Newport, RI; USS *Lake Champlain* (CVS-39), Mayport, FL; VW4 NAS Jacksonville, FL; NAF Naples, Italy; Submarine Base, New London, CT; VR21 Barbers Point, HI; CAG-19 Lemoore, CA.

Made deployments March 1965 to January 1966 aboard USS *Bon Homme Richard* (CV-31) and October 1966 to May 1967 aboard USS *Ticonderoga* (CV-14). Graduated from Finance School, Washington, DC and transferred to Defense Attache Office, American Embassy, Rabat, Morocco.

Other assignments include Naval Security Group, Bremerhaven, Germany; USS *Durham* (LKA-114), 1971-76, making three WestPac cruises; Navy Finance Center, Clevleland, OH; USS *America* (CV-66), 1980.

A memorable experience was being aboard the Champ for Mediterranean Cruise and the fire in the port of Marseilles, France in July 1957.

Retired as DKCS on March 1, 1982. His medals include the Navy Achievement, seven Good Conducts, Navy Expeditionary, National Defense, Armed Forces Expeditionary, Vietnam Service, Humanitarian Service, Navy Unit Commendation, Navy Meritorious Unit Commendation, Sea Service Deployment, Vietnam Gallantry Cross Unit Citation and Vietnam Campaign.
He married Yoko Peterson in 1947 and worked 14 years for Civil Service at PSA Jacksonville, FL. He is now fully retired.

ROBERT "BOB" PFEIFFER, born July 14, 1941 in Cincinnati, OH and enlisted in the Navy Reserves his senior year in high school, September 1958, and went to boot camp at Great Lakes in November 1959.

He was assigned to VX1, Key West, FL, where he served until February 1962, attaining the rate of aviation machinist mate 3rd class. He served with VS-22 at Quonset Point which was attached to the carrier *Lake Champlain* (CVS-39). While serving with VS-22 he made ADR2. In May 1964 he reported to VT3 NAAS Whiting Field in Milton, FL, serving there until his discharge in June 1965.

His most memorable experience was participating in the Cuban Blockade while serving aboard *"The Champ."*

Retired in February 2001, at 59-1/2, after working 36 years for Xtek Inc. Married Mary Saulsbury on Sept. 17, 1960. They have two children (both served with the Navy) and five grandchildren.

WAYNE V. PORTER, born Jan. 15, 1933 in Vona, CO and joined the USN in April 1950. Duty assignments include US Naval Training Center, San Diego, CA, Seaman Recruit, Co. 82; USS *Mount Olympus* (AGC-8), ship's company, LCVP Coxswain, 1st Div.; USS *Lake Champlain* (CVA-39), ship's company, Gunnery 2nd Div.
His memorable experiences were aboard the *Lake Champlain,* crossing the Equator and becoming a shellback; also, a severe storm in November 1953 (when the *"Champ"* was returning to the States after the Korean War) that kept the crew battened down and in life jackets for almost two days.

Discharged Dec. 15, 1953 with the rank of SN. His medals include Good Conduct Medal, Korean Service Medal, UN Medal, Navy Occupation Service Medal, National Defense Service Medal and Commendation for General Excellent Performance of Duty aboard Ship.

Following retirement, he spent 30 years working for the Newton Fire Department, Newton, KS, retiring in December 1992 with the rank of captain. He married Janet Jacobsen in 1954 and had five children: Farley, Fayne, Farrell, Fawn and Faber. Janet died in 1971. He married Sabina Paul in 1972 and they live in Newton, KS. They have 10 grandchildren.

JACKIE LEWIS PORTWOOD, born May 10, 1935 in Decatur, IL. He enlisted in the USN June 11, 1952 and was stationed at FASRON 2 Quonset Point, RI; USS *Lake Champlain;* USS *Coral Sea* (CVB-43); USS *Sequoia* (AG-23); President yacht; USS *Chardon* PC564; USS *Cambrig* (APA-38).

His memorable experience was getting to see different countries and meeting shipmates. He was discharged Oct. 9, 1959 as seaman. Awards include the National Defense and European Occupation medals.

Married Marie Dec. 10, 1953 and they have children: Pamela, Jack and Mark. A retired truck driver, he lives in Decatur, IL.

JOHN E. PRINTY, born Sept. 1, 1930 in Dover, NH and joined the USN in October 1948. Duty assignments include Patrol Squadron 27 and 4, NAS Whidbey Island, WA; Ftr. Sqdn. 22, NAS, Jacksonville, FL; All Weather Attack Sqdn. 33, NAS, Atlantic City, NJ and NAS Quonset Point, RI; USS *Saratoga* (CVA-60); USS *Forrestal* (CVA-59); Air Antisubmarine Squadron 31, NAS Quonset Point, RI; USS *Wasp* (CVS-18); USS *Lake Champlain* (CVS-39), ship's company, NAS, Quonset Point, RI; USS *Independence* (CVA-62), ship's company, NOB, Norfolk, VA.

Shore Duty: NAF, Annapolis, MD; Service Sqdn. 108, NAS Brunswick, ME; NATTC, Jacksonville, FL and NAS, Cecil Field, FL.

He took part in the last two months of the Korean War in Ftr. Sqdn. 22 aboard USS *Lake Champlain* in TF-77. His memorable experience was aboard the *Lake Champlain* as the recovery ship for Space Mission Gemini V when they recovered the two astronauts, Pete Conrad and Gordon Cooper.

Retired Aug. 1, 1969 with rank of CWO (W-2). His medals include five Good Conducts, China Service, European Occupation Service (Navy), National Defense w/star, Korean Service w/Battle Star (US), UN Service Medal, Korean PUC and Korean Service Medal (issued by ROK); Honor Graduate at Navy Training Command COP Leadership School in 1961; Honor Graduate at Field Command DASA Weapons School (Officer Course) 1966.

Following retirement, he spent 24 years working for Atwell, Vogel and Sterling (later known as Equifax Commercial Services). Married Eileen Brady in 1952 and had 11 children: Mary, Colleen, Kevin, Timothy, Brian, Stephen and five children who died at birth or shortly afterward. They also have 13 grandchildren.

JOSEPH M. RACKL, joined USNR Niagara Falls Air Station, NY in 1955. Active duty at NAS Quonset Point, RI, 1956; VA-72 1st Attack Squadron to get a 4D Sky Hawk aircraft.

Transferred to NAS Cecil Field, Jacksonville, FL, 1957-59; attended Air Prep School, Norman, OK, 1959; Aviation Ordinance School, Jacksonville, FL, 1959; USS *Lake Champlain*, Quonset Point, RI, 1959; took part in Freedom 7 Space Program 1960 and picked up Allen Shepard; transferred to USS *Enterprise* in 1961 for commissioning, became plankowner and took part in naval blockade of Cuba.

Awarded Life Saving Commendation, Cannes, France 1963. Received an honorable discharge in July 1963. Rejoined Reserve Station, NARDIV 731, Buffalo, NY in 1963 and discharged in 1971 as aviation ordinance man first class.

Joined Otis Elevator Company in 1964 and retired in 1998. He married the former Roberta Cascio in 1960, Buffalo, NY. They enjoy summers in Buffalo, NY and winters in Cocoa Beach, FL. They have three daughters and five grandchildren.

WILLIAM E. RANDALL, born Sept. 20, 1926, Cortland, NY and enlisted in the USN in June 1944. Duty assignments include Sampson Navy Center; US Navy Armed Guard; Gunnery School, Little Creek, VA; and SS Fort Niagara (tanker), October-December 1944.

First crew of the USS *Lake Champlain*, assembled at the Newport, RI Training Center in January 1945, and was aboard for one and a half years. Discharged in June 1946 as gunner's mate 3rd class.

Following his retirement, he was a small business owner and self-employed in the area. He was appointed by Governor Pataki of New York to the Board of Friends of the Oxford (NY) Veterans Home. He is a life member of the Veterans of Foreign Wars and remains active in it. Married to Iva H. Sherman in 1949, whose husband was killed in the Invasion of France in 1944. She had a small daughter. They had three children, four grandsons and seven great-grandchildren.

JAMES W. RINEHART, born March 22, 1943, Baltimore, MD and joined the USN, V-2 Div. in June 1961. He served aboard the CVS-39 at Quonset Point, RI and participated in the Cuban crisis.

Discharged in November 1963 as ABEAN (E-3). Married 39 years to wife Judy. They live in Churchville, MD and have two children and four grandchildren. He retired as sergeant, Maryland State Police and now works part-time as deputy sheriff.

JOHN ROBBEN, born Feb. 27, 1930 in New York City, NY. A 1952 graduate of Fordham University, he enlisted in the Navy on Oct. 27, 1952. After completing boot camp at Bainbridge, MD, he reported aboard the USS *Lake Champlain* on Feb. 24, 1953 and served 17 months aboard as Commander Joseph A. Kelly's Chaplain's Aide.

Returned to inactive duty on July 24, 1954. Medals earned include the China Service, Naval Occupation, National Defense, UN Medal w/Korea Clasp, Korean Service Medal w/Battle Star, Navy Combat Action and Korean PUC.

Most memorable experience was climbing Fujiyama while on R&R in Japan with Don Caulfield, Dick Murphy, Alan Pengally, Jack Sauter and Ken Wilcox.

He's author of *Coming To My Senses,* and numerous articles and OP-ED essays in national publications and is working on a memoir of his Navy life aboard the *Champ.*

Following naval service he joined the family's toy business in 1954, becoming president of RobToy, Inc. in 1974. His children now own the company.

He married Margie Burger on Jan. 2, 1954. They have five children: Susan, Janet, Ellen, John and Robert, and 14 grandchildren.

THOMAS J. ROOS, born June 28, 1931, Pittsburgh, PA and joined the USN, USNS R Div. March 26, 1956. Assignments include Great Lakes, IL and USS *Lake Champlain* (CVS-39).

Memorable experience was the Mediterranean Cruise in 1957. He was discharged Dec. 12, 1957 as FP3.

He and his wife Lucille live in Pittsburgh, PA and have three children: Christine, Tim and Brian. He was a steamfitter, Local 449 and is now retired.

IVISON D. ROWLAND, born April 15, 1934, East Orange, NJ and reared in Montclair, NJ. He volunteered for the draft in 1955 and was fortunate to time it with a rare period of Navy induction.

Boot camp was at Bainbridge during the winter of 1955-56, followed by 11 weeks of Hospital Corps School at the same base. One of the high

points of this period was participating with the base choir in making a recording of *Eternal Father, Strong to Save...* for submission to the TV Program *Navy Hog.*

He reported aboard the *Lake Champlain* while the ship was in Brooklyn Navy Yard drydock. The sight of the hull resting on wood blocks with "Yard Birds" all around was very impressive to a young sailor. He made the Gitmo cruise in pre-Castro 1956 and spent Thanksgiving as 6th Fleet backup during the Suez Crisis. Sailed Ex-Mayport in January 1957 for the Mediterranean – visiting all the usual ports plus Istanbul, Salonika and the infamous Marseilles fire in July.

Favorite times were working flight quarters and playing music all night in sick bay.

Married to long-time sweetheart Janice while CVA-39 was still in Brooklyn. He wrote many pounds of letters home while working nights in sick bay.

Returning home in September 1957, he earned a BS degree from Rutgers University, reared and educated four children and had a productive life in railroading with PRR-PC and Conrail. Retiring in 1990 to Malvern, PA, he enjoys his nine grandchildren, trips to the beach, motoring and NASCAR.

THOMAS ROYCRAFT, served in Night Fighter Squadron VC-4 and was assigned to the USS *Lake Champlain* (CV-39) for the Korean Cruise.

Memorable experience was crossing the Equator on May 30, 1953; also, the detachment to K-6 near Payongtac, South Korea to serve with VMFN-513.

Most regretful was the loss of LTjg R.S. Bick and L.C. Smith ATC, who were killed in action over Korea.

Second tour of duty on the *Champ* was from 1963-65 while assigned to Helicopter Anti-Submarine Sqdn. Five at Quonset Point, RI.

Transferred to the Fleet Reserve in July 1965 as an AEC with Good Conduct Medal, WWII Victory Medal, Korean Service Medal, National Defense Medal and the Navy Occupation Medal (European).

JOHN B. SANGER, born July 16, 1931 in Philadelphia, PA. He enlisted in the USN Jan. 22, 1951 and went through boot camp at Great Lakes, IL. He had shore duty at Naval Gun Factory, Fort McNair, Washington, DC for 16 months.

Assigned to the USS *Lake Champlain* (CVA-39) in August 1952, he served during the Korean Deployment and two

Mediterranean cruises as Ship's Company, Fox Division, until November 1954 when he was transferred at sea by helicopter to the USS *Coral Sea* (CVA-43) for return to the States.

Discharged Dec. 28, 1954 as FT3. His medals include the Korean Service w/Battle Star, Navy Commendation, Navy Combat, China Service, United Nations, Korean War Medal, Korean Presidential Unit Citation, Navy Occupation w/Euro and Asia Clasps, Good Conduct and National Defense.

Memorable experiences were shore patrol duty in Manila with next day round-up of Liberty Party and climbing cargo net to report onboard.

The *Champ* was berthed at the Philadelphia Naval Shipyard in the late 1960s awaiting end of service. He was proud and privileged to see her every day.

After discharge from the USN he went to work at Skip and Bart Trucking for four years. Started working at the Philadelphia Naval Shipyard in September 1958 and retired from there in January 1989.

Married Theresa Gadzinski in April 1951 and they have seven children: Kathleen, John, Terri, Michael, Valerie, Kenneth and Kevin. They also have six grandchildren: Theresa "T.J.", Marc, Candace, Marisa, Fil and Alexa.

JACK SAUTER, born Dec. 15, 1929. He served in the NYNG, 107th Inf., September 1947-June 1950. He enlisted in the USN Aug. 2, 1950 and went to boot camp at Great Lakes NTC, IL; Airman Primary School, Memphis, TN, Nov. 12, 1950; Aviation Electronics School, January-July 1951; Fleet Airborne Electronics School (Atlantic) Norfolk, August-September 1951.

Other assignments include Composite Sqdn. 12, Quonset Point, RI, September 1951-June 1954; USS *Midway* (CVB-41), August-October 1952; USS *F.D. Roosevelt* (CVB-42), January 1953; USS *Lake Champlain* (CVA-39), April-December 1953. He flew 21 AEW and ASW missions with CAG-4 Task Force 77.

Most memorable experience occurred in September 1953 when starboard folding wing failed to lock and they returned to ship on hydraulics and prayers.

Discharged June 8, 1954, as AT1, CAC. He served in USNR until June 1960. His medals include the Air Medal, Navy Commendation, China Service, European Occupation, UN Service w/Korea Clasp, Korean Service Medal w/star, Korean PUC, Good Conduct. National Defense w/star, Expert Rifle, Navy Unit Citation, Naval Reserve, Navy Combat Ribbon and Combat Aircrewman.

Following naval service he built an insurance agency with State Farm Ins. in Flushing, NY, 1956 to retirement in 1995. His book about his naval service, *Sailors In The Sky*, was published in 1995; also articles in major magazines; editor of *Champ* since 1994 and presently writing a travel book.

Married Marianne Hockemeyer May 1, 1954 and they have three children: Karen, Laurette and Keith.

DONALD C. SCHUNK, born Aug. 7, 1934 in Detroit, MI, and graduated from De La Salle High School and Wayne State University in Detroit. Drafted into the Navy in November 1955 and went to boot camp at Great Lakes, IL.

All time was spent aboard the *Champ* from Mayport, FL to Brooklyn Navy Yard to Guantanamo Bay, Cuba then the Mediterranean cruise with the 6th Fleet. The two years aboard *Champ* were among the defining periods of his life. This period was marred by the tragic loss of life in a fire aboard ship in Marseille, France. He was discharged in September 1957 and although only ranked a seaman first class and assigned to the Aviation Fuel Division, he always felt honored to be a part of the *Champ* and its crew and history.

After several endeavors he went to work in Detroit for Chrysler Corp. and eventually became a Chrysler dealer in St. Louis, MO for 27 years, retiring in 1999. He now lives in Las Vegas, NV with his wife Betty. Married 44 years they have three sons, four grandchildren and one great-grandchild.

JAMES SCORSE, born Feb. 2, 1934, Rochester, NY. Joined the USN in December 1951 with assignments at Great Lakes, Norfolk Radar School, USS *Midway*, USS *Lake Champlain* OI Division.

He participated in the Korean Campaign, was discharged in January 1955 with the rate RD3.

James has one son, two daughters and eight grandchildren. Employed 21 years with CAA/FAA/DOT and is now retired, lives in Dana Point, CA, and enjoys riding his Gold Wing.

THOMAS W. SCOTT, born March 20, 1937, Enola, PA and joined the USN in December 1955. Assignments include SK School, Newport, RI; Bainbridge, MD (Ships Company); USS *Lake Champlain*.

Memorable experience was ship's fire in France and cruises to the Mediterranean and North Atlantic. He was discharged in December 1958 as SK2.

He lives in Nokomis, FL, is a general contractor and trying to retire. He's married and has six children and nine grandchildren.

KENNETH THEODORE SCHWEDA, born Aug. 27, 1940, Chicago, IL. He joined the USN Aug. 27, 1956 and served as electrician's mate, E Division. Assignments include USS *Lake Champlain* (CVA-39/CVS-39); USS *Independence* (CVA-62); USS *Saratoga* (CVA-60).

Participated in Middle East tensions 1957 and 1958-60. Memorable experience was the explosion and fire in Marseille, France (1957) and collision with ORE freighter in 1960, USS *Saratoga*.

Discharged Aug. 26, 1962 as EM2/c. His awards include the Good Conduct, National Defense and Navy Expeditionary Medal.

He lives in Palos Heights, IL and has six children and 11 grandchildren. Worked 40 years for Rheem Mfg. Co. in engineering and sales and just recently retired.

JOHN R. SELLERS, born May 22, 1920 in Oneida Castle, NY. He enlisted in the USN as MM2/c. Assignments include NRS Albany, NY; NTS Newport, RI; RS New York; RS Norfolk, VA; USS *Maintonomah*; RS New Orleans; RS Chickasaw, AL; USS *Zeal*; San Francisco, CA; ATB Little Creek, VA; USS *Lake Champlain* (CV-39); USNTADC Williamsburg, VA and several other assignments.

After his discharge on Aug. 29, 1945 as MM1/c, he went into government work as a contract specialist with the federal government. He lived in Japan for a time with the family working in conjunction with the Japanese and American government. After retiring he moved to Missouri.

John passed away on Aug. 1, 2000 and is survived by his wife Margaret, daughter Margo, son Garth, granddaughter Carrie and two great-grandchildren, Dallas and Casey.

NOTE: Margaret and John married on Feb. 3, 1943 in the Episcopal Church in New Orleans, LA with two sailors as witnesses. The family would like to find these two sailors.

HARRY G. SEYFERT, born Jan. 17, 1942, Danville, FL. Joined the USNR July 5, 1960 and began active duty March 20, 1963, serving in OE Division. Assignments include Service School Command; Electronics Tech "A" School, Great Lakes, IL; USS Lake Champlain (CVS-39).

Participated in Gemini-Titan Mission 2, primary recovery vessel, Operation Steel Pike I, Springboard II, III. Memorable was having two collisions within 35 days; three trips to Bermuda; two trips to Puerto Rico; one trip to western Mediterranean Sea and later USNR annual training in Mediterranean and Philippines.

Discharged from active duty March 19, 1965 as ETN2 and USNR, January 1991 as CWO4. His medals include the Naval Reserve, Meritorious Service and Naval Reserve Service (30 years).

He lives in Danville, IL where he is an electronics instructor, VOTEC, and looking forward to retirement in two years. He has two children, Patricia Downey and Stephen Seyfert (also a Navy veteran), and two granddaughters.

JOSEPH D. SHAY JR., born Feb. 20, 1943, Brooklyn, NY and moved to Lindenhurst, Long Island, NY in June 1953. Graduated from Lindy High, Class of 1960 and joined the Naval Reserve Dec. 10, 1960 and served with a submarine reserve division in Brooklyn.

Received two weeks submarine training in New London, CT, early in 1961, followed by an eight week course which he didn't complete. He reported to active duty June 20, 1962 at the Brooklyn NRS, Brooklyn

Navy Yard, assigned to the USS Lake Champlain (CVS-39) and transferred to Quonset Point, RI to await his ship.

The ship arrived in port and he reported aboard and was assigned to 1st Division. His memorable moments aboard the *Champ* include taking part in the blockade of Cuba; turning 21 in 1963, missed ships movement and was flown to DC; one day sail out of Bermuda when President Kennedy was assassinated.

Scheduled separation was June 19, 1964, however, due to budgetary expenditures all crew separating to June 30, 1964 were separated upon arriving in port March 28, 1964. He left active service as a seaman and with the Good Conduct Medal.

Joseph went to work at Fairchild Space and Defense, Camera and Instrument Division in April 1964. He left Fairchild in June 1969 for the Nassau County Sheriff's Department where he rose through the ranks to captain. He retired in his 30th year.

He married Karan Morgan and divorced in 1995. He has three children: Timothy (deceased at age 36), Dennis and Tara. Dennis is married and has given him two lovable grandchildren, Dakota Joseph and Skylar Maren.

ED SHETTER, born Aug. 18, 1937, Gettysburg, PA. He enlisted in the USN Sept. 26, 1955 and went to boot camp at Bainbridge, MD and Radioman Class A School, January to July 1956.

Served aboard the USS *Lake Champlain* July 1956 to December 1957 and participated in Barrier Force Atlantic, airborne Early Warning Wing, Fleet Air Argentia, Newfoundland in staff communications, December 1957 to August 1959. He was discharged Sept. 9, 1959.

Married Glenda Miller Feb. 14, 1960 and they have 10 children and 20 grandchildren as of July 2002. His daughter Laura Knight served in Search and Rescue, PO3, Norfolk, VA; son Chris, Ensign, USN, attending Flight Officer's School, Pensacola, FL; son-in-law Rae Knight, PO3, USS *Cole* (DDG-67); son-in-law Adam Wine, Master Chief, USCG, Great Lakes Command.
Ed still lives in Gettysburg, PA and in retirement is active in church and doing volunteer work with the Gettysburg National Military Park.

O.V. "BUD" SIMPSON, born Feb. 12, 1930, Empire, AL and enlisted Aug. 12, 1948 in the USNEV Program. Rate HN, Aug. 12, 1948 to Aug. 12, 1949; USNR Inactive, Aug. 12, 1949 to Aug. 1, 1954; discharged June 15, 1958 to USNR and went on retired status in 1990 with the rank of CDR.

Recruit training was at USNTC Great Lakes, IL, 1948; Hospital Corps School, Great Lakes, 1948; USNH, Pensacola, FL, 1949; University of Pittsburgh School of Dentistry, commissioned Ensign in senior year, 1954-55; USNH St. Albans, NY, 1955-56.

Served aboard USS *Lake Champlain* (CVA/CVS-39) July 1, 1956 to June 15, 1958; Reserve Active Duty, June 15, 1958 until July 1, 1990; USNR (Ret), CDR, July 1, 1990. He trained at RTC, Great Lakes, IL, Hospital Corps School and USNH/St. Albans, NY.

Memorable experiences include attending the funeral of Ed Wolf, LCDR (VF Squadron) then had dinner with him two weeks later; fire aboard *Lake Champlain;* encounter with Errol Flynn (Majorca); and birth of daughter, Diana (Sept. 6, 1957) while *"Champ"* was in Dardanelles and seeing her six weeks later.

He has a full time family practice of dentistry with emphasis on "special needs" cases (debilitated cases, disability cases, mental illness and Medicaid).

Bud and his wife Lois have three children: David, Diana and Larry.

EDWARD JOHN SOWA, born June 13, 1930, Nanticoke, PA. He joined the USN Aug. 10, 1950 and served with Attack Squadron 45.

Assignments include NAS Jacksonville, FL; USS *Coral Sea* and USS *Lake Champlain*. Most of his duty was overseas in the Mediterranean.

Discharged June 10, 1954 with the rate aviation ordnanceman third class. His medals include the Korean Service Medal w/star, UN Service Medal, National Defense Service Medal and Navy Occupation Service Medal w/Euro Clasp.
Married Theresa Kiviatkowski Oct. 23, 1954 and they have three children: Brenda and twin sons, Andre and Alan. Employed as shoe factory foreman, 1954-68 then with P&G as papermaking technician. Retired from P&G in 1992. Edward passed away April 16, 2002.

CHARLES R. SPAMER, born Dec. 19, 1934 in Baltimore, MD and joined the USN in November 1952. Assignments include USNTC Great Lakes, IL; USS *Bennington* (CVA-20); USS *Lake Champlain* (CVA-39); *Coral Sea* (CVA-43) and USS *Forrestal* (CVA-59).

Shore duty as instructor, Norfolk, VA; Gunnery School, Newport, RI; instructor NOB Norfolk, VA; NAS Jacksonville, FL; N. Severn Naval Station, Annapolis, MD; YP, Brooklyn Naval Yard; instructor, Fort McHenry, MD; instructor on landing crafts and cargo handling, Little Creek, VA; Instructor School, Norfolk, VA.

He took part in the Korean War aboard USS *Lake Champlain* in the 1st Division. His memorable experience was aboard the *Champ* as the recovery ship for space mission Gemini V when they recovered the two astronauts, Pete Conrad and Gordon Cooper.

Retired in December 1971 with the rate BMC. His medals include five Good Conduct medals, European Occupation Service, National Defense w/star, Korean Service w/star and UN Service Medal.

Following retirement, he spent 17 years at the Maryland State Penitentiary as a correctional officer. Married Maxine Helen Kuhn in 1956 and they have three children: Elizabeth Ann, Charles Jr. and Jay. They also have two grandchildren and one great-grandchild.

RICHARD E. SPELINA, born Dec. 7, 1940, Brooklyn Naval Hospital. He joined the USN Jan. 23, 1958 and went to boot camp at Great Lakes, IL.

Other assignments include NAAS Chase Field, Beeville, TX, April to July in 1958; Prep School, Norman, OK, July to September 1958; NAS

Pax River, MD, September 1958 to March 1959; USS *Lake Champlain* April 1959 to December 1961.

Memorable experience was being on the recovery ship for Commander Sheppard Mercury Program. He was discharged Dec. 6, 1961 with the rate ADR3. He received the Good Conduct Medal.

Married Stephanie Collins Feb. 25, 1973 and they live in Central, SC. They have three children: Merritt, Peter and Tyler. Employment: independent owner/operator, trucking; supervisor for city of Clemson, SC.

ARLIN SPRAGG, born March 3, 1931, Al Pena, MI and joined the service April 11, 1949. Trained at Great Lakes, IL and served aboard USS *Soley* (DD-707); USS *Lake Champlain* (CVA-39); Ships Company, Engineering Division (air conditioning and refrigeration, engine room).

In November 1949 aboard the USS *Soley* he participated in Cold Weather Exercise, Arctic Ocean and in 1953 aboard the *Champ* in Korea.

Memorable experience was while on the *Soley* and being washed overboard in Arctic Ocean when thrown by heavy seas through life line and grabbed life line by finger tips and toes while going through.

Discharged in April 1950 with the rate MMR3 and was recalled in April 1952 until April 1954. His medals include the National Defense Service Medal, Korean Service Medal w/star, UN Service Medal, Navy Occupational Medal, Good Conduct and European Occupation.

Married in 1952, he and Marjorie recently celebrated 50 years. Their children are Karen, Robert, Tamyra and Lori. They also have 12 grandchildren and five great-grandchildren. He was owner/operator of a concrete block and cultured marble mfg. business and is now retired. They live winters in Largo, FL and summers in Hubbard Lake, MI.

LARRY STONEBRAKER, attended Eagle Rock High, Glendale College and Los Angeles Trade Tech. College in California. Served aboard YTB large tug #538; YTS small tug #96 and #94; and converted LCM #1 and #3 (auxiliary tug), Charleston, SC.

Served aboard USS *Lake Champlain* (CVS-39), 1960-62, engineman 3/c, A Div.; Ships Company, home port Quonset Point, RI. Participated in Alan Shepard recovery, Cuban blockade, Russian sub surveys, Midshipmen Cruise, dependent cruises and President Kennedy support to Europe.

Discharged in June 1962 at Quonset Point, RI to Naval Reserve in Long Beach, CA and discharged from there in 1966. His medals include the Good Conduct, National Defense, Expert Rifle, Ships Battle Award 2Es, engineering and ships company.

Worked several different jobs, then after 22 years retired Oct. 10, 2000 as building inspector, city of Los Angeles. Married 38 years he lives with his wife Sandy in Glendale, CA. They have two daughters, Ronna and Dana, one granddaughter and one grandson.

KEITH SWEAZY, born Aug. 30, 1932, Elkhart, IN. He enlisted Feb. 18, 1952 and went to boot camp and MM School at Great Lakes NTC. He served aboard the USS *Lake Champlain* in Korea, 1952-53.

Memorable experience was serving with his brother Walter in the *Champ* and both of them playing on the baseball and basketball teams. Discharged in 1953 with the rate MML3. He received all the usual medals given for Korea.

Keith and Alice (Griffin) have been married 30 years and have five children. He did woodworking for RV Ind. and retired on his 70th birthday. His home is in White Pigeon, MI.

ROBERT L. SWEETMAN, born April 1, 1938, Manitowoc, WI and enlisted in the USMC July 30, 1956. Assignments include Parris Island, SC MCRD; USS *Lake Champlain* (CVS-39); NCO Leadership School, 2nd Marine Div., Camp Lejeune, NC.

Memorable experience was Oct. 21, 1960 at the Newport, RI, firing range when the "Lakes" Marine Detachment copped the 100% qualification banner for the second year in a row. Out of 47, the detachment had 22 experts and 22 sharpshooters.

Cpl. Sweetman was discharged July 29, 1962. His medals include the Good Conduct Medal and Rifle Expert.

Robert and Nancy have been married 42 years and live in Big Bend, WI. They have four children: Robin, Susan, Deborah and Robert Jr. After 32 years in law enforcement he retired as police chief, a position he held for 20 years.

FRANK TALARICO, born June 5, 1929 in Red Bank, NJ and joined the Navy June 30, 1946. Duty assignments as a gunner's mate, aboard the USS *Oregon City* (CA-122); USS *Randolph* (CV-15); USS *Kearsarge* (CV-33); LSU Squadron 1&3; USS *Begor* (APD-127); USS *Floyds Bay* (AVP-40); Deep Sea Diving School, Washington DC; Explosive Ordnance Disposal School, Indian Head, MD.

Promoted to Ensign in 1960 and assigned to the USS *Lake Champlain* (CVS-39) as "G" Division Officer from 1960-62; Explosive Ordnance Disposal Unit 2, Charleston, SC; USS *Skill* (MSO-471), MAC Vietnam; NAF Sigonella Sicily. Shore duty included Naval School Explosive Ordnance Disposal, Indian Head, MD, as training officer.

He took part in Korea on board amphibious landing ships and the USS *Begor* (APD-127) and served as explosive ordnance disposal officer in Vietnam. Memorable experience was being aboard the *Lake*

Champlain on May 5, 1961 during recovery of Alan Shepard in the Mercury capsule; also memorable was disarming a fully armed 984 lb. chemical horn contact sea mine with a charge of 506 lbs. of cast TNT in hostile waters in Vietnam on Dec. 31, 1966.

Retired Aug. 1, 1971 with the rank of LCDR. His medals include the WWII Victory Medal, Korean Service Ribbon, UN Service Ribbon, Navy Occupation Service Medal, Bronze Star Medal w/Combat V, four Good Conduct Medals, Bronze Star on National Defense, Vietnam Service Medal and Ribbon w/Device, Presidential Unit Citation, Navy Unit Citation w/star, Combat Action Ribbon, RVN Cross of Gallantry and the Navy Commendation Medal.

Following retirement, he worked as a Safety Professional at Walt Disney World, Seminole County Government and Cape Kennedy. Married to Debra Jean Stevens in 1958. He's now retired and living in Orlando, FL.

NORM K. TAUBE, born July 22, 1940 in Kankakee, IL. He joined the USNR and went to boot camp in Great Lakes, IL in May 1959. Norm was then assigned to the USS *Lake Champlain* (CVS-39) in July 1959 to the V-4 Aviation Fuel Division.

In February 1961, Airman Taube, continued in the active reserve at Grosse Isle NAS in Michigan to be assigned to the active reserve VS-733. In October 1961 the squadron was activated and he served at NAS South Weymouth, MA as a parachute rigger until discharged in October 1962. He was honorably discharged from the US Navy in 1964.

He later became a respected Detroit Police motorcycle officer retiring in 1985 to northern Michigan. His proud achievements include his sons: Mark, Randy and Todd, along with his four grandchildren: Zach, Bethni, Isaac and Max. He is currently working as security at a renowned golf and ski resort in northern Michigan.

Taube's good times shared with shipmates will always be memorable. Yet, he is now sharing his MOST memorable moments with his loving wife Gail.

TIMOTHY B. "TIM" THORNTON, born Feb. 20, 1942, Charleston, SC. He joined the USN April 4, 1961, ABE, V2 Arresting Gear. Boot camp was at Great Lakes, IL; ABE A School, Philadelphia, PA.

He served aboard the USS *Champlain* from October 1961 to April 1965. Memorable experience was participating in the Cuban blockade; two collisions; and a storm that folded up first 50 feet of both flight decks, catwalks from bow. Discharged April 4, 1965 as ABE3, Barrier PO.

Married Roberta in 1973 and they have two children, Brooks and June. He's a civil engineer and lives in Tarpon Springs, FL.

GEORGE D. TOTH, born Dec. 18, 1941, Pontiac, MI. He attended all the schools in Pontiac from elementary to high school and after attending Michigan State University at Oakland for six months he enlisted in the USN Regular June 12, 1961. Boot camp was at Great Lakes, IL; Aviation Electronic School, NATTC Memphis, TN, 1961-62; NAS Guantanamo Bay, Cuba, 1962-63.

In September 1963 he transferred to VS-32, USS *Lake Champlain* and made numerous cruises. Memorable was the Cuban Missile Crisis; Gemini II recovery and the NYC Goodwill Cruise in 1965. The *Lake Champlain* was bought with war bonds in 1944 and named after Lake Champlain in New York State. They spent about a week there where the ship was open for tours and it was a lot of fun.

Discharged in June 1965 as electrician and metal model maker. Awards include the Navy Expeditionary and Armed Forces Expeditionary medals.

Employed 36 years with General Motors, he retired in 2001. Single, he lives in Waterford, MI.

CARL R. ULMER, born Nov. 26, 1929 in Philadelphia, PA and enlisted in the USN Sept. 10, 1948. Assignments include USS *Midway* (CV-41), USS *Lake Champlain* (CVA-39), Willow Grove NAS and Columbus, OH, NAS.

He participated in European Occupation and the Korean War. Memorable was shore patrol in Manila, P.I., June 3, 1953.

Discharged July 14, 1952 with the rate AT3. His medals include the European Occupation, Good Conduct Medal, National Service, United Nation and Korean Service Medal.

Retired from military electronics, he lives in Philadelphia, PA with his wife. They have a daughter and two sons.

DAVID JOHN "D.J." VOSSEN, born Feb. 6, 1944 in St. Paul, MN, on and Enlisted in USNR in 1961. He had duty aboard the *Princeton* and *Lake Champlain* where he was boat coxswain and starboard crane operator; Navy Boat School in Philly; and Little Creek, VA. Home port for the *Champ* was in Quonset Point, RI.

He participated in Dominican Republic action and Cuban Missile Blockade and Haiti hurricane relief and rescue (Hurricane Flora).

Memorable experience was being involved in collision with freighter in Chesapeake Bay (6 months in dry dock); collision with Destroyer in Atlantic maneuvers (more dry dock); and abandoning sinking 40 foot utility boat during downed helicopter rescue in Caribbean.

Discharged Oct. 17, 1964 as BM3. His medals include Expedition medals in Dominican Republic, Cuban Blockade; Good Conduct Medal and Presidential Unit Citation.

Married Geri Homan in 1965 and they live in Amery, WI. They have four children: Joe, Jeremy, Sadie and Joshua; and four grandchildren: Aaron, Alex, Alanna and Adam. He's spent 30 years as brick layer, dairy farmer, train derailment specialist and since 1993 has been employed with Noma Cable Tech Co. (located in Toronto Ontario Canada) as U.S. Sales Rep.

NOTE: he would like to honor a deceased veteran of the USS *Lake Champlain* who was his friend and shipmate: John Albert "Pukey" Foreman, BM3 3rd Div., (CVS-39). He was born in Springfield, IL, where he was firefighter as was his father. His younger brother Tom is a retired Navy chief. John passed away from heart failure in 1988 and is buried in Veterans Cemetery in Springfield, IL. He was a great friend and sailor.

PHILLIP C. WALKUP, born Feb. 23, 1941 in Beverly, MA, and joined the USN in July 1961. Duty assignments included boot camp Great Lakes, IL; USS *Lake Champlain* (CVS-39), 1962-64.

Memorable experience was the Cuban Missile Crisis, collision with the USS *Decatur* and a collision with a Norwegian freighter.

Discharged in July 1967 with rank of MR2 at the Salem Reserve Center. He lives in Beverly, MA and works for SIGARMS in the quality control department as chief inspector. He has two children, Christene and Amy, and two grandchildren, Kayla and Jared.

GERALD WEINSTEIN, born in March 1933, Point Pleasant, NJ, and joined the Navy in October 1952. He served one year as storekeeper at the BOQ at NAAS, Kingsville, TX. After Fire Control Technician School he joined the USS *Lake Champlain* at Gitmo in 1954 for three years and two Sixth Fleet cruises.

In October 1956 at RCA he worked at Cape Canaveral and downrange missile tracking stations. He then joined General Dynamics as a launch team member for the first successful US ICBM and Centaur launches. In 1965 he served on the GE Apollo team at Cape Kennedy and at Grumman in New York. In 1975 he worked for GE at Hanscom Field, Bedford, MA, designing tactical intelligence systems. In 1979 he was at GE Aerospace in Valley Forge, PA, designing and managing National Intelligence Systems. In Northern, VA in 1990 he was the operations and engineering manager at an intelligence center during the Gulf War.

He retired in 1996 to write about the Apollo Program. He and wife, Joanne, are blessed with a family of 19, most recently with the birth of their eighth grandchild on Dec. 31, 2000. Jerry and Joanne reside at Summerfield, FL.

ARTHUR A. "SANDY" WEST, born Dec. 22, 1929 in Quincy, FL, and joined the Navy in January 1952 after BS in Forest Mgt. Boot camp was at San Diego, then Electronics Class A&C Schools at Treasure Island.

Reported to USS *Lake Champlain* (CVA-39) ship's crew as ETSN in April 1953, before Gitmo shakedown/Korean cruise. Two subsequent Mediterranean cruises on *Champ* before December 1955 and discharge as ET1.

Earned BEE, UofFL, 1957. Joined General Electric Co. in 1957 for a 33 year career in military electronics (including surface ship sonar, submarine combat control systems) in Syracuse, NY, retiring from executive level management ranks in 1990. Registered PE, New York State; MBA, SyracuseU, 1973.

In retirement, 10 year business manager, InterReligious Council and overlapping 10 years (and counting) business manager (volunteer), Syracuse Symphony Orchestra; tax counselor; golfing and fishing. Married to Peggy Lewis, American Embassy girl friend in Athens, Greece for 45 years. They live in Jamesville, NY and have three children and five grandchildren.

EDWARD R. WHITAKER, born July 16, 1935, Louisville, KY. He joined the USN Sept. 8, 1953, as a seaman in 7th Div. Assignments include Bainbridge, MD; Norman, OK, Aviation School; USS *Lake Champlain* (CVA-39); and Rhine River Patrol, Manheim, Germany.

Memorable experience was being Oklahoma Golden Gloves Champ in 1954; All-Navy Runner-up in 1955; USS *Lake Champlain* boxing team, 1954-55; Featherweight Champ Area Commands Conf., 1956; Featherweight Champ Southeastern Area Commands, 1957 and All-Army Tournament, Washington DC, 1956. He was discharged Sept. 6, 1957.

Married Laurel Seeuskie in 1960 at St. Louis Bertrand Church and they live in St. Bernice, IN. They have four children: Ed Jr., Dave, Beth and Tom. Employed 32 years with Boilermakers Local 374, Hammond, IN, and is now retired and enjoying his seven grandchildren.

A. RICHARD WILLIS, born June 29, 1935, Bangor, ME and enlisted July 7, 1952 in the USN. Assignments included NTC Bainbridge, MD; USS *Palau* (CVE-122), Fire Fighting School, Philadelphia Navy Yard, PA; Engineman School, Great Lakes NTC, IL; USS *Lake Champlain* (CVA-39).

Memorable experience was visiting 15 different countries; taking part in a five ship convoy to Japan ferrying Marine fighter squadron to Korea; passage through Panama Canal; one Caribbean and two Mediterranean cruises.

Discharged June 15, 1956 as END3. His medals include Good Conduct, Navy Occupation, National Defense, UN Service, Korean Service and Korean War Service (ROK).

Married Maxine Cray and they have two sons, one daughter and four grandchildren. He's employed with City Sheriff Dept., Security Dept.,

Nuclear Power Plant. He lives in Ellsworth, ME, and enjoys hunting, fishing, camping and traveling.

HARRY E. WILSON, born Jan. 29, 1932, Brooksville, KY and moved to West Carrollton, OH in 1940. He joined the USN Dec. 12, 1950 in Minneapolis, MN; trained at Great Lakes, then to the USS *Midway* OI Div. He attended TAD Radar School, CIC, Fargo Bldg., Boston, MA.

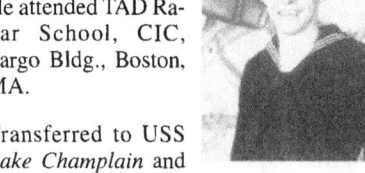

Transferred to USS *Lake Champlain* and went to Japan and Korea. Back from Korea, the ship operated out of Mayport, FL and was the first ship to have Mayport for homeport. Memorable was when CDR Veach and Wilson brought down 15 to 20 aircraft in 1-1/2 to 2 hours in very heavy fog using Height-finding radar.

Discharged Sept. 12, 1954 in Jacksonville as radarman 3/c. His medals include the Good Conduct, National Defense, UN Service Medal, European Occupation and Korean Service Medal w/star.

He and Alma "Jackie" have been married 43 years and have one son, four daughters and 10 grandchildren. He lives in West Carrollton, OH and owns his own business, Wilkie's Auto Service.

EDWARD H. WINSLOW III, born Dec. 28, 1933, Boston, MA and enlisted in the USN Nov. 10, 1954. Boot camp was at Bainbridge, MD; Airman Prep School, Norman, OK; NAMTC Point Mugu, CA; PR School, Lakehurst, NJ; VF-81, *Lake Champlain* (CVA-39) and *FDR* (CVA-41, V-6 Div.

Memorable event was the fire on the *Champlain* in 1957 at Marseille, France.

Discharged Oct. 30, 1958 as PR2. His medals include the Good Conduct and National Defense.

Married 41 years, he has two sons and two grandsons. Retired after 40 years employment with United Shoe Mach Corp. He lives in Beverly, MA, plays golf and works at ER Dept, Beverly Hospital.

CHARLES E. WOLFE, born June 7, 1935 and joined the USN in 1952. He went to boot camp at Bainbridge, MD, then went aboard the USS *Lake Champlain* out of Jacksonville, FL for two years and participated in the Korean War.

Discharged in 1960 as PO3. He loved sea duty and would have stayed in if he could have gotten sea duty again. His medals include the Good Conduct Medal, Purple Heart and National Defense.

He married Frances Carver in 1959 and they have four beautiful children: Chris, Charlotte, Charles and Craig. He was a truck driver for a flooring company in Cherry Hill, NJ for 25 years. He passed away Dec. 30, 2001. He was a very proud veteran who would have loved to re-enlist on Sept. 11, 2001 – God bless all the wonderful vets. *Submitted by his widow, Mrs. Frances Wolfe.*

ROBERT E. WOMACK, born Aug. 20, 1928, Hollow Rock, TN and graduated Castle Heights Military Academy, Lebanon, TN, May 15, 1946. He enlisted in US Navy, June 20, 1946 with recruit training at Bainbridge, MD; Electronics School at Great Lakes, IL and NRL, Washington, DC. Assigned to Electronics Shop, US Submarine Base, New London, CT until end of enlistment in 1948.

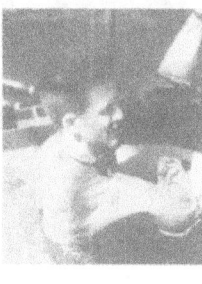 

Active reserve status until recall to active duty in May 1950. Instructor at NRTC, Jackson, TN until May 1952; USS *Lake Champlain* (CVA-39) Pre-Commissioning Detail, Norfolk, VA; and Guantanamo Bay Underway Training Cruise.

Transferred to USS *Coral Sea* (CVA-43), then recalled to USS *Lake Champlain* for Korean service cruise and served until January 1954.

Attended Damage Control School (Atomic Defense) instructor, Treasure Island, CA until discharged in May 1957. An honor graduate of Electronics Technician Class A and B Schools, graduate of Instructor Training Course, Atomic Defense (Officers) Course, RADIAC Instruments Maintenance Course. His decorations include Navy Good Conduct w/2 stars, WWII Victory, Korean Service w/Battle Star, Japanese Occupation Service, UN Service, Korean Presidential Unit Citation, and Korean Service Medal (issued by ROK). He left the service as chief electronics technician (E-7).

He was Leading Petty Officer for Communications and Navigational Aids Equipment Maintenance on the "Champ" and assisted in a study resulting in redesign of the ship's mast and UHF/VHF antenna display.

He worked in nuclear research at General Electric's Vallecitos Atomic Laboratory, Lawrence Livermore Laboratory, and Babcock & Wilcox's Lynchburg Research Center a total of 33 years, developing remotely controlled equipment for handling and characterizing radioactive materials, and was consultant in this field for 10 years, retiring in 1996 to do the things he really enjoys, golf and music. He is a graduate of San Jose State University, and Past Chairman of the Remote Systems Technology Division of the American Nuclear Society, and holds 15 US Patents.

He married Louise Crawley in 1951. They have a son Thomas, a daughter Vicki, and three grandchildren.

HARRY WOOD, born March 17, 1943, Newark, NJ and enlisted in the USN in March 1960. Assignments include Naval Air Test Center, Patuxent River, MD and USS *Lake Champlain*.

He participated in the Cuban Missile Blockade and while at Patuxent River was plane captain to Alan Boan who later flew on Apollo 12 and walked on the moon.

Discharged in March 1964 as ADJ3. He lives with his wife Sandra in Kenilworth, NJ, and works as director of maintenance. They are the parents of two daughters, Sallie and Lisa.

EDWARD J. ZAWACKI, born 1933. While in training, he served aboard the PC-1182 during 1950. His next assignment was in 1952 aboard the USS *Salerno Bay* (CVE-110) and toured the Caribbean Sea in 1954. Ed stayed aboard a barracks ship for a time to put the *Salerno Bay* out of commission. The *"Sally-B"* served her country well!

Following that tour of duty, he served aboard the USS *Lake Champlain* (CVA-39) in 1954. His first tour on that ship was, again, the Caribbean Sea. But the *"Champ"* was now heading to the Mediterranean for the first of two tours. She saw Beruit, Lebanon, France, Italy, Greece, and a bunch of other countries in between.

Ed did his share to protect the *"Champ."* One night during a storm at sea, a vicious wave destroyed a metal curtain of a hangar deck. He was washed under a plane, but eventually managed to secure the deck. Another time, gas began leaking from a pipe in the hangar deck. Ed doused the planes in the immediate area with flame-retardant foam, saving them from possible explosion. He was honorably discharged as a 3rd class boatswain's mate.

In 1961 he married Patricia Oleskiewicz and built a home in Meriden, CT. Following the Navy, he worked for SNET for 34 years. Ed and Pat have two children, Bonnie and Edward Jr. Today, Ed is an avid bass fisherman and gardener. He can steer a canoe though the roughest of seas and makes a mean pizza!

ARISTOTLE "TELLY" ZEYOS, born March 3, 1938, Manchester, NH. He joined the USN Jan. 7, 1957 and assigned to AE, V-6 Div., USS Lake Champlain and FASRON-9 NAS Cecil Field.

His whole time aboard the Champ was memorable. He was discharged Dec. 15, 1960 with the rate AN.

Retired as master electrician, he lives with his wife Joanne in Manchester, NH. They have three children: Nicole, Daniel and Jonathan. He drives a school bus to keep busy.

KENNETH M. ZOLNA, born Dec. 9, 1940, Cleveland, OH and enlisted March 11, 1958 in the USMC and assigned to Marine Detachment CVS-39. Assignments were at Parris Island from June 1958 to September 1958, 1st Bn., 2nd Mar., 2nd Mar. Div., October 1958 to February 1959 and sea detachment, 1959 to 1961.

Memorable experience was being part of a crew on the Champ's record fire shoot, 45 leathernecks emerged from the record shoot with 100% qualifications.

Discharged Aug. 25, 1961 as corporal (E-4). His medals include the Good Conduct, Expert Rifle, Bar and 45 Cal.

Married Mary Ottinger April 16, 1967 and they live in Valrico, FL. They have one son Jeffry. Retired from NYNEX in 1995 (Verizon) and now working at Raytheon Aircraft at Tampa International Airport.

(L-R): John Printy (who helped immensely in putting this book together) and wife, Al Hudson and wife

1953

Singapore 1953

F3D Skyniht Korea 1953

1962

1953 Korea

On Liberty - Canne, France 1957

Chief Roush and PHM Richardson with birthday cake, 1945

John Williford and Walton McCoy on Liberty-Tokyo, June 1953

Dan Hornstein, BKR 1/C presenting ENS. R.G. Ford, VBF-150, with cake celebrating the one thousandth landing aboard the USS Lake Champlain

29 June 1953, P.O. Club - Yokasuka, Japan. Jack, George, Mel, and Scottie

Admiral Burke on inspection Lake Champlain

Tony Traiano

December 1945

V-3 Div. Feb 20-61, taken after award for record crunch-free aircraft movements

1945

"R" Division, Compartment B-307-L 1954 - Pounds, Cobb, Cirillo, Waramont, Mikle, Long, Alsept, Szamatulski, Brown, McHugh, Livzey, Smith, Macey. (Photo courtesy of Bob Livzey)

Gemini Astronauts Cooper and Conrad aboard Champ, Aug 1965

Gemni V spacecraft on Champ Aug. 1965

Catholic Mass on the hangar deck -Oct. 1953

Bakeshop CV-39, 1945

Fire on the flight deck, June 1953

Reunion Pensacola

Hong Kong 1953-Rich Murphy, Andy Stein and Jack Santer

Reunion Pensacola

Reunion Pensacola

INDEX

A
Adams 30
Ader 6
Allor 65
Alsept 117
AMERIKA 7
ANTIETAM 54, 75
ARGUS 9
Athens 46
Austin 12, 70

B
Balch 30
Barcelona 46
Barcliff 11, 12
Batchell 30
Bates 68
Beirut 46
Benedict 54
Bennington 71
Bick 42
BIRMINGHAM 7, 8
Black 30
Blovin 62
Bolam 54, 62
Bolan 53
Bolem 54
BOXER 24, 28, 34, 71, 72
Boxmeyer 64
BREMERTON 28, 34, 35
Brewer 31
Brickson 30
Brooklyn Navy Yard 20
Brown 117
Broyles 36
Brumbach 36
Bryant 62
Burgess 53, 62, 64
Burke 116

C
Campion 63
Cannes 46
Carroll 59
Castro 51
Chambers 7, 8
Champs-Elysées 20
Chapin 6
Chappell 66
Chastain 12
Chatterton 49
Chevalier 48
Cirillo 117
Clark 31, 38, 50, 71
Clayton 59, 62, 70
Cobb 50, 117
Cole 27, 30
Collett 48
Compton 30
CONFIANCE 11
CONNECTICUT 6
Connor 61
Conrad 53, 54, 75, 117
Cooper 53, 75, 117
CORAL SEA 26, 27
Cox 51, 74
Crandall 48
Crosby 27
Curtiss 6, 7

D
Danielson 66
Davis 36
DECATUR 53
Decatur 64, 74
Dunn 81
Dunning 8
Düsseldorf 8

E
EAGLE 9
Edmonds 8
Ellis 68
Ellyson 7
Ely 7, 8
English 62
ENTERPRISE 10, 11
ESSEX 10, 12, 24, 50, 51, 53, 54, 57, 59, 71, 74
Essey 50

F
Fant 50
Field 62
Fields 20
Fisher 39
Flately 46
Flatley 62
Forney 72
FORRESTAL 43, 46, 55, 56, 73
Fort Myer 6
Francis 34
FRANKLIN D. ROOSEVELT 55
Fuller 67
Fultz 68
FURIOUS 8, 9

G
Gaillard 51, 74
Garrison 63
Gayler 64
GEMINI 5 53
Genoa 46
Gercnack 30
Gerritsen 66
Gibraltar 46
Gillen 63
Gillott 50
Glass 68, 69
Goodman 33
Great Britain 6
Green 30
Gumpper 30

H
Halsey 19, 20
Hammock 50
Hannigan 46, 62
Harper 19
HERMES 9
Hewitt 19
Hoare 63
Holden 41
HORNET 10, 56, 59
Hornet 71
Hornstein 115
Houser 71, 72
Hudson 31, 112
Humble 62

I
INGRAHAM 26
INTREPID 11, 54, 56, 57, 59
Isenberg 62
Izmir 46

J
J.F.KENNEDY 54
James 33
Johnson 24, 28, 36
Jones 12
JUPITER 9

K
Katz 12
Kearsarge 71
Kelly 40, 41, 43
Kennedy 66, 74
Keown 31
Kilduff 62, 70
Kilgrove 34
Kimball 6
Kinnear 72
Koch 57
Koons 51, 74
Korea 5
Kruitoff 30

L
LAKE CHAMPLAIN 11, 12, 17, 19, 20, 21, 22, 24, 25, 26, 27, 28, 31, 32, 35, 38, 39, 41, 42, 43, 45, 49, 50, 51, 52, 53, 54, 55, 56, 57, 59, 63, 64, 65, 68, 69, 70, 71, 72, 73, 74, 75, 76, 78, 80
Lake Champlain
LANGLEY 9
L'Aviation Militaire 6
Leeman 62
Lemmon 22
LEXINGTON 10, 11, 56
Leyte 24
Livzey 117
Long 117
Longino Jr. 62
Lowenstoft 63
Lubich 51, 59, 75, 76
Luker 50, 62
Lynch 41

M
Macey 117
MANCHESTER 35
Manningham 51, 74
March 41
Marseilles 46, 49, 73
Martin 57, 59
Mayport 24, 26, 49, 50, 53, 71, 73
McCain 67
McCoy 115
McCreary 68
McDonald 53
McDonough 11
McHugh 117
McKean 59
McRee 63
Mexico 8
Michener 37, 41, 72
MIDWAY 10, 12, 55, 56
Mikle 117
MISSISSIPPI 8
Mitchell 9
MOALE 26, 32
Monaghan 76
Morrison 62
Mosley 50
Motika 30
Mount Fuji 34
Moynihan 57
Mundorff 24, 41, 62, 80
Murphy 41, 50, 56, 119
MUSASHI 8
Myers 35

N
Naples 46
Nault 31
Nazak 65
NEVADA 56
NEW JERSEY 31, 35
Norfolk 7, 11, 12, 17, 22, 24, 27, 34, 54, 64, 70, 73, 74, 78
NORTH CAROLINA 8
North Island, San Diego, CA 7
Notre Dame 49
Null 50

O
ORISKANY 41, 71, 73
OSTFRIESLAND 9

P
Page 27, 39
Palma de Majorca 46
Pasquale 30
PATWING TWO 12
Pearl Harbor 12
Peloquin 31
Penland 50, 62
PENNSYLVANIA 7
Peterson 51
PHILIPPINE SEA 24, 28, 71
Polmar 62
Pounds 117
PRINCETON 24, 28, 34, 71
Printy 59, 112
PURDY 20, 26

Q
QUEEN MARY'S 20, 21
Queen of Bermuda 64

R
Raddatz 74
Ramsey 12, 16, 17, 21, 22, 62, 70
Randolph 71
RANGER 10, 11
Reeves 30
Rhodes 46
Richardson 115
Rickover 6
Robben 25, 41, 56, 77
Rodgers 8
Rooney 41, 72
Roush 115
Royal Flying Corps 8

S
SABINE 26
San Diego, California 11
SARATOGA 10, 11, 56
Sauter 5, 59, 62, 119
Savisky 67
Schweda 78
Scotland 11
Sea King 74
Shepard 51, 64, 74, 76, 77, 80
Shepard Jr. 74
Sims 9
Skauvagg 74
Smith 30, 42, 117
Southerland 41, 62, 80
SS United States 64, 70
ST.PAUL 35
Stein 39, 119
Suez Canal 26, 28
Sullivan 35
SUMNER 26
Sweazy 59
Sweeney 25
Szamatulski 117

T
Talarico 78, 80
Taylor 35
The Bridges At Toko-Ri 41, 72
The Champ 27
TICONDEROGA 57
Towler 8
Traiano 116
TRIUMPH 24
Truman 23
Turley 50

U
UNITED STATES 24

V
Valencia 46
VALLEY FORGE 11, 24
VINDEX 8
Vitztum 42

W
Wallace 34
Walls 32
Waramont 117
WASP 10, 50, 71, 73, 74
Webb 50
Weymouth 50, 51, 62, 74
White 12, 63, 65
Williams 36
Williford 56, 115
Willoughby Spite 7
Wilson 65
Wiseman 28
Womack 80
Woods 32, 36
Wright 6, 7, 8

Y
YAMATO 8
YARMOUTH 8
YORKTOWN 10, 11, 56, 71
Young 50, 62

CVA-39 recovering aircraft, 27 July, 1953; the last day of the Korean War. Taken by Jack Sauter from the rear compartment of an AD4W Skyraider landing.©

www.ingramcontent.com/pod-product-compliance
Lightning Source LLC
Chambersburg PA
CBHW081200230426
43666CB00016B/2875